BCL - 3rd ed.

The Future of Nonmetropolitan America

The Future of Nonmetropolitan America

Studies in the Reversal of Rural and Small Town Population Decline

Niles M. Hansen
University of Texas

Lexington Books
D.C. Heath and Company
Lexington, Massachusetts
Toronto   London

0569114

60658

Library of Congress Cataloging in Publication Data

Hansen, Niles M.
    The future of nonmetropolitan America.

    1. Economic zoning – United States. 2. Industries, Location of –
United States. 3. United States – Economic conditions – 1961–   –Case
studies.   I. Title.
HC110.Z6H35   330.9'73'092   73-8515
ISBN 0-669-87106-0

Copyright © 1973 by D.C. Heath and Company

Published simultaneously in Canada.

Printed in the United States of America.

International Standard Book Number: 0-669-87106-0

Library of Congress Catalog Card Number: 73-8515

Contents

List of Maps   ix

List of Tables   xi

Preface   xv

Chapter 1   Introduction   1

Chapter 2   Factors Determining the Location of Economic Activity in   7
            Metropolitan and Nonmetropolitan Areas

    Population Trends   7
    Relative Advantages of Metropolitan Areas   8
    Residential Location Preferences   10
    The Emergence of Urban Fields   12
    Industrialization of Rural Areas   13
    Summary and Conclusions   15

Chapter 3   The Role of Highways   19

    Introduction   19
    Highways and the Appalachian Regional Development   21
      Program
    The Role of Highways in the Present Context   25
    Summary and Conclusions   31

Chapter 4   Changes in Employment Structure   33

    The Nature of the Data   33
    Employment Change: One-digit SIC Code Sector Level   36
    Employment Change: Two-digit SIC Code Level for   40
      Manufacturing
    Employment Change: Two-digit SIC Code Level for   52
      Services
    Summary and Conclusions   54

Chapter 5   Minnesota and Wisconsin   57

    Employment Change   57
    Minnesota   61
    Central Wisconsin   66
    Northern Wisconsin   71
    Summary and Conclusions   73

Chapter 6   The Ozarks   77

             Employment Change   77
             Arkansas   80
             The Ozarks: A Summary View   83
             A Note on the McClellan-Kerr Waterway and   85
             Nonmetropolitan Development

Chapter 7   The Tennessee Valley   91

             Employment Change   91
             Tennessee   94
             Northern Alabama   103
             Northeastern Mississippi   106
             The Role of the Tennessee Valley Authority   107

Chapter 8   Colorado and New Mexico   111

             Employment Change   111
             New Mexico   114
             Colorado   117
             Summary and Conclusions   123

Chapter 9   Vermont and New Hampshire   125

             Employment Change   125
             Accessibility and Growth   130
             Chittenden County: A Special Case   133
             Recreation, Second Homes and the Environment   135
             Summary and Conclusions   139

Chapter 10   Northern Georgia and Central Texas   141

             Northern Georgia   141
             Central Texas   148

Chapter 11   Migration and Income Change in Turnaround Counties   153

             The Nature of the Data   153
             Nonmetropolitan Migration   153
             Migration Flows with Regional SMSAs   155
             Migration Flows with the Rest of the United States   156
             Summary and Conclusions   157

Chapter 12   Summary and Conclusions   159

Notes   169

Index   185

About the Author   189

List of Maps

5-1   Gain in Wisconsin Manufacturing Jobs   68

5-2   Nonresident   Usage   of   Wisconsin   69
           Recreational Facilities on the Peak Day of
           an Average Summer Weekend, 1970

9-1   Driving Times to New England Locations —   132
           from Montreal, Boston, and New York City

List of Tables

1-1	Persons by Poverty Status, by Type of Residence, 1969	3
2-1	Actual and Preferred Place of Residence of Americans Sixteen Years of Age and Older (Percent)	11
3-1	Average Distance of Counties from Interstate Highways or Limited-access Divided Highways, by Population Change Group and Distance from SMSA	26
3-2	Average Distance of Counties from Interstate Highways or Limited-access Divided Highways, by Population Change and Regional Groups	27
3-3	Average Number of Multilane Highways, by Population Change Group and Distance from SMSA	29
3-4	Average Number of Multilane Highways, by Population Change and Regional Groups	30
4-1	Estimated Percent Distribution of Paid Civilian Wage and Salary Employment by Coverage Status Under the Social Security Program: March 1969	34
4-2	Employment in Hancock County, Mississippi, First Quarter, 1970, as Reported in *County Business Patterns*	35
4-3	Absolute and Percentage Employment Change by Sector (One-digit SIC Code) in Selected Counties from Six Regions, by Population Change Category, 1964-69 and 1959-69	38
4-4	Absolute and Percentage Employment Change by Manufacturing and Service Sector (Two-digit SIC Code) in Turnaround Counties in Six Regions, 1964-69 and 1959-69	41
4-5	Manufacturing Employment Change by Sector in Turnaround-Acceleration Counties, Ranked by Absolute Employment Change	50
4-6	Manufacturing Employment Change by Sector in Turnaround-Reversal Counties, Ranked by Absolute Employment Change	51

4-7   Service Employment Change by Sector in Turnaround   53
       Counties, Ranked by Absolute Employment Change

5-1   Absolute and Percentage Employment Change by Sector   58
       (One-digit SIC Code) in Selected Minnesota and Wisconsin
       Counties, by Population Change Category, 1964-69 and
       1959-69

5-2   Minnesota's Industrial Growth by Area, 1968-1969-1970   63

5-3   Net Migration of Population in Central Wisconsin   67
       Turnaround Counties, 1950-60 and 1960-70

6-1   Absolute and Percentage Employment Change by Sector   78
       (One-digit SIC Code) in Selected Ozarks Counties, by
       Population Change Category, 1964-69 and 1959-69

6-2   Average Hourly Earnings and Percent of Total   82
       Manufacturing Employment by Major Industry Groups,
       United States and Arkansas, 1969

6-3   Selected Comparison Indicators, United States and Ozarks   84
       Region

6-4   Mean Weighted Employment Ratios (1967-71 to 1959-66),   88
       Arkansas and Oklahoma

6-5   Mean Weighted Employment Ratios (1967-71 to 1959-66),   88
       Arkansas and Oklahoma, SMSA Counties Excluded

6-6   Mean Weighted Employment Ratios (1967-71 to 1959-66),   88
       Arkansas, SMSA Counties Excluded

6-7   Mean Weighted Employment Ratios (1967-71 to 1959-66),   88
       Oklahoma, SMSA Counties Included

7-1   Absolute and Percentage Employment Change by Sector   92
       (One-digit SIC Code) in Selected Tennessee Valley
       Counties, by Population Change Category, 1964-69 and
       1959-69

7-2   New Industrial Plants and Expansions in the TVA Area: 108
       Establishments Added or Expanded, Electric Energy

Required, Employment and Payrolls Created, and
Investment, Manufacturing Groups Ranked by 1963-68
Average Weekly Earnings for the United States, 1959-68

8-1   Absolute and Percentage Employment Change by Sector   112
       (One-digit SIC Code) in Selected Colorado and New Mexico
       Counties, by Population Change Category, 1964-69 and
       1959-69

9-1   Absolute and Percentage Employment Change by Sector   126
       (One-digit SIC Code) in Selected Vermont and New
       Hampshire Counties, by Population Change Category,
       1964-69 and 1959-69

10-1   Nonmetropolitan Counties from Which At Least 5 Percent   142
       of the Work Force Commutes to Work Places in the Atlanta
       SMSA, 1970

10-2   Absolute and Percentage Employment Change by Sector   144
       (One-digit SIC Code) in Selected Georgia Counties, by
       Population Change Category, 1964-69

10-3   Absolute and Percentage Employment Change by Sector   150
       (One-digit SIC Code) in Selected Central Texas Counties,
       by Population Change Category, 1964-69

11-1   Variation in 1 Percent Social Security Sample Estimates for   154
       Given Sample Sizes

12-1   Public Cost for Creating Each New Job for Rural Workers   166

Preface

During the past several decades the entire population increase of the nation has been absorbed by urban areas. By 1970 nearly three quarters of the total population was living in cities of 2500 or more persons. Moreover, of the fifty largest Standard Metropolitan Statistical Areas, all but one showed substantial growth during the 1960s. Meanwhile, more than one third of the counties in the United States, mostly rural, lost inhabitants.

Urbanization is of course a worldwide phenomenon. Economic activities are attracted to cities because of the economies of agglomeration associated with concentration, and people are drawn to cities because they offer improved incomes and a diversity of career and life-style options. Nevertheless, the centripetal forces at work in the urbanization process are tending to be offset — at least in part — by several countervailing tendencies. One is the widespread feeling that the quality of living in big cities is deteriorating. In this perspective the city is associated with increasing congestion, slums, violence, welfare costs, and suburban sprawl. On the more positive side there are two centrifugal forces favoring nonmetropolitan areas. One is the extension of "urban fields," that is, interdependent rural-urban living spaces extending up to a hundred miles or more from metropolitan cores. The other is the decentralization of manufacturing from metropolitan to nonmetropolitan areas. These phenomena are examined at length in the present study.

In the past Americans gave little thought to the distribution of the nation's population and economic activity. Whatever the validity of the traditional faith in the market system, it has become increasingly apparent that there is now widespread public sentiment for the development of small towns and cities as an alternative to present metropolitan growth trends. This has been borne out by public opinion polls and by recent congressional and executive actions.

This book attempts to draw together the disparate forces at work in the evolving spatial structure of overall national economic growth and to point up the often clouded issues surrounding the development of a national urban and regional growth policy. Emphasis is given to nonmetropolitan regions that grew in population during the 1960s after previous decline, and particularly to the causes of their turnaround, in the hope that some new light may be shed on the conditions under which reversal of rural decline may be expected to take place as a consequence of either spontaneous trends or deliberate public policy.

The growth of turnaround regions is examined in a national context. Thus the first three chapters and the last chapter are primarily devoted to national patterns rather than to turnaround regions. Moreover, the chapters that deal directly with turnaround counties compare them with groups of counties that have been consistently declining, stagnant, or consistently growing in terms of population change. Nevertheless, the turnaround counties uniquely exemplify the opportunities and problems apparently inherent in the forces favoring nonmetropolitan growth in a largely urban society.

The author is indebted to numerous persons for their assistance in preparing this volume. The scores of state and local officials and university personnel interviewed in the regions concerned preclude individual identification, although it would not have been possible to carry out the study without their generous cooperation. The contributions of my colleagues in the Center for Economic Development, University of Texas, are also gratefully acknowledged. Peggy Worthington's work on the Interstate Highway System and that of Curtis Toews on the McClellan-Kerr Waterway were particularly helpful. Dann Milne and Vic Niemeyer also provided valuable support throughout. Carol Pfrommer's exceptional field work and her critical evaluations of preliminary chapter drafts contributed immensely to whatever merit this research possesses. The migration data presented in chapter 11 were processed by David Hirschberg (Bureau of Economic Analysis, U.S. Department of Commerce), whose cooperation on various projects over the past several years has been invaluable. The very able secretarial work of Sandra Hooper, Pamela Pape, and Rita Ellison was also very important.

Finally, the combined efforts would not have been possible without the support of the Office of Research and Development, Manpower Administration, U.S. Department of Labor. In this regard I am particularly indebted to Howard Rosen, Lawrence Asch, Harry Burton, Joseph Epstein, and Ellen Sehgal.

It is hoped that this study will be useful to economists, geographers, planners, and others concerned with regional development and manpower policies, and that the questions posed may enable them to improve such deficiencies as remain here.

The Future of Nonmetropolitan America

1 Introduction

This study is primarily concerned with nonmetropolitan development in the context of an essentially urban, and still urbanizing, society. Although economists have formulated abstract models — usually based on unrealistic assumptions — of optimal spatial resource allocation, there seem to be few places where the people (or at least those who count themselves among the articulate segments) believe themselves to be living under these conditions. City dwellers have their urban crisis and country residents find no end of information on how disadvantaged they are relative to their more affluent cousins. In the early 1970s the legislative pendulum appears to be swinging in favor of "doing something" for rural areas, which still retain a strong sentimental advantage in terms of worldliness. (Christmas cards invariably remind us that a Mediterranean stable or a Vermont landscape is where *it* is all together. The city has no existence in this world view.)

The concept of rural America is by no means precise. Given the great variety of population settlement and density patterns which prevails in this country, to say nothing of attitudes and life styles, it is often rather arbitrary to classify one place or group of people as "rural" and another as "urban." Nevertheless, quantitative analyses of regional problems must rely on some conventional distinctions. Following common practice, those adopted here are defined by the Bureau of the Census. Thus the rural population includes persons living in the open country or in towns with fewer than 2500 inhabitants. The urban population includes all persons living in urbanized areas or, outside of urbanized areas, in places with 2500 or more people. An urbanized area — a concept adopted by the Bureau of the Census in 1950 — contains at least one city of 50,000 or more people (or twin central cities with a combined population of at least 50,000) and is divided into a central city (or cities) and the remainder of the area, or the urban fringe. However, it is now more customary to differentiate metropolitan and nonmetropolitan residence categories in terms of Standard Metropolitan Statistical Areas. There are a number of criteria for defining an SMSA but essentially it must have one city of at least 50,000 inhabitants, and it includes the county of such a central city and those adjacent counties which are found to be metropolitan in character and economically and socially integrated with the county of the central city.

The case for development policies for rural or nonmetropolitan areas usually is based on two not unrelated phenomena. First, nonmetropolitan counties have consistently had lower per capita personal incomes. In 1968 the value was $2614

1

for all nonmetropolitan counties, whereas the corresponding value for metropolitan counties was $3811.[1] As the data in table 1-1 indicate, nonmetropolitan areas experience a disproportionate number of persons living in poverty. For all races, 17.1 percent of the nonmetropolitan population, as compared with 9.5 percent of that in SMSAs and 13.4 percent of that in central cities, was in poverty status in 1969. However, although about a third of all blacks were below the poverty level, this was also the case for over half of the blacks living in nonmetropolitan areas.

Another rationale for rural development policies concerns loss of population. In the past fifty years the national population has increased from 106 million to 203 million and the urban population from 54 million to 149 million. The rural population has remained steady, at around 54 million. However, the farm sector of rural population has declined from 32 million in 1920 (or three fifths of the rural total) to fewer than 10 million today (less than one fifth of the rural total). The rate of farm outmigration remains high, although because of the reduced farm population base the annual number of outmigrants has declined from 1 million per year in the 1950s to about 600,000 in the 1960s. Continuing outmigration of the farm population is a result of declines in agricultural employment, especially where nonfarm jobs have taken up the slack. In some areas the outmigration of young adults has produced a phenomenon relatively rare in American history, namely, a natural decrease in population. In 1950 only 2 counties experienced natural population decrease, and in 1960 there were only 38. In 1970, however, more than 500 counties fell in this category. In particular, there have been fewer births than deaths in large groups of contiguous counties in Missouri, Kansas, Nebraska, Illinois, and Texas. It has been remarked that "this is more a startling symbol of distortion of the normal age composition than it is a problem in itself. But it usually reflects conditions in which great difficulty is being experienced in obtaining new sources of employment or in retaining the present population level."[2]

Although some counties have shown deterioration in their ability to hold people and others have continued previous growth patterns, there is a sizeable group of nonmetropolitan counties which have demonstrated remarkably improved population retention. It is the purpose of this volume to analyze the nature of this growth and its significance for policies that might be applied to other areas. As discussed in the following chapter, it is not assumed here that population growth is necessarily desirable or that population decline is necessarily bad. Nevertheless, an examination of the factors behind the reversal of stagnation or decline has obvious relevance to the formulation of national manpower and growth policies encompassing all kinds of urban and rural places.[3] Indeed, it is our contention that this reversal can only be understood in the context of a national system of forces involving both metropolitan and nonmetropolitan areas.

The selection of counties to be studied was made on the basis of a

Table 1-1
Persons by Poverty Status, by Type of Residence, 1969

Residence Type	All Races			White			Black		
		Below Poverty Level			Below Poverty Level			Below Poverty Level	
	Total	Number	Percent of Total	Total	Number	Percent of Total	Total	Number	Percent of Total
United States	199,849	24,289	12.2	175,231	16,668	9.5	22,349	7,214	32.3
Metropolitan	130,017	12,320	9.5	112,440	8,200	7.3	15,824	3,855	24.4
Central City	57,781	7,760	13.4	44,392	4,527	10.2	12,439	3,068	24.7
Metro Ring	72,236	4,560	6.3	68,049	3,674	5.4	3,384	786	23.2
Nonmetropolitan	69,831	11,969	17.1	62,791	8,468	13.5	6,525	3,359	51.5

Source: Bureau of the Census, *Current Population Reports*, "Consumer Income," P-60, No. 76, table 3.

classification system of population retention made available by Calvin Beale of the Economic Research Service, U.S. Department of Agriculture. In this system each county was placed in one of three groups: (1) counties having inadequate and declining population retention ability; (2) counties having improved retention ability; and (3) counties experiencing population growth and net inmigration in both of the past two decades.

In the first of Beale's groups were four subgroups. Two of these, termed *Stagnant Gainers* in the present study, either (a) gained population in the last two decades but at a lower rate in the 1960s or (b) gained in both decades but had net inmigration in the 1950s and net outmigration in the 1960s.

The other two subgroups in Beale's first group respectively (a) lost population in both decades but at a higher rate in the 1960s and (b) lost population in the 1960s after gaining in the previous decade. To this subset we have added a subset from Beale's second group, namely, (c) counties that lost population in both decades but at a lower rate in the 1960s. It was felt that their "improved retention" did not compensate for the fact that they were still declining. These three subgroups taken together are termed *Losers*. (This purely technical term is in no way intended to impugn the character of their residents.)

For the sake of brevity, counties in Beale's third group are referred to as *Consistent Fast Gainers.*

The two kinds of counties that are the focus of this study are subgroups of Beale's second group. The first, termed *Turnaround-Reversal,* consists of counties that gained population in the 1960s after losing in the 1950s. The second, termed *Turnaround-Acceleration,* consists of counties that gained population in both decades but grew rapidly in the 1960s after relative stagnation and net outmigration in the 1950s.

No attempt is made to examine all turnaround counties in the United States. Rather, on the basis of map studies, the author used his judgment to select six groups of such counties, each containing a relatively large number of contiguous turnaround counties; thus the cases investigated involve whole regions that have reversed decline or overcome stagnation, rather than a county here and a county there. The regions studied are northern Vermont and New Hampshire, the Tennessee Valley, the Ozarks, central Wisconsin and Minnesota, the Colorado and New Mexico Rockies, and central Texas.[4]

Throughout this study the turnaround counties are compared with nonmetropolitan counties in the Loser, Stagnant Gainer, and Consistent Fast Gainer categories. Counties in these groups were selected by virtue of their being in the same Bureau of Economic Analysis (BEA) economic areas as the turnaround counties. These areas, rather than states or some other geographic areas, were chosen because they are the most meaningful delineations of economic areas. Because the choice of BEA areas is critical to the entire study it is appropriate briefly to consider their nature.

The Regional Economics Division of the Bureau of Economic Analysis (U.S.

Department of Commerce) is engaged in a program of regional measurement, analysis, and projections of economic activity. To facilitate this program BEA has defined economic areas on the basis of the nodal-functional area concept. Thus, to each urban center are attached the surrounding county units where economic activity is focused directly or indirectly on that of the center. Insofar as possible, each BEA area combines the place of work and place of residence of employees. There is therefore a minimum of commuting across BEA area boundaries. Each area approaches self-sufficiency in its residentiary industry. That is, even though each area produces goods and services for export, most of the services and some of the goods required by the residents and firms of the area are provided within the area.

The BEA areas correspond fairly closely to the closed trade areas of central place theory, in which the number and type of firms and their size and trade areas are bounded by the relative transportation costs from hinterland to competing centers. Each area approaches closure with respect to residentiary industries that include general and convenience retail and wholesale trade activities and those other services which, because they are difficult to transport, are most efficiently consumed in the vicinity of their production. On the other hand, the areas remain largely open to the movement of transportable commodities and to nontransportable special services, such as education at Cambridge and recreation at Miami.

The first step in the specific delineation of BEA areas was the identification of economic centers. SMSAs were chosen where possible because of their obvious significance as wholesale and retail trade centers and as labor market centers. However, not all SMSAs were made centers, because some are part of larger metropolitan complexes, as in the New York area. In rural parts of the country where there were no SMSAs, cities in the 25,000 to 50,000 population range were chosen as centers, provided that two criteria were met: first, the city had to be a wholesale trade center for the area, and second, the area as a whole had to have a minimum population of about 200,000 persons, although some exceptions were made in sparsely populated areas. Once centers were identified, intervening counties were allocated to them on the basis of comparative time and distance of travel to them, the interconnection between counties because of journey to work, the road network, and other linkages and geographic features. In cases where commuting patterns overlapped, counties were included in the economic area containing the center with which there was the greatest commuting connection. In more rural parts of the country, where journey to work information was insufficient, distance of travel to the economic centers was the major factor in establishing the boundaries of economic areas.

In a few instances in the present study departures were made from including all counties in BEA areas in which turnaround counties fell. If only one or two turnaround counties were in a BEA area it would not be included. In a few very large BEA areas not all counties were included. The area centering in San

Antonio, for example, extends from the Gulf of Mexico to West Texas. It was clear that not all of these counties were comparable to the turnaround counties lying in the center of this vast BEA area. In general, however, the BEA delineations were respected in selecting the nonturnaround counties included in this study. Before detailed attention is given to the nature and significance of the growth of turnaround counties, the following chapter considers in a very general fashion the major forces that seem to be influencing the location of population and activity within and between metropolitan and nonmetropolitan areas. The issues raised in this examination constitute the basis for the subsequent analysis.

2

Factors Determining the Location of Economic Activity in Metropolitan and Nonmetropolitan Areas

This chapter makes no attempt to list all of the factors that can or do enter into decisions affecting the location of economic activity.[1] They may range from analysis carried out in the context of highly refined profit maximization models to choices based on personal likes or dislikes, with most cases falling somewhere in between. Rather, it is primarily concerned with issues related to the growth of previously declining or stagnating nonmetropolitan areas; these issues are taken up again in later chapters to the extent that they are relevant to specific areas.

Population Trends

The Bureau of the Census recently published a map showing population trends by counties from 1940 to 1970. The map shows counties that have gained population only in the last decade, those that have gained in the last two decades, and those that have gained in all of the last three decades. Counties that have lost population in corresponding periods also are indicated.

To generalize rather broadly, consistent population gains have been registered in the northeastern megalopolitan region (including nearly all of New York State), the Great Lakes urban-industrial region, the Piedmont Crescent, Florida, the Gulf Coast, the West (particularly Arizona, California, Nevada, Oregon, and western Washington), and numerous metropolitan areas in other parts of the nation.

Population losses have characterized northern New England, central Appalachia, the southern Atlantic coastal plains, central and southern Georgia, Alabama and Mississippi (excluding the Gulf Coast), the Mississippi Valley, and much of the prairie and plains areas from Canada to Mexico. Counties that have lost population only in the last decade generally are either in or bordering on these areas.

Counties that have gained population in the last decade after extended periods of decline or stagnation tend to be concentrated in a few areas. They include northern Vermont and New Hampshire, central Wisconsin and Minnesota, the Tennessee Valley (broadly defined to include numerous counties in all states bordering on Tennessee except Arkansas and Missouri), the Ozarks and adjacent areas, central Texas, and central Colorado and New Mexico.

7

Relative Advantages of Metropolitan Areas

What have been the reasons for these phenomena? First, the growing metropolitan areas benefit from external economies of agglomeration[2] as well as from cultural and geographic amenities, and these factors provide the impetus for self-sustained future growth. It has been estimated that whereas less than forty years ago nearly 30 percent of the labor force needed to be located close to natural resources, today only 7 percent are resource-bound. Thus, the great preponderance of workers now are potentially "footloose" or must locate in proximity to consumers who themselves are relatively footloose, and economic opportunity is associated less with land and natural resources and more with the presence of capital and human skill.[3]

It should be emphasized that the advantages of larger urban areas cannot be simply explained by the traditional economic base approach because it really never came to grips with the dynamics of the process by which an area amasses overhead capital and by which it acquires new export bases. Similarly, classical location theory, including central place theory, relied too heavily on static analyses with "other things equal." As Wilbur Thompson points out:

The economic base of the larger metropolitan area is, then, the creativity of its universities and research parks, the sophistication of its engineering firms and financial institutions, the persuasiveness of its public relations and advertising agencies, the flexibility of its transportation networks and utility systems, and all the other dimensions of infrastructure that facilitate the quick and orderly transfer from old dying bases to new growing ones. A diversified set of current exports — "breadth" — softens the shock of exogenous change, while a rich infrastructure — "depth" — facilitates the adjustment to change by providing the socio-economic institutions and physical facilities needed to initiate new enterprises, transfer capital from old to new forms, and retrain labor.[4]

In contrast, whatever advantages relatively stagnant nonmetropolitan areas may have in terms of a stable, cheap, and abundant labor force, of adequate and relatively cheap land, and of easy access to work and recreation areas, they still often have a host of disadvantages to overcome. Cheap land and low tax rates may be more than offset by low levels of public services. There may be relatively few business contacts with other producers, suppliers, or auxiliary business services. Although labor may be plentiful, adapting untrained workers to the firm's needs may prove expensive. The local market will probably not be significant, and firms frequently find it advantageous to locate near competitors rather than at a distance. Bad connections with long-distance transportation may create higher transfer costs. Nonmetropolitan areas also tend to be lacking in cultural and educational facilities and personnel, and there is often a great deal of mistrust of industrialization in rural areas, including the wariness of local "leaders" who do not wish to see the status quo altered.

Because these problems are familiar, it is perhaps more appropriate here to dwell on the relatively ignored question of the structure and functioning of nonmetropolitan financial markets. For example, data from North Dakota and Minnesota indicate that:

> The hypothesis that rural area savings provide part of the capital for industrial-urban development . . . seems to be supported in the evidence. . . . The sizable net correspondent balances of the Twin Cities commercial banks provide substantial capital to aid in the acceleration of the development of the urban area. In this way, the Minneapolis-St. Paul area specifically appears to be dependent upon rural North Dakota and Minnesota capital flows to help finance economic growth. Further, this flow seems to be more a function of the system than economic incentives.[5]

Another study of Minnesota banking data during the 1960s shows that the correspondent system is providing a flow of funds to the urban correspondent banks but not a reverse flow in terms of rural participation loans.[6] An analysis of local savings in central Appalachia likewise indicates that in 1967 the region had a $109 million gross capital outflow.[7]

The credit situation is especially bad with respect to long-term financing. Small unincorporated firms and many small corporations are highly dependent on commercial banks for their long-term capital requirements. Moreover, they frequently must rely on personal, informal contacts rather than intermediation in perfect capital markets.[8]

While part of the difficulty with financing rural enterprise is lack of competitive local demand, there are indications that the nature of the local financial community also is at fault. This raises the issue of the efficiency of the banking system. As Shane points out, banks must be judged by how well they transfer surplus community funds into actual investment projects. If they are not successful "the costs are measured in jobs not available and income not earned."[9] In this context, comparisons of efficiency can be measured by relative loan-to-deposit ratios rather than earnings on capital.[10]

There is convincing evidence that the loan-to-deposit ratios of rural banks are less than those of urban banks. The principal reasons that have been advanced for this phenomenon are risk aversion on the part of small rural banks (especially unit banks), and institutional factors detrimental to rural areas.

The portfolios of nearly all rural unit banks are tied to agriculture. Because they are less diversified than urban banks, it is rational for them to have a smaller proportion of total assets in loans.[11] However, a branch bank (or a holding company affiliate) would not have to face this problem. A particular branch office does not have to diversify its portfolio so long as the system of which it is a part diversifies. Indeed, there is considerable evidence that branch offices in fact have higher loan-to-deposit ratios whether they are the only banks in their towns or are competing with other branch offices or unit banks.[12]

The advantages of branch banking also extend to competitive performance characteristics. Bigness does not necessarily imply monopoly, and a few firms in a branch banking system may well compete more statewide than would individual unit banks, each with its own local monopoly.[13]

Finally, it must be emphasized that among the greatest barriers to the provision of adequate rural development financing are the attitudes of many bankers in rural areas. Low wages and salaries make it difficult to retain competent personnel in many rural banks,[14] but an even more important problem is that bankers simply are not growth minded. Instead of vigorous competition in the marketplace for new economic activity, there is too often only conservative, personal intermediation, serving only to confirm and reinforce the local power structure and economic stagnation. The introduction of statewide branching in all states would create pressure for reform, but the more efficient use of local resources for local job creation may require more cogent means for replacing entrenched mediocrity with progressive financial leadership.

Although the foregoing discussions indicate in a very general way that metropolitan areas have many advantages over nonmetropolitan areas with respect to attractiveness to industry, it does not necessarily follow that the public's residential preferences correspond to the directions in which economic activity has been drawn. Indeed, there are indications to the contrary.

Residential Location Preferences

A Gallup Poll survey released in 1968 found that 56 percent of the respondents would prefer living in rural areas or small towns if jobs were available. In comparison with a poll taken two years earlier, the proportion of persons expressing a preference for city or suburban living dropped by seven percentage points.[15]

The data in table 2-1 where obtained from a probability sample carried out by Opinion Research Corporation using a questionnaire designed by the staff of the Commission on Population Growth and the American Future.[16] About seventeen hundred persons were interviewed. While only 12 percent of the respondents resided on farms or in open country not on farms, 34 percent would prefer to live in such areas. At the other end of the spectrum, over twice as many respondents lived in large cities compared with those who would prefer to live there, and twice as many lived in suburbs of large cities compared with those who would prefer to live there. It is not surprising therefore that 52 percent of the respondents thought that the federal government should discourage or should not encourage further growth of large metropolitan areas. Similarly, 58 percent felt that the federal government should encourage people and industry to move to smaller cities and towns.

Of course, most people "are not in reality free to live just anywhere. The vast majority are employees who must live where there are jobs, and the location of jobs is not their choice. The concentration of the country's population is the result of employer-created job patterns that the people have had to follow."[17]

Table 2-1
Actual and Preferred Place of Residence of Americans Sixteen Years of Age and Older (Percent)

	Actual Residence	Preferred Residence
Farm	5	14
Open County Not on a Farm	7	20
Small Town	20	19
Small City	13	11
Medium-size City	14	10
Large City	16	7
Suburb of Medium-size City	14	12
Suburb of Large City	12	6

Source: Commission on Population Growth and the American Future.

Although the present distribution of jobs and people is largely the result of market forces, other factors also have created a bias toward metropolitan areas. Wilbur Thompson has pointed out that most semi-skilled production workers have implicitly abandoned any influence they might have had on the location of their jobs by quoting a spatially invariant wage through their unions.

If blue-collar, middle-income workers should happen to prefer small towns or medium-size cities as places to live and to fish, such a preference is irrelevant as a locational factor. What could be most relevant is that the wives of the corporate managers prefer the theater. Under unionism, managers become increasingly free to locate where *they* would like to live . . . the manager (not owner) group now chooses the place to live and work, with income and education rather than birthplace and family ties determining that choice.[18]

Reinforcing this skill bias through which managers and professional people lock the semi-skilled production workers into their preferences for metropolitan areas is an age bias in migration. The more affluent, the better educated, and the young are the more mobile persons who not only have preferred cities but have not hesitated to move to them. With time and aging many city people may prefer the environment of nonmetropolitan areas, but they will tend not to move because of heavy financial and psychic investments in home, friends, and local institutions and the shorter remaining life span over which the costs of moving must be recaptured.[19]

Despite these considerations, there are indications of forces at work that may bring preferred and actual places of residence more into harmony for increasing numbers of people. A Wisconsin survey suggests that what most people actually prefer is the best of both worlds, that is, rural or semi-rural living within commuting distance of a metropolitan area.[20] Indeed, nationally one of the main characteristics of the residential use of heretofore "empty areas" appears to be that the sites are within one hundred miles or are certainly no more than two hundred miles from at least one major urban center.[21] Another factor that may be bringing jobs and residential location preferences more into line is the decentralization of many manufacturing activities. Thus, it appears that reversal of population decline in nonmetropolitan areas cannot be treated in isolation because it involves interrelations between nonmetropolitan and metropolitan areas. On the one hand growth may result from the high income elasticity of demand of city people for leisure-oriented activities, coupled with increased mobility. On the other hand, nonmetropolitan areas may also grow as a consequence of the location of activities spun off from larger cities. These phenomena will now be considered in turn in some detail.

The Emergence of Urban Fields

The wider community of interests increasingly emerging in American living patterns has been noted by numerous scholars. John Friedmann and John Miller, for example, have pointed out:

It is no longer possible to regard the city as purely an artifact, or a political entity, or a configuration of population densities. All of these are outmoded constructs that recall a time when one could trace a sharp dividing line between town and countryside, rural and urban man. From a sociological, and, indeed, an economic standpoint, what is properly urban and properly rural can no longer be distinguished.[22]

Thus the city is no longer so much a physical entity as a pattern of localizations and connecting flows of people, information, money, commodities, and services. A number of concepts have been suggested to encompass this expanding scale of urban activity, but the most satisfactory perhaps is that of an "urban field," which has been defined in the following terms:

Looking ahead to the next generation, we foresee a new scale of urban living that will extend far beyond existing metropolitan cores and penetrate deeply into the periphery. Relations of dominance and dependency will be transcended. The older established centers, together with the intermetropolitan peripheries that envelop them, will constitute the new ecological unit of America's post-industrial society that will replace traditional concepts of the city and metropolis. This basic element of the emerging spatial order we shall call the "urban field."[23]

The urban field, in this view, represents a fusion of metropolitan areas and nonmetropolitan peripheral areas into core areas each with a minimum population of 300,000 persons and extending outward for approximately one hundred miles, that is, a driving distance of about two hours. In the past metropolitan growth has tended to draw off productive population and investment capital from hinterland areas, but in the future centrifugal forces will reverse this pattern. For one thing, the hinterlands have space, scenery, and communities that are increasingly attractive to metropolitan populations. Demand for these resources is being generated by rising real income, greater leisure, and increasing mobility. Personal income in 1972 has been estimated at $920 billion, a gain of almost 50 percent in a five-year period. Over 40 million Americans now work under employment conditions entitling them to three-week vacations. Federal law now provides five three-day weekends each year, and a trend toward a four-day work week is clearly in evidence, with about two thousand companies now following this precedure. Earlier retirement has been encouraged by improved pension plans and higher Social Security benefits.[24] Access to nonmetropolitan hinterlands has been vastly improved; for example, when the Interstate Highway System is complete an estimated 3.5 to 7.5 million acres will be opened for development.[25]

Dollar sales of leisure equipment (an estimated $105 billion in 1972) have increased by 52 percent over the past five years, reflecting an accelerating desire to "get back to nature." A survey by the Department of the Interior indicates that three quarters of the American population nine years of age and older is involved in some form of outdoor recreation. The most popular outdoor activities, with the shares of the relevant populations who participate, are: picnicking (49 percent), swimming (46 percent), playing outdoor sports (36 percent), attending sports events (35 percent), walking for pleasure (30 percent), fishing (29 percent), boating (24 percent), bicycling (22 percent), camping (21 percent), nature walks (18 percent), and hunting (12 percent). Moreover, about two million American families own second homes used for vacationing, and the number is increasing each year by from one hundred and fifty thousand to two hundred thousand units. In addition, about seventy two thousand "motor homes" are expected to be manufactured in 1972, up from thirteen thousand two hundred only four years ago. About one third of the total mileage driven in private automobiles is devoted to getting to and from vacation areas.[26] Clearly, satisfying leisure-time desires already represents a major opportunity for many nonmetropolitan areas, and growth prospects in this regard have few parallels.

Industrialization of Rural Areas

There has been considerable interest in recent years in programs that would induce greater industrialization of nonmetropolitan areas, and it is common to identify "industry" with manufacturing. However, it is essential to keep in mind that over the past two decades goods-related employment has dropped from 50 percent of nonagricultural employment to only 38 percent; manufacturing employment has declined from 34 percent of the nonagricultural total to 26 percent. Meanwhile the share accounted for by service-related employment has increased from 50 to 62 percent.[27] Moreover, there is abundant evidence that tertiary industry shows less ability or willingness to disperse than does manufacturing.

Nevertheless, many rural areas have experienced considerable growth of manufacturing employment in recent years. This has been particularly true in the South, where it grew at an annual rate of 4.0 percent between 1960 and 1970, compared with only 1.1 percent elsewhere. The South increased its share of national manufacturing employment from 22 to 26 percent over the decade. The absolute increase in southern manufacturing employment was 1489 thousand, which was greater than the increase of 1416 thousand in the rest of the nation. The nonmetropolitan South gained 753,000 manufacturing jobs between 1960 and 1970, while the metropolitan South was gaining only 736,000. The nonmetropolitan annual growth rate in manufacturing was 4.8 percent, compared with 3.5 percent for metropolitan areas. Whereas the nonmetropolitan South accounted for 38 percent of total southern employment in 1970, it accounted for 45 percent of manufacturing employment. In contrast, nonmetropolitan areas had only 33 percent of service employment.[28]

Thomas Till, in a highly detailed analysis of rural industrialization in the South from 1959 to 1969, found that total nonfarm employment in counties more than fifty miles from an SMSA grew by 674,000, or 49 percent.[29] This compares with an almost identical 50 percent growth rate in SMSAs. The "distant" nonmetropolitan counties grew in manufacturing employment by 61 percent, compared with an SMSA growth rate of 44 percent. The distant county absolute increase in manufacturing employment (309,000) was almost half that of the SMSAs (702,000). However, population growth in the distant counties was only 3.5 percent (compared with 22.4 percent for SMSAs), because of large declines in farm employment.

Till examined manufacturing employment change at the two-digit Standard Industrial Classification (SIC) level for a sample of distant counties that represented 47 percent of all relevant counties and 65 percent of their total nonfarm employment. From 1959 to 1969, apparel, electrical machinery, and transportation equipment accounted for the greatest gains in distant county employment. Nevertheless, apparel, lumber and wood products, and food and kindred products were still the dominant sectors in 1969, as they had been in 1959. In general, the growth of nonfarm employment in the distant counties was predominantly in nationally slow-growth industries. Whether or not competitive gains despite a slow-growth industry mix can continue to be made is questionable. However, because the rural South's attractiveness seems to lie largely in its large pool of underemployed and relatively unskilled labor, the growth of labor intensive and low-wage sectors will not bring the incomes of rural southerners up to the levels of the nation as a whole. Of course, it is possible that the objective and subjective advantages of living in smaller places are sufficient to compensate many of the workers for their lower money incomes. This is a subject that needs considerable research but has received almost none.

It should be emphasized that the growth of manufacturing employment in the rural South — and indeed in other rural areas of the country — is quite consistent with Wilbur Thompson's "filtering down" theory of location.

In national perspective, industries filter down through the system of cities, from places of greater to lesser industrial sophistication. Most often, the highest skills are needed in the difficult, early stage of mastering a new process, and skill requirements decline steadily as the production process is rationalized and routinized with experience. As the industry slides down the learning curve, the high wage rates of the more industrially sophisticated innovating areas become superfluous. The aging industry seeks out industrial backwaters where the cheaper labor is now up to the lesser demands of the simplified process.[30]

And it is of course small towns and rural areas that constitute the lowest rung of the filtering process. Thus Thompson argues that a filtering down theory of industrial location goes far in explaining why the

smaller, less industrially advanced area struggles to achieve an average rate of growth out of enlarging shares of slow-growth industries, which were attracted by the area's low wages. It would seem that both the larger industrial centers from which, and the smaller areas to which, industries filter down must run to stand still (at the national average growth rate); the larger areas do, however, run for higher stakes.

The economic development of the smaller, less developed urban area would seem to require that it receive each successive industry a little earlier in its life cycle, to acquire the industry at a point in time when it still has both substantial job-forming potential and high-skill work. Only by upgrading the labor force on the job and by generating the higher incomes (fiscal capacity) needed to finance better schools can the area hope to break out of its underdevelopment trap.[31]

In brief, then, until nonmetropolitan areas, particularly those not in proximity to SMSAs, are able to capture firms earlier in the life cycles of their industries, they will continue in too many cases to run along the treadmill of trading dying industries for mature, low-skill, low-wage industries.

Summary and Conclusions

Recent growth in total national employment has been accounted for primarily by expansion of service-related activities, which for the most part tend to locate in or near metropolitan areas. It has been argued that those industries that have tended to leave metropolitan areas have been characterized by relative stagnation or decline; they frequently seek cheap, nonunion labor in areas with surplus agricultural populations. Rapidly expanding sectors, on the other hand, have favored metropolitan areas because of their numerous external economies of agglomeration. Of course, these generalizations are not ironclad; there obviously are a wide variety of contrasting situations within and between metropolitan and nonmetropolitan areas.

Brian Berry has presented evidence showing that "the degree of metropolitan labor market participation is the key variable in the 'regional welfare syndrome,' indexing the gradient of urban influence on surrounding areas."[32] The degree of this participation continues to increase as transportation improvements contribute to greater mobility. This is not to say, of course, that the prospects for employment opportunities in nonmetropolitan areas are necessarily bleak. If the life styles of most Americans are increasingly "urban" in many respects, it also is true that city dwellers increasingly manifest a desire for the amenities of the countryside. What is emerging is a new scale of life and work that transcends the customary bifurcations between rural and urban, metropolitan and nonmetropolitan. This process will be accentuated in the future by the advent of a whole new spectrum of communications permitting significantly less dense population settlement. Present cities and transportation networks reflect such factors as the need to be near energy sources or to move people and objects. In the future more emphasis will be given to moving information, and in principle it will be possible to work, shop, receive intellectual and cultural achievements, and "visit" with relatives, friends, and business associates at one's home. If the limited survey data we have are correct, these developments correspond to prevalent residential location preferences.

For the more immediate future a hard look must be taken at the varying prospects for nonmetropolitan America. Many small towns and rural areas will continue to benefit from industrial decentralization and from increased mobility and the high income elasticity of demand for leisure-oriented activities. However, many displaced farm workers are not benefiting from increases in rural nonfarm jobs. Many firms moving to nonmetropolitan areas bring workers with them; some attract workers from other areas or "cream" the local labor market. Because of past underinvestment in human resources, displaced farm workers are not the cream of the labor market, and relatively little is being done to prepare them for the more attractive nonfarm jobs.[33]

Inadequate investment in human resources has occurred in many rural areas not only because of inadequate local funds but also because available funds have been squandered on attempts to attract industry. Instead of building better schools and using public amenities to attract firms, many communities have extended direct financial inducements. Some have even gone so far as to grant tax moratoria to new firms, thereby sacrificing many of the gains that industrial development was supposed to bring. Firms attracted by tax incentives often tend to be labor intensive (employing mostly women) and slow-growing, and to pay low wages. Frequently they pull out when other communities offer more favorable tax concessions.

State legislatures have also been prone to single out manufacturing plants for special tax breaks. However, as one examination of this phenomenon points out:

> The practice of making special tax concessions to new industry can have baneful effects on our federal system by setting in motion a self-defeating cycle of competitive tax undercutting and irrational discriminations among business firms. Therefore, states should avoid policies calculated to provide special tax advantages or concessions to selected groups of business firms, and frame their business tax policies along general rather than special benefit lines.[34]

It must be admitted that not all nonmetropolitan areas have significant growth potential, and it may be more sensible to organize an orderly retreat than to fan false hopes for future growth. The Great Plains, for example, have had heavy outmigration for several decades, and quite a few counties within or near this area declined in population during the past decade after having grown previously. There are those who view population decline with alarm, and numerous bills are before Congress to provide special assistance to these "distressed" areas. However, it is difficult to compare the situation in the Great Plains, the Upper Great Lakes, northern New England and other relatively prosperous areas having heavy outmigration with the situation in areas such as central Appalachia, South Texas, the southern Atlantic Coastal Plains, and the Mississippi Delta. In the Great Plains, for example, outmigrants have generally been well prepared to take advantage of economic opportunities in other areas. Of course, the population left behind has a relatively high proportion of older people and it is often difficult to maintain essential services for a widely dispersed population. On the other hand, agriculture is viable and there is relatively little poverty. In addition to savings and farm income there is considerable income from the federal government in the form of farm subsidies and Social Security benefits. There also are viable small towns, although they probably should be developed as service centers for rural hinterlands rather than as "growth centers" capable of halting and even reversing outmigration. Economic theory maintains that outmigration should raise the value of the marginal product of the remaining labor force, other things being equal. This is because each of the remaining workers has more of the nonlabor resources of a given area with which to work. And, in fact, the evidence indicates that population adjustments in the Great Plains reflect successful adaptations not only for outmigrants but also for the people left behind. The greatest acceleration of nonmetropolitan income in the country has taken place in the Great Plains, rising from an annual rate of change of 2.9 percent in the 1950s to 6.2 percent in the 1960s.[35]

Finally, transportation, and in particular highway transportation, has not been considered here because its role is discussed in some detail in the following chapter.

3 The Role of Highways

Introduction

The role of highways as a stimulus to regional economic development has been subject to varying interpretations and evaluations. Probably no one would deny that economic development requires an "adequate" transportation system, but there is no consensus concerning the priority that should be attached to highway construction in development programs.

The notion that the expansion of directly productive activities is a direct result of improved transportation facilities can be traced back to Adam Smith's argument that division of labor is limited by the extent of the market.[1] It would therefore follow that improved transportation should produce more rapid economic growth by helping to expand the market and bring about greater specialization of labor.

In general, improvement in transport conditions permits a reduction in the total resources required to produce and distribute a given volume and pattern of output per time period. Highways enable goods and people to be transferred between and within producing and consuming centers. Highway construction also tends to alter relative factor cost by lowering shipment cost and reducing the time and resources required to move inputs into the area or outputs out of the area. Highways also serve as a public good to be enjoyed by those living in or traveling through an area. Improved or newly constructed highways make possible faster, safer, cheaper, and more dependable transportation. The availability of good roads in the region may well be enough to encourage expansion of existing industry or location of new firms in the region.[2]

The importance of highway transportation also has been linked to the growth center concept, which has played a major part in the regional development strategies of many countries, including the United States. The rationale for a growth center strategy rests heavily on the observation that the spatial concentration of economic activity often provides firms with collective benefits that they would not receive in isolated locations. These take the form of external economies of agglomeration, as distinguished from the internal economies that a firm may generate from the expansion of its own organization. It has been argued that lagging regions can be most efficiently developed by concentrating public and private investment in a relatively few growth centers, and that "spread effects" from induced-growth centers will eventually bring

19

greater prosperity to the surrounding hinterland areas.[3] An analysis of the mechanism through which alleged spread effects operate maintains:

It appears that if there is one critical factor necessary to the concept of a positive spread effect it must be associated with the transportation network, with the technology of communications and with the types of subsidies and supports given to different types of transportation. Communication and transportation services create a framework within which the private sector makes its capital budget decisions. And once in place, the various transportation systems shrink economic distance and by so doing warp and modify market organization.[4]

However, not everyone would agree that highways are so essential to economic development. Some recognize their importance but put more emphasis on their permissive role. Albert Hirschman, for example, finds that the development process involves a complex interaction between human and material resources, with transportation presenting an opportunity for developing other resources.[5] E.K. Hawkins has similarly noted that while transportation improvements may release working capital for more productive use as fixed capital elsewhere, there first must be suitable productive opportunities in potential markets.[6] Citing evidence on the determinants of plant location decisions, John Kuehn and Jerry West conclude that "although transportation is often given as a factor . . . it is only one among many quantifiable factors and subjective considerations. Research results stress the multiplicity of industrial location motives. Highways can trigger further investment activity, but so can other forms of investment."[7]

Howard Gauthier suggests that those who emphasize the developmental role of highways and other forms of transportation may be influenced by Walt Rostow's identification of the railroads as the critical investment sector in the take-off stage of economic growth in the United States, and by Holland Hunter's similar contention that there was a causal linkage between low-cost transportation and economic development. However, he points to more recent evidence that railroad growth after 1830 did not precede the growth of other sectors but rather followed them. Indeed, "the railroad was not indispensable to American growth and . . . in fact transportation capacity in the United States, until the turn of the century, could have been provided by existing waterways. In terms of a causal association, the railroads were built to demand and not in advance of demand."[8]

Beside those who have either espoused the primal role of transportation in the development process, or else emphasized its permissive nature, are those who have argued that too much emphasis on transportation may have a negative effect on long-run growth if it absorbs resources that have more profitable alternative uses. Although accessibility may be a problem, economically lagging regions may have even greater needs for better education and training, more rational use of natural resources, a better industry mix, and less traditional attitudes toward work and migration. In previous studies the present writer has expressed sympathy with this position.[9] Moreover, there is a great deal of recent evidence indicating that the geographic distribution of federal outlays favors less-developed rural areas with respect to per capita transportation outlays but not with respect to per capita outlays for human resource development.[10]

Still, political support for highway construction as a high priority item in development programs remains strong. Some maintain that the lumpiness, longevity, and externalities involved in highway building make calculation of future costs and benefits extremely hazardous. However, the very absence of criteria and sanctions may endear such investments to planners and government officials because they are difficult to prove wrong before they are undertaken and may never become obvious failures.[11] On the other hand it has been argued that highways should not be judged purely on their narrowly economic function, because they may be an integral part of investment in human resources. Thus "If children cannot get to a school for lack of decent transportation, if a pregnant mother cannot get to a hospital for lack of a decent road, if a breadwinner cannot get to a job because the job 30 miles away cannot be reached in a reasonable time, then is such an investment in people or an investment in concrete?"[12] Because these complex issues have been raised frequently in connection with it, the Appalachian Regional Development Program merits at least brief consideration at this point.

Highways and the Appalachian Regional Development Program

The activities of the Appalachian Regional Commission (ARC) — which was created by the Appalachian Regional Development Act of 1965 — represent both an unprecedented effort to develop a large, lagging region of this country and a novel experiment in the reform of intergovernmental relations.[13] In general, the Appalachian experience has been a laboratory for experimenting with institutions and programs that combine (1) respect for national goals; (2) respect for regional and local differences; and (3) broad state and local participation in formulating plans to meet state and local needs.

Before the creation of the ARC, states and local communities were faced with a maze of agencies, regulations, and forms, and it frequently was impossible to put together coordinated plans. To secure federal funding, state agencies had set up direct relationships with counterpart federal agencies, in effect bypassing governors who might have been able to establish priorities and coordinate projects in such a manner as to pursue their attainment efficiently. The Appalachian Regional Development Act gave governors a potentially strong voice in establishing how and where federal funds would be spent in their respective states, and it provided a single federal official with whom they could deal on a wide range of grant programs. Through this procedure the states became brokers between local areas and federal agencies with program funds.

Because of the key role assigned to the governors, it was hoped that state agencies that had operated independently would coordinate their efforts in the planning process. Instead of piecemeal and uncoordinated action, it was now possible to consider systematically which areas have real growth potential and what kinds and amounts of investments they should receive.

The overall objectives of the ARC are to provide every person in the region with the health and skills needed to compete for the opportunities wherever he chooses to live, and to help Appalachia make its own contributions to national growth through the development of the region's full economic potential. However, there purposely has been no attempt to arbitrarily set quantified goals for the region, because it is too vast and varied for this to be tenable. Instead, it has been left largely to each state and area to establish its own objectives within these general goals.

From its birth the ARC has represented a compromise between political expediency on the one hand and more dispassionately determined objectives and the best means for attaining these objectives on the other. For example, many critics of the Appalachian program, myself among them, argued at the outset that far too much emphasis was given to highway construction and far too little to human resource development, the most basic need of Appalachia's people.

In what was probably the most thoroughgoing critical analysis of the Appalachian highway program, John Munro pointed out that of the initial $1.1 billion federal authorization for the total Appalachian program, $840 million was allocated to highway construction over a five-year period, while $252 million was allocated to a number of other social and economic programs over a two-year period. Bringing the two types of programs down to a two-year basis and adding matching state funds, he calculated that about $480 million was to be spent on highways and approximately $281 million on eleven other major categories. But, he argued, "the need for and probable effects of the development of a highway system have never been meaningfully set forth."[14] He further maintained that the system was largely a product of political desires and that little real attention was paid to the development potential of the areas served by the highway corridors chosen to "fill in" the "gaps" in the Interstate System, which directly serves eighteen of the twenty Standard Metropolitan Statistical Areas in Appalachia. Research on the causal relations between highway improvement and economic development was neglected, even though there is evidence that transportation investment has not been a good initiator of economic development in depressed areas. In general, he concluded that the Appalachian highway system "has not been located with reference to planned future growth,"[15] and that the fact that criteria for the construction of the system were developed after funds for the program were authorized is a commentary on the quality of the planning behind the system.

In 1969 I interviewed a number of persons who were instrumental in developing the Appalachian program. In general, it appeared that the "movers and shakers" whose initiative in fact led to the realization of the ARC were by no means unaware of the region's human resource development needs. However, at the time when the commission was created there was considerable opposition from the Office of Economic Opportunity to duplication of its efforts within the framework of the ARC. In addition, the ARC relied heavily on state planning, whereas the OEO relied more on planning at the federal level. It was largely for these reasons that so much emphasis was placed on the development highway system to sell the Appalachian program to Congress. Moreover, one of the most influential of the economists advising the President urged that highways be given priority because Congress could not be sold on another "poverty program." In many respects, then, the highway program was the political price paid for having any commission at all. Fortunately, once the commission was off the ground it proceeded to give considerable attention to the region's human resource needs. It can still legitimately maintain that appropriation cutbacks caused by the Vietnam involvement have caused a serious setback in the highway program, but delays in this regard have probably been more than compensated for by the real gains that have been made in funding and executing health, education, and job-training programs and projects. In any case, there is strong support for the highway program within the ARC, primarily on the ground that it is the matrix within which the human resource investments will prove their effectiveness (e.g., roads are necessary to get children to schools and health facilities as well as to enlarge commuting fields and thereby give workers more opportunities to employ their skills and training without migrating).

In a rebuttal (too detailed to examine at length here) to many of Munro's criticisms of the Appalachian highway system, Ralph Widner, then executive director of the ARC, concluded:

The central part of Appalachia, where half of all the highway investments are concentrated, has a population density in excess of that of the United States as a whole, even though it is unurbanized. It is precisely because this population, though dense, is dispersed that the highway system is a necessary compenent of a regional development program. A transport net is essential in order to bring the several million persons in Appalachia within range of centers where jobs and services can be developed.

There are some low density areas in the Appalachian Highlands traversed by two Appalachian corridors. These corridors are designed to link Charleston, West Virginia, and Baltimore and Cincinnati and intervening points with Baltimore. The highways will open up a large area of Appalachia as an amenity region for the metropolitan areas on either side. Because the area has a low density should it be made impossible for people to use it or get to it? And should that rule out a connection between Charleston and Washington?

Finally, it is true that in many underdeveloped countries and in some of the peripheral regions of the United States, transportation investments have not *by themselves* initiated economic development.

It has never been argued that transportation investments *by themselves* will bring about economic growth in Appalachia.

But we firmly believe that transportation investments combined with other investments in human and physical capital are essential to bring about development in Appalachia. History will prove whose judgment is accurate.

Statistics now begin to indicate that the transportation decision in Appalachia was a valid one. Significant new industrial locations have begun to occur along the development corridors in the most poverty-stricken areas of Appalachia, and commutation patterns are increasingly being strengthened and enlarged.[16]

Widner cites evidence that the corridor in eastern Kentucky, the poorest part of Appalachia, was already showing signs of economic growth. However, a General Accounting Office (GAO) study of a county in the corridor, chosen because it had the typical characteristics of economically distressed areas, questions the success of the highway and other development efforts that have been made in the war on poverty.[17] The GAO investigated Johnson County's progress from fiscal 1965 to fiscal 1969 and found that the federal government had spent $21.5 million in grants, or $243 per year per resident, plus $6.7 million in loans. Despite this infusion of funds, little was accomplished. Among the improvements, one major industrial plant was established, providing about three hundred jobs. There also was considerable upgrading of classroom facilities and the quality of primary and secondary schools. Assistance programs such as food stamps, welfare, health services, and low-rent housing were found to have helped maintain a minimum standard of living, but a continuing need for this kind of aid is anticipated as long as the area is unable to extricate itself from economic depression and chronic unemployment.

A large proportion of federal aid was directed toward economic development, and about half of these funds was used to construct twenty-three miles of highway through the county. Although the highway may eventually bring substantial benefits, it was pointed out that:

"the mountainous terrain, the limited accessibility to supply sources and markets and the relatively unattractive living conditions make it difficult to induce industry to locate in the area. The makeup of the local work force — to a large extent lacking in education and technical skills needed for industrial employment and composed of older persons — may also limit the attraction of industry."[18]

Federal manpower programs trained workers with little prospect that local jobs would be available at the end of the training period. (In response to the GAO study, the superintendent of a well-known vocational school in Johnson County averred, "We're training people here. We don't have any choice about where they go. We've got more people than jobs. Either you shoot them, put them on welfare or train them for jobs somewhere else."[19])

The GAO report suggested that improved planning and coordination of federal programs was necessary, but it also found that no federal agency had overall responsibility to coordinate a wide range of programs in a specific locality. The two agencies most concerned with the development of Johnson County — the ARC and the Economic Development Administration — were urged to become more active in coordinating and planning, and in studying how to attract more industry to rural areas, respectively. The ARC replied that there were statutory and other obstacles to full and effective coordination that would make it difficult for the commission to assert primary responsibility for coordination. The EDA replied that the real cause of poverty in Johnson County was the emphasis on social programs at the expense of development program funds.[20] One is indeed inclined to agree with Harry Caudill's observation that the programs of the Great Society have "aimed at helping Appalachia's poor without inconveniencing any of Appalachia's rich."[21] And unfortunately the fate of Appalachia's poor is shared by too many other Americans.

The Role of Highways in the Present Context

The most massive public works project in the history of mankind, officially known as the National System of Interstate and Defense Highways, was authorized by Congress in the mid-1950s. It was, as one observer noted, "conceived as a concrete response to the Red Menace."[22] Whatever the equation of pavement with patriotism, the system's potential for the development of many areas cannot be denied. (Although, if the Department of Transportation's budget for research into the developmental aspects of the system is a reflection of its true importance in this regard, the pessimists have won going away.)

The particular interest of the system here is that it was largely constructed during the past decade. Population changes in the counties being studied may therefore reasonably be tested against its introduction. A number of major limited-access highways were built concurrently with the Interstate System. Because their economic impact would be similar to that of Interstate Highways, they also are included in the present analysis.

Table 3-1 shows the average distance from an Interstate Highway or other limited-access, divided highway (primarily toll roads) of counties in each of the county categories and regions discussed in chapter 1. In computing these values a county was given a value of 1 if it contained an Interstate Highway or four-lane toll road. 2 if it was one county away from such a road, 3 if it was two counties away, and so forth. The number of counties in each cell is shown in parentheses.

The average value for all counties was 2.15. Consistent Fast Gainers were closest to the relevant highways, with a value of 1.53. Losers were the farthest, with a value of 2.29. Stagnant Gainers had the average value for all counties. Turnaround-Acceleration counties (1.90) were somewhat closer than the overall average, but Turnaround-Reversal counties (2.21) were more distant.

It may be seen that regional variation in the values presented in table 3-2 is greater than variation among the population change classes. On a regional basis the values range from 1.52 in the case of northern Vermont-New Hampshire to 2.56 in the case of central Minnesota-Wisconsin. Nevertheless, in every region

Table 3-1

Average Distance of Counties from Interstate Highways or Limited-Access Divided Highways, by Population Change Group and Distance from SMSA

	1	2	3	4 or More	All Counties
Turnaround-Reversal	1.85 (68)	2.27 (74)	2.56 (43)	2.47 (15)	2.21 (200)
Turnaround-Acceleration	1.59 (29)	1.89 (27)	2.57 (14)		1.90 (70)
Losers	(1.76 (51)	2.20 (70)	2.56 (50)	3.30 (20)	2.29 (191)
Stagnant Gainers	2.00 (16)	1.83 (12)	2.14 (7)	3.40 (5)	2.15 (40)
Consistent Fast Gainers	1.36 (22)	1.75 (8)	2.50 (2)		1.53 (32)
All Counties	1.74 (186)	2.14 (191)	2.53 (116)	3.00 (40)	2.15 (533)

except central Texas the consistent Fast Gainers are closest to the highways, and even in central Texas this group is closer to the average for the region. Moreover, Losers in each region are farther from the highways than the respective regional averages. Turnaround-Acceleration counties are closer to the regional average in every case, although the regional pattern is mixed with respect to Turnaround-Reversal counties.

The data in table 3-1 aid considerably in interpreting these results. They show the average distance from an Interstate Highway or limited-access, divided highway of counties in each of the county categories according to how far counties are from an SMSA. A value of 1 indicates that a county is contiguous with an SMSA, 2 means the county is in the next tier out, and so forth. With two relatively minor exceptions (Turnaround-Reversal counties in the 4 or more group and Stagnant counties in the 2 group), the average distance from a relevant highway consistently increases with distance from an SMSA. The explanation seems fairly straightforward. The Interstate System (and limited-access highways) tends to connect major centers of population, that is, SMSAs. A county bordering an SMSA therefore has a higher probability of being traversed by, or in proximity to, an Interstate Highway than does a county in a distant hinterland area.

The significance of this phenomenon in the present context is best seen by examining the data for each population change class in table 3-1. (A chi-square test based on a contingency table using distance of county from SMSA and the five population change classes led to a rejection of the independence hypothesis at the .001 significance level.)

Table 3-2

Average Distance of Counties from Interstate Highways or Limited-Access Divided Highways, by Population Change and Regional Groups

	Ozarks	Colorado New Mexico Rockies	Central Texas	Central Minnesota-Wisconsin	Northern Vermont-New Hampshire	Tennessee Valley	All Counties
Turnaround-Reversal	2.05 (77)	2.45 (11)	2.00 (6)	2.88 (24)	1.75 (8)	2.18 (74)	2.21 (200)
Turnaround-Acceleration	1.60 (5)	2.50 (6)	1.00 (2)	2.39 (23)	1.33 (9)	1.64 (25)	1.90 (70)
Losers	2.11 (56)	2.59 (22)	2.33 (12)	2.66 (38)	2.00 (2)	2.13 (61)	2.29 (191)
Stagnant Gainers	1.67 (3)	2.67 (6)		2.43 (14)	1.00 (1)	1.88 (16)	2.15 (40)
Consistent Fast Gainers	1.20 (5)	2.20 (5)	1.67 (3)	1.71 (7)	1.00 (1)	1.27 (11)	1.53 (32)
All Counties	2.02 (146)	2.52 (50)	2.04 (23)	2.56 (106)	1.52 (21)	2.01 (187)	2.15 (533)

First, a high proportion — about two thirds — of counties in the Consistent Fast Gainer category are adjacent to SMSAs. It is probably this rather than proximity to the Interstate System that accounts for their growth. Such an interpretation is consistent with Dick Netzer's contention that:

A significant amount of new investment in manufacturing plants in the outer parts of urban areas is not along the lines of new freeways but along *existing,* rather second-rate, highway transportation facilities. Similarly, this is true of much suburban residential development: if transportation is responsible, then it is highway investment in the 1920's and 1930's that accounts for housing in the 1960's.[23]

Similarly, of the remaining population change categories, the Turnaround-Acceleration group has the least average distance to a relevant highway, but it also has the highest proportion of counties in the 1 and 2 groups with respect to distance from an SMSA. A comparable pattern is discernible for the remaining groups. Thus the Loser group differs from the other groups not so much because of distance from a relevant highway but rather because it has a high proportion of counties in the 3 and 4 or more groups with respect to distance from an SMSA.

Because our primary concern is the turnaround counties, it is instructive to consider the difference between the Turnaround-Acceleration and Turnaround-Reversal groups. It will be recalled that the former were not actually declining during the 1950s, whereas the latter were. The accelerated growth of the former appears to be related to their proximity to SMSAs (although counties in the 1 and 2 groups in the Turnaround-Acceleration category are closer to highways than are those in the Turnaround-Reversal group). The Turnaround-Reversal group, on the other hand, has a relatively high proportion of counties at some distance from SMSAs (as has the Losers group). Moreover, within each of the columns the average distance from a highway in Turnaround-Reversal counties does not differ substantially from that in all counties. Thus the explanation for their population reversal does not appear to be related to proximity to highways or SMSAs, but rather must be sought elsewhere.

It might be argued with respect to the data in tables 3-1 and 3-2 that if an Interstate Highway or other limited-access, divided highway crosses only a corner of a county the bulk of its people and economic activity may not really be "on the highway," or at least no more so than are the people and economic activity of a neighboring county that may be just missed by the highway. It may also be argued that two counties may both be on a relevant highway, but if one is traversed by several such highways this should be taken into account. Because of the large number of counties involved it is hoped that problems of this nature "average out" so that valid group comparisons can be made. Nevertheless, tables 3-3 and 3-4 present data analogous to those in tables 3-1 and 3-2. The values in the latter tables however, refer, to the average number of multilane highways per

Table 3-3
Average Number of Multilane Highways, by Population Change Group and Distance from SMSA

	1	2	3	4 or More	All Counties
Turnaround-Reversal	1.85 (68)	1.81 (74)	1.72 (43)	1.87 (15)	1.81 (200)
Turnaround Acceleration	2.66 (29)	2.52 (27)	2.71 (14)		2.61 (70)
Losers	2.16 (51)	1.79 (70)	1.74 (50)	1.75 (20)	1.87 (191)
Stagnant Gainers	2.38 (16)	2.83 (12)	3.14 (7)	1.80 (5)	2.58 (40)
Consistent Fast Gainers	2.36 (22)	3.00 (8)	0.50 (2)		2.41 (32)
All Counties	2.17 (186)	2.02 (191)	1.91 (116)	1.80 (40)	2.03 (533)

county. "Multilane highways" include not only those in the Interstate System and other limited-access, divided highways, as in the previous tables, but also other four-or-more-lane highways, whether divided or not.

The row totals in table 3-3 indicate that the population change categories fall into two distinct groups. Three categories have a relatively high average number of multilane highways: Turnaround-Acceleration counties (2.61), Stagnant Gainers (2.58), and Consistent Fast Gainers (2.41). In contrast, the corresponding values for the other two categories are relatively low: Turnaround-Reversal (1.81) and Losers (1.87). Again there is more variation among regions than among the population change categories. The range for the regions goes from 1.64 for the Colorado-New Mexico Rockies to 3.76 for northern Vermont and New Hampshire (see table 3-4).

The data in table 3-3 are similar to those presented in table 3-1. There is an overall direct relationship between degree of proximity to an SMSA and average number of multilane highways, although this is not the case for several of the population change categories considered separately. The three categories with the highest averages are again those with the greatest proportion of counties near an SMSA. The lowest categories, Turnaround-Reversal and Losers, have a relatively low average number of multilane highways even when only counties adjacent to an SMSA are considered. The same holds for columns 2 and 3. Although lack of highways may have some connection with the decline of Losers, the evidence clearly suggests that such a lack does not preclude growth. The Turnaround-Reversal counties grew despite being in the worst situation with respect to number of multilane highways.

Table 3-4
Average Number of Multilane Highways, by Population Change and Regional Groups

	Ozarks	Colorado-New Mexico Rockies	Central Texas	Central Minnesota-Wisconsin	Northern Vermont-New Hampshire	Tennessee Valley	All Counties
Turnaround-Reversal	1.69 (77)	1.45 (11)	1.50 (6)	2.29 (24)	2.88 (8)	1.74 (74)	1.81 (200)
Turnaround-Acceleration	3.00 (5)	1.67 (6)	1.50 (2)	2.30 (23)	4.11 (9)	2.60 (25)	2.61 (70)
Losers	2.14 (56)	1.59 (22)	2.00 (12)	2.08 (38)	2.50 (2)	1.54 (61)	1.87 (191)
Stagnant Gainers	2.66 (3)	1.83 (6)		2.57 (14)	7.00 (1)	2.56 (16)	2.58 (40)
Consistent Fast Gainers	1.80 (5)	2.00 (5)	1.33 (3)	2.57 (7)	7.00 (1)	2.64 (11)	2.41 (32)
All Counties	1.93 (146)	1.64 (50)	1.74 (23)	2.27 (106)	3.76 (21)	1.91 (187)	2.03 (533)

Summary and Conclusions

Highway construction usually has high priority in regional development programs, and in some quarters it is still felt that highways cause development. Kentucky, for example, has 647 miles of toll roads in addition to the Interstate System and other multilane, divided roads. (Although Kentucky ranks forty-fourth nationally in per capita income, only 7 of its 120 counties are more than one county removed from an express-type highway.) However, tolls have been coming in at rates much lower than expected. In 1969 this led to considerable resistance to proposed new toll roads that would have had to be subsidized by the state. In response, then Governor Louie Nunn "described the roads as 'developmental.' He said the general economic growth which would follow the roads would help pay for them both through increased tax revenues and decreased welfare rolls as jobs become available."[24] It may be too soon to expect results yet the fact remains that four out of every ten Kentuckians still live in poverty conditions, a slightly higher percentage than in 1964. Moreover, less than a third of the poor population lives in the eastern part of the state, which has received highway and other assistance through the Appalachian development program.[25]

Although no doubt there are isolated success stories, emphasis on the causal efficacy of highways with respect to development has diminished in favor of greater emphasis on their permissive role. This has been the case not only in the scholarly literature but also in some development programs, notably that for Appalachia.

The evidence presented in this chapter suggests that differing change patterns among the county categories under consideration are not explainable in terms of proximity to major highways or in terms of number of major highways in a county. Where highways appeared to have an important role in growth, proximity to SMSAs was found to be even more influential. Although counties in the Loser category appeared to be at some disadvantage with respect to highways, lack of highways did not preclude the growth of Turnaround-Reversal counties. Because a high proportion of the latter are in the Ozarks region, it is noteworthy that the results obtained here are consistent with those of Kuehn and West concerning highways and regional development in the Ozarks. Their findings "do not indicate that highways have been crucial factors in economic development within the Ozarks Region."[26] They conclude:

Success in economic development efforts is not assured by construction of more or better highways. As suggested by others who have studied the role of transport, the probability of success is dependent on existence of prior dynamism in the region. The investment in highways must be a part of a cluster of change.[27]

Moreover, analyses of the geographic distribution of federal investments do not indicate that the bottleneck to the growth of lagging nonmetropolitan areas has been a relative lack of highway outlays. If such areas have been shortchanged, it is rather in terms of human resource investments so necessary to the "cluster of change."

To summarize the findings of this chapter with respect to the turnaround counties, it appears that the growth of the Turnaround-Acceleration group is related to their relative closeness to SMSAs. Although proximity to SMSAs or highways may account for the growth of some Turnaround-Reversal counties, a more general explanation must be sought elsewhere.

4

Changes in Employment Structure

The Nature of the Data

This chapter analyzes changes in employment structure in the five groups of nonmetropolitan counties defined in chapter 1. The data are derived from *County Business Patterns,* which is published annually by the Department of Commerce. As table 4-1 shows, the data represent all wage and salary employment of private nonfarm employers covered by Social Security and of nonprofit membership organizations under compulsory Social Security coverage, as well as all employment of religious, charitable, educational, and other nonprofit organizations covered under the elective provisions of the Federal Insurance Contributions Act. The *County Business Patterns* reports are a by-product derived from employment and payroll information reported on Treasury Form 941, Schedule A, supplemented by a special survey of multiunit companies.

Data for the following types of employment covered in whole or in part by the Social Security program are not included in the basic tabulations: governmental employees, self-employed persons, farm workers, and domestic service workers reported separately. Railroad employment subject to the Railroad Retirement Act and employment on oceangoing vessels are also omitted. Governmental and farm employment are clearly the most important omissions.

In accordance with federal law, data that disclose the operations of an individual employer are not published. The number of reporting units in a kind of business and their distribution by employment-size class are not considered a disclosure, and these items may appear in instances where other items of information, such as employment, are withheld. Data are not shown separately for any industry that does not have at least one hundred employees or ten reporting units in an area — county, state, or United States — covered by the tabulation. However, data for an unpublished industry are included in the total shown for the broader industry group of which it is a part. Also, data for some reporting units that could not be classified by detailed kind of business are included in the tabulations in a broader category.

Although disclosure problems are infrequent at the state and national levels, they are common at the county level. An estimation procedure was therefore necessary. Data for the number of reporting units and the number of employees by employment-size class are given for the one-digit and two-digit Standard Industrial Classification (SIC) sectors at the state and national levels. This

33

Table 4-1

Estimated Percent Distribution of Paid Civilian Wage and Salary Employment by Coverage Status under the Social Security Program: March 1969

Employment Group	Percent
Total, paid civilian wage and salary employment[a]	100.0
Covered by Social Security	90.3
In *County Business Patterns* scope	76.0
Not in *County Business Patterns* scope	14.3
Agriculture	1.2
Domestic service	1.8
Government	10.4
Railroad employment[b]	0.9
Not covered by Social Security	9.7
Agriculture	0.1
Domestic service	0.7
Government	8.0
Other	0.9

[a]Excluded from these data are self-employed persons who comprise about 10 percent of all paid civilian employment.

[b]Jointly covered by Social Security and railroad retirement programs.

Source: Department of Health, Education, and Welfare, Social Security Administration, Office of Research and Statistics, Division of Statistics, April 28, 1970.

permitted the calculation of average firm sizes, in terms of employment, for the respective SIC categories and employment-size classes. (Examination of the data indicated that median employment-size class values were usually too large in relation to the computed average values at both the nonmetropolitan county and national levels.)

Because there were seldom more than two or three disclosure problems per county at the one-digit SIC level, it was possible to refine the estimation procedure further. In such cases an estimate was first made for the smallest of the undisclosed sectors. The estimate was added to the disclosed sector total, and the resulting sum was then subtracted from the county total, with the balance being attributed to the larger undisclosed sector. This method may be illustrated by reference to the *County Business Patterns* data in table 4-2, which refers to Hancock County, Mississippi.

The first sector, agricultural services, forestry, fisheries, and the last, unclassified establishments, are undisclosed. The first has only one reporting unit, and it is in the 1 to 3 employment-size class. Adding the estimated value of 2 to the disclosed sector total and subtracting this sum from 3900 (the county total) leaves a residual of 70, which is attributed to unclassified establishments. (This value may be compared with the value of 84 which would have been

Table 4-2

Employment in Hancock County, Mississippi, First Quarter, 1970, as Reported in *County Business Patterns*

SIC Code	Industry	Number of Employees, mid-March Pay Period	Taxable Payrolls, Jan.-Mar. ($1000)	Total Reporting Units	Number of Reporting Units By Employment Size Class							
					1 to 3	4 to 7	8 to 19	20 to 49	50 to 99	100 to 249	250 to 499	500 or more
	Total	3,900	8,032	220	108	45	36	21	6	1	2	1
...	Agricultural Services, Forestry, Fisheries	(D)	(D)	1	1	—	—	—	—	—	—	—
...	Contract Construction	248	298	33	16	9	5	2	1	—	—	—
15	General Building Contractors	141	195	11	4	3	2	1	1	—	—	—
17	Special Trade Contractors	(D)	(D)	19	10	6	2	1	—	—	—	—
...	Manufacturing	2,155	6,059	15	4	3	3	1	—	1	2	1
19	Ordnance and Accessories	(D)	(D)	1	—	—	—	—	—	—	1	—
34	Frabricated Metal Products	(D)	(D)	1	—	—	—	—	—	—	1	—
346	Metal Stampings	(D)	(D)	1	—	—	—	—	—	1	—	—
36	Electrical Equipment & Supplies	(D)	(D)	2	—	—	1	—	—	—	—	1
367	Electronic Components & Accessories	(D)	(D)	1	—	—	1	—	—	—	—	—
3679	Electronic Components, NEC	(D)	(D)	1	—	—	1	—	—	—	—	—
—	Administrative and Auxiliary	(D)	(D)	4	1	1	1	1	—	—	—	—
...	Transportation and Other Public Utilities	136	248	10	7	—	1	1	1	—	—	—
49	Electric, Gas and Sanitary Service	(D)	(D)	3	1	—	1	—	1	—	—	—
...	Wholesale Trade	61	87	7	4	—	2	1	—	—	—	—
...	Retail Trade	495	487	67	33	11	15	8	—	—	—	—
54	Food Stores	104	108	12	6	3	—	3	—	—	—	—
55	Automotive Dealers & Service Stations	91	129	19	13	3	2	1	—	—	—	—
554	Gasoline Service Stations	31	26	13	11	1	1	—	—	—	—	—
58	Eating and Drinking Places	161	110	13	2	1	8	2	—	—	—	—
...	Finance, Insurance, Real Estate	154	214	19	8	8	1	2	—	—	—	—
...	Services	579	543	56	30	10	7	5	4	—	—	—
73	Miscellaneous Business Services	(D)	(D)	4	1	1	—	1	1	—	—	—
...	Unclassified Establishments	(D)	(D)	12	5	4	2	1	—	—	—	—

Source: *County Business Patterns, Mississippi, 1970.*

attributed if the averaging method had been applied directly to the reporting units in unclassified establishments (i.e., (5 X 2) + (4 X 5) + (2 X 12) + (1 X 30) = 84.)

This residual method of calculation was generally not possible at the two-digit SIC level because of the large number of undisclosed values. For example, in the case of Hancock County there are four reporting units listed at the two-digit level. They include one in ordnance and accessories in the 250 to 499 employment-size class, one in fabricated metal products in the 100 to 249 class, and two units in electrical equipment and supplies, in the 8 to 19 and 500 or more classes, respectively. Adding the four average values for these classes gives a value of 2137. This estimate is no doubt too high, because there are only 2155 employees in all fifteen manufacturing reporting units. It is assumed, however, that although such biases might seriously affect the analysis of one or a few counties, they will not seriously impair comparisons of employment change among large groups of counties.

The period from 1959 to 1969 was used to minimize distortions that might have been caused by the business cycle. However, it was not until 1964 that separate *County Business Patterns* information became available for counties in Georgia, Illinois, Kansas, Kentucky, Missouri, North Carolina, Texas, and Virginia which previously had been combined with contiguous counties. For this reason the following analyses involve the 1964-69 period as well as the longer interval.

Employment Change: One-Digit SIC Code Sector Level

Table 4-3 presents absolute and percentage change in employment for each one-digit SIC code sector by population change category for all of the counties in the study. The 1964-69 figures include all counties, whereas the 1959-69 figures include only those counties for which data were available for 1959. In central Texas 1959 data were available for only one county of the 24 included in the study. Data for 1959 were available for 109 of the 147 Ozarks counties and 166 of the 186 Tennessee Valley counties. On the other hand 1959 data were available for all but two counties in the Colorado-New Mexico Rockies and for all counties in northern Vermont and New Hampshire and central Minnesota and Wisconsin.

The 1959-69 percentage change data show that counties in the Loser category had the lowest total employment growth. They had the greatest losses in mining and unclassified employment as well as the lowest percentage and absolute gains in all sectors except agriculture. The 1964-69 data present a similarly bleak picture, although the gain in service employment is the highest of any category, a phenomenon that will be considered later when service employment change is analyzed at the two-digit level.

At the other end of the spectrum, counties in the Consistent Fast Gainer category had the greatest percentage increase in total employment for both the 1959-69 and 1964-69 periods. During the former period they had the highest growth rates in transportation; wholesale trade; retail trade; finance, insurance, and real estate (FIRE); and services. They were next highest in construction. Their rate of growth from 1964 to 1969 was the highest in agriculture, transportation, wholesale trade, and retail trade. It was next to highest in manufacturing.

The Stagnant Gainer counties ranked fourth in total employment percentage gain in both periods. Their growth rate was not first in any sector between 1959 and 1969, although growth in construction was the highest from 1964 to 1969. In general they ranked relatively low in most sectors, often leading only the Losers. Their relatively better showing in the 1964-69 period may be accounted for by the inclusion of a large number of counties from central Texas, the Ozarks, and the Tennessee Valley, for which 1959 data were not available.

For the 1959-69 period the Turnaround-Reversal counties ranked highest in rate of growth in agriculture, mining, and manufacturing and next to highest in growth of total employment, wholesale trade and FIRE. The key to their relatively rapid growth in total employment was manufacturing, because absolute growth in agriculture and mining was small. In absolute terms manufacturing accounted for over half of the total employment increase in the Turnaround-Reversal group, or 122,727 out of a net gain of 226,404 jobs. For the 1964-69 period this group did not rank lowest with respect to rate of change in any sector, but it did rank next to lowest in the construction, transportation, and retail trade sectors. It ranked highest in the mining, manufacturing, FIRE, and unclassified sectors. It also ranked just behind the Consistent Fast Gainer category in rate of growth of total employment. As in the 1959 to 1969 period, when absolute levels of employment increase are examined, it is apparent that the high rate of growth in total employment was due to the growth of manufacturing employment, since the other sectors of rapid percentage increase involved relatively few jobs in absolute terms. Between 1964 and 1969 total employment had a net increase of 176,434, of which 94,729 was accounted for by manufacturing.

The importance of manufacturing growth is much less apparent in the Turnaround-Acceleration counties than in the Turnaround-Reversal group. During both the 1959-69 and the 1964-69 periods the Turnaround-Acceleration counties ranked third in rate of increase in manufacturing employment and below the rate of manufacturing growth for all counties. In terms of rate of growth they did relatively well in construction, ranking first in 1959-69 and second in 1964-69; in retail trade, where they ranked second in both periods; and in services, where they ranked second in 1959-69 and a strong third in 1964-69.

The overall picture gained from the data in table 4-3 is consistent with the

Table 4-3

Absolute and Percentage Employment Change by Sector (One-digit SIC Code) in Selected Counties from Six Regions by Population Change Category, 1964-69 and 1959-69

	Total	Agricultural Services, Forestry, Fisheries	Mining	Contract Construction	Manufacturing
Absolute Change, 1964-69					
Loser	89,924	269	-2,025	5,948	34,961
Stagnant Gainer	108,753	140	765	9,966	51,397
Turnaround-Reversal	176,434	894	2,200	9,741	94,729
Turnaround-Acceleration	151,081	396	-552	12,590	63,015
Consistent Fast Gainer	73,784	411	-175	5,344	30,717
Percentage Change, 1964-69					
Loser	21.4	8.7	-11.2	30.1	20.4
Stagnant Gainer	29.5	13.4	8.5	54.3	28.1
Turnaround-Reversal	36.6	28.5	21.2	40.8	43.7
Turnaround-Acceleration	33.8	17.7	-8.5	53.3	33.1
Consistent Fast Gainer	37.3	35.7	-14.5	50.4	35.1
Absolute Change, 1959-69					
Loser	87,605	650	-3,715	3,382	45,341
Stagnant Gainer	121,055	318	-496	7,848	56,465
Turnaround-Reversal	226,404	1,876	2,426	11,790	122,727
Turnaround-Acceleration	202,441	878	-524	16,524	83,715
Consistent Fast Gainer	100,562	281	-10	6,005	43,158
Percentage Change, 1959-69					
Loser	26.1	34.4	-22.0	20.2	36.1
Stagnant Gainer	40.3	42.7	-6.2	50.0	36.8
Turnaround-Reversal	58.9	98.5	31.8	64.4	72.9
Turnaround-Acceleration	52.8	51.5	-8.2	90.7	49.8
Consistent Fast Gainer	71.5	25.2	-1.0	82.0	65.6

Table 4-3 (Continued)
Employment Change

	Transportation and Other Public Utilities	Wholesale Trade	Retail Trade	Finance, Insurance, and Real Estate (FIRE)	Services	Unclassified Establishments
Absolute Change, 1964-69						
Loser	986	3,340	16,200	3,644	26,092	422
Stagnant Gainer	3,627	3,983	17,129	3,515	18,109	140
Turnaround-Reversal	4,262	4,413	24,071	6,372	28,809	844
Turnaround-Acceleration	4,784	3,498	29,671	5,893	31,580	378
Consistent Fast Gainer	3,048	2,983	15,236	1,831	14,090	258
Percentage Change, 1964-69						
Loser	3.8	16.0	16.8	21.3	55.4	23.9
Stagnant Gainer	20.8	23.6	25.9	24.2	43.5	12.6
Turnaround-Reversal	18.2	19.9	23.1	37.3	48.7	34.9
Turnaround-Acceleration	21.8	15.5	33.1	29.8	46.5	26.3
Consistent Fast Gainer	31.0	33.6	38.3	23.2	46.8	33.3
Absolute Change, 1959-69						
Loser	571	2,119	15,037	4,492	26,000	-1,186
Stagnant Gainer	4,735	4,213	19,740	5,384	23,335	-502
Turnaround-Reversal	5,219	6,073	30,974	8,834	37,366	-934
Turnaround-Acceleration	6,538	5,309	36,295	9,490	44,460	-766
Consistent Fast Gainer	4,240	4,065	18,898	3,920	20,009	-26
Percentage Change, 1959-69						
Loser	2.6	12.1	19.3	34.7	72.7	-40.0
Stagnant Gainer	34.2	30.7	36.7	50.4	80.5	-31.1
Turnaround-Reversal	25.0	32.7	35.5	67.4	83.5	-23.4
Turnaround-Acceleration	33.4	26.1	45.5	60.7	87.2	-30.7
Consistent Fast Gainer	61.3	62.3	66.1	87.1	111.3	-2.6

general arguments presented in chapter 2, as well as with the findings of chapter 3. The Consistent Fast Gainer group, as might be expected from their relative proximity to SMSAs, not only has the highest rates of growth in total employment but also ranks particularly high in those sectors that are most "urban" in nature, i.e., transportation, wholesale and retail trade, FIRE, and services. The turnaround counties have next highest growth rates in total employment, yet the reasons differ between the two groups. In chapter 3 it was pointed out that the growth of the Turnaround-Acceleration counties was probably better explained by their proximity to SMSAs than by highways, and that the explanation for the growth of the Turnaround-Reversal group was to be found elsewhere than in highways or proximity to SMSAs. The employment change data indicate that Turnaround-Acceleration counties have done relatively well in growth of non-goods-producing jobs. Although the growth of some of these sectors has been relatively high for the Turnaround-Reversal group, the major source of its expansion has been manufacturing. In contrast, the Stagnant Gainers and Losers have had low total employment growth, and they rank low in most sectors.

Employment Change: Two-Digit SIC Code Level for Manufacturing

Table 4-4 shows employment change in the Turnaround-Reversal and Turnaround-Acceleration categories by two-digit SIC code for manufacturing and services, which are key sectors in terms of the discussion in chapter 2. As pointed out earlier in this chapter, estimates of employment where there were disclosure problems were more difficult at the two-digit level than at the one-digit level, and the various subsectors shown in table 4-4 do not of course sum to the manufacturing and services totals shown in table 4-3. Nevertheless, the data reveal clear patterns in the structure of employment change.

The Turnaround-Reversal counties had considerably greater absolute growth and rate of change of manufacturing employment than did the Turnaround-Acceleration counties for both the 1964-69 and the 1959-69 periods. Moreover, for most manufacturing sectors the Turnaround-Reversal counties had higher rates of growth in both periods. It is particularly noteworthy that in no manufacturing sector did the Turnaround-Acceleration counties have a higher rate of growth than did the Turnaround-Reversal counties for both periods. The strong performance of the Turnaround-Reversal group in manufacturing was largely a result of strong gains in four sectors. Between 1964 and 1969 employment in electrical equipment and supplies increased by 18,594; in rubber and plastics by 16,775; in apparel and other textile products by 15,083; and in transportation equipment by 14,686. Together these sectors accounted for 65,138 of the total increase of 107,934. They also accounted for 84,583 of the total manufacturing

Table 4-4

Absolute and Percentage Employment Change by Manufacturing and Service Sector (Two-digit SIC Code) in Turnaround Counties in Six Regions, 1964-69 and 1959-69

	Manufacturing	Ordnance and Accessories	Food and Kindred Products	Textile Mill Products	Apparel and Other Textile Products
Absolute Change, 1964-69					
Turnaround-Reversal	107,934	1,814	7,370	4,189	15,083
Turnaround-Acceleration	59,541	6,224	1,209	4,007	2,686
Percentage Change, 1964-69					
Turnaround-Reversal	49.2	46.5	40.7	17.4	28.1
Turnaround-Acceleration	32.3		5.2	17.7	16.8
Absolute Change, 1959-69					
Turnaround-Reversal	136,594	5,500	7,629	6,914	28,885
Turnaround-Acceleration	79,137	2,719	3,932	2,428	5,714
Percentage Change, 1959-69					
Turnaround-Reversal	79.9	2,594.3	46.9	33.9	81.3
Turnaround-Acceleration	48.4	77.5	19.4	10.0	44.9

Table 4-4 (Continued)
Six Regions

	Lumber and Wood Products	Furniture and Fixtures	Paper and Allied Products	Printing and Publishing	Chemicals and Allied Products
Absolute Change, 1964-69					
Turnaround-Reversal	−649	4,237	2,580	1,524	5,780
Turnaround-Acceleration	−238	1,872	1,673	2,270	2,933
Percentage Change, 1964-69					
Turnaround-Reversal	−2.9	82.8	55.2	69.7	191.6
Turnaround-Acceleration	−2.4	26.3	13.6	35.5	41.9
Absolute Change, 1959-69					
Turnaround-Reversal	−5,031	6,888	2,348	1,967	4,191
Turnaround-Acceleration	−1,133	2,409	4,361	0	4,145
Percentage Change, 1959-69					
Turnaround-Reversal	−19.8	298.4	60.1	124.1	94.1
Turnaround-Acceleration	−10.9	36.6	45.4	0.0	71.6

43

Table 4-4 (Continued)
Six Regions

	Petroleum and Coal Products	Rubber and Plastics Products, NEC	Leather and Leather Products	Stone, Clay, and Glass Products	Primary Metal Industry
Absolute Charge, 1964-69					
Turnaround-Reversal	−185	16,775	2,034	−105	4,676
Turnaround-Acceleration	0	2,553	1,649	443	6,516
Percentage Change, 1964-69					
Turnaround-Reversal	−53.9	444.4	13.7	−1.3	124.6
Turnaround-Acceleration	0.0	58.1	15.8	8.9	120.9
Absolute Charge, 1959-69					
Turnaround-Reversal	0	18,586	5,600	1,826	3,536
Turnaround-Acceleration	0	4,201	1,614	878	7,394
Percentage Change, 1959-69					
Turnaround-Reversal	0.0	1,273.0	53.1	33.9	80.6
Turnaround-Acceleration	0.0	153.2	15.4	19.4	164.0

Table 4-4 (Continued)
Six Regions

	Fabricated Metal Products	Machinery except Electrical	Electrical Equipment and Supplies	Transportation Equipment	Instruments and Related Products
Absolute Change, 1964-69					
Turnaround-Reversal	5,777	6,960	18,594	14,686	3,189
Turnaround-Acceleration	3,482	1,108	11,971	−41,106	2,580
Percentage Change, 1964-69					
Turnaround-Reversal	109.8	92.6	176.9	117.9	401.1
Turnaround-Acceleration	45.4	5.9	75.0	−80.6	105.6
Absolute Change, 1959-69					
Turnaround-Reversal	6,553	9,476	20,480	16,632	3,493
Turnaround-Acceleration	5,553	8,539	18,914	2,067	4,510
Percentage Change, 1959-69					
Turnaround-Reversal	198.2	197.2	406.2	158.4	711.4
Turnaround-Acceleration	99.3	76.1	209.8	26.4	882.5

Table 4-4 (Continued)
Six Regions

	Miscellaneous Manufacturing Industries	Tobacco Manufactures	Services	Hotels and Other Lodging Places	Personal Services
Absolute Change, 1964-69					
Turnaround-Reversal	2,506	-1,317	28,784	1,687	897
Turnaround-Acceleration	923	159	29,439	3,357	288
Percentage Change, 1964-69					
Turnaround-Reversal	55.3	-72.8	47.9	24.5	9.4
Turnaround-Acceleration	36.6	62.8	44.5	54.0	3.4
Absolute Change, 1959-69					
Turnaround-Reversal	3,052	173	36,896	3,535	2,173
Turnaround-Acceleration	718	-4	42,755	5,854	1,142
Percentage Change, 1959-69					
Turnaround-Reversal	91.5	108.8	80.2	75.0	28.7
Turnaround-Acceleration	26.3	-.9	87.3	164.2	15.8

Table 4-4 (Continued)
Six Regions

	Miscellaneous Business Services	Auto Repair, Services, and Garages	Miscellaneous Repair Services	Motion Pictures	Amusement and Recreation Services, NEC
Absolute Change, 1964-69					
Turnaround-Reversal	420	221	21	0	1,044
Turnaround-Acceleration	1,306	602	498	0	1,339
Percentage Change, 1964-69					
Turnaround-Reversal	74.8	14.1	12.7	0.0	67.7
Turnaround-Acceleration	75.5	40.8	117.1	0.0	58.7
Absolute Change, 1959-69					
Turnaround-Reversal	855	739	34	0	1,393
Turnaround-Acceleration	2,143	1,012	660	0	2,474
Percentage Change, 1959-69					
Turnaround-Reversal	78.5	72.8	22.3	0.0	137.9
Turnaround-Acceleration	240.5	100.0	250.9	0.0	215.8

Table 4-4 (Continued)
Six Regions

	Medical and Other Services	Legal Services	Educational Services	Museums, Botanical, Zoological Gardens	Nonprofit Membership Organizations
Absolute Change, 1964-69					
Turnaround-Reversal	13,107	353	1,397	0	9,400
Turnaround-Acceleration	9,023	263	6,739	36	5,155
Percentage Change, 1964-69					
Turnaround-Reversal	77.0	100.8	54.4	0.0	248.5
Turnaround-Acceleration	41.0	25.5	81.2		105.2
Absolute Change, 1959-69					
Turnaround-Reversal	16,964	452	1,828	0	9,686
Turnaround-Acceleration	14,257	546	9,340	36	4,396
Percentage Change, 1959-69					
Turnaround-Reversal	147.2	180.0	100.0	0.0	348.5
Turnaround-Acceleration	88.6	72.9	176.0		100.0

employment increase of 136,594 in the Turnaround-Reversal counties between 1959 and 1969, although they ranked differently. During this period the biggest absolute gain was in apparel and other textile products (28,885), followed by electrical equipment and supplies (20,480), rubber and plastics (18,586), and transportation equipment (16,632). The apparel sector alone accounted for 21 percent of the total absolute growth in manufacturing.

In view of Wilbur Thompson's thesis that rural areas tend to receive low-wage, slow-growth industries spun off by the cities it is appropriate to consider the apparel sector in greater detail. Between 1960 and 1970 this sector grew in employment by 12 percent nationally, whereas employment in nonagricultural industries grew by 33 percent, in manufacturing by 15 percent, and in nondurable goods by 12 percent. Thus, although apparel employment grew at the same rate as nondurable goods employment it was nonetheless a relatively slow-growing sector in a larger context. It came off even worse with respect to average weekly hours of work and average hourly earnings. In 1970 production workers in the private sector worked an average of 37.2 hours and earned $3.23 per hour. In manufacturing they worked an average of 39.8 hours and earned $3.36 per hour. In the nondurable goods sector they worked an average 39.1 hours and received an average $3.08 per hour. In contrast, apparel workers on the average worked only 35.3 hours and received average hourly earnings of only $2.39.[1] Clearly the importance of the apparel sector in the growth of manufacturing employment in the Turnaround-Reversal counties is consistent with the Thompson thesis. In contrast, this sector was not nearly so important to manufacturing growth in the Turnaround-Acceleration counties. For the 1964-69 period it accounted for only 2686 of the total manufacturing increase of 59,541; for the 1959-69 period it accounted for only 5714 of the total increase of 79,137.

The electrical equipment and supplies sector was one of the fastest growing in both the Turnaround-Reversal and Turnaround-Acceleration groups. For the 1964-69 period it accounted for 17 percent of the total manufacturing increase in the former group and for 20 percent of the comparable increase in the latter. For the 1959-69 period it accounted for 15 percent of the manufacturing increase in the former and for almost a quarter of the increase (24 percent) in the latter. In contrast to the apparel sector, the electrical equipment sector grew in employment by 30 percent nationally between 1960 and 1970, just behind the rate for nonagricultural industries but twice the rate of manufacturing and almost twice the 18 percent rate of employment growth for durable goods. In 1970 production workers in this sector worked an average of 39.9 hours and received average hourly earnings of $3.29. The comparable values for the durable goods sector in general were 40.3 hours and $3.56.[2] Nevertheless, the electrical equipment and supplies sector still was close to the comparable values for total employment in the private sector and in manufacturing (see above). It would therefore be difficult to call this sector marginal in any sense.

The other two sectors that account for the major share of Turnaround-Reversal manufacturing growth — rubber and plastic products and transportation equipment — were not so important in the Turnaround-Acceleration counties. The rubber and plastic products sector grew in employment nationally by 51 percent between 1960 and 1970; in 1970 the average weekly hours worked was 40.3 and average hourly earnings was $3.20. The transportation equipment sector grew by only 16 percent, but average hours worked in 1970 was 40.3 and average hourly earnings was a relatively high $4.07.[3]

After the four major sectors just discussed, absolute employment growth in the Turnaround-Reversal counties was greatest in the machinery (except electrical) and food and kindred products sectors. (This was the case for both periods.) The former grew nationally in employment by 33 percent between 1960 and 1970, whereas the latter did not show any increase.

As pointed out above, the Turnaround-Acceleration counties had their greatest absolute increase in the electrical equipment and supplies sector. This was the case for both the 1959-69 and the 1964-69 periods (see table 4-5). Of the eight leading Turnaround-Acceleration sectors in 1959-69 in terms of absolute growth, five were also among the top eight covered by 1964-69 data. For the 1959-69 period the two leading Turnaround-Acceleration sectors — electrical equipment and machinery — together accounted for over one third of total manufacturing growth in this group of counties. Moreover, the national growth rates for these sectors were twice that for manufacturing and the same as that for all private sector nonagricultural industries. The remaining leading sectors were mixed with respect to national growth rates and average hourly earnings. For the 1964-69 period the leading electrical equipment sector accounted for 20 percent of the total manufacturing increase, but the next three sectors, which were very slow-growing nationally, accounted for 28 percent. These differences between the two periods are of course partly caused by regional differences in data availability for 1959. It is also worth noting that similar differences occur between the two periods for the Turnaround-Reversal group. The leading sector for the 1959-69 period was slow growing nationally, but it was followed by two fast-growing sectors (which together accounted for 30 percent of the total manuafacturing gain). However, the two leading sectors for the 1964-69 period were fast growing nationally and accounted for about one third of the total manufacturing increase, whereas the next three sectors were slow growing nationally (see table 4-6).

To generalize, manufacturing employment in both turnaround groups grew considerably faster than the national 1960-70 growth rate of 15 percent, even when only the 1964-69 period is considered. (This is true with respect to the estimates in table 4-3, based on one-digit SIC code sectors or the two-digit estimates shown in table 4-4.) However, both in absolute increase and rate of change the growth of manufacturing was much more important to the Turnaround-Reversal counties than to those in the Turnaround-Acceleration

Table 4-5
Manufacturing Employment Change by Sector in Turnaround-Acceleration Counties, Ranked by Absolute Employment Change

Sector	Absolute Change	Percent Change	National Employment Change (Percent)[a]	National Average Hourly Earnings, 1970[a]
			1959-1969	
Electrical equipment and supplies	18,914	210	30	3.29
Machinery, except electrical	8,539	76	33	3.77
Primary metal industries	7,394	164	06	3.94
Apparel and other textile products	5,714	45	12	2.39
Fabricated metal products	5,553	99	22	3.53
Instruments and related products	4,510	882	30	3.34
Paper and allied products	4,361	45	18	3.44
Rubber and plastic products, NEC	4,201	153	51	3.20
MANUFACTURING	79,137	48	15	3.36
			1964-1969	
Electrical equipment and supplies	11,971	75	30	3.29
Primary metal industries	6,516	121	06	3.94
Ordnance and accessories	6,224		13	3.61
Textile mill products	4,007	18	04	2.45
Fabricated metal products	3,482	45	22	3.53
Chemicals and allied products	2,933	42	28	3.69
Apparel and other textile products	2,686	17	12	2.39
Instruments and related products	2,580	106	30	3.34
MANUFACTURING	59,541	32	15	3.36
Nonagricultural industries (private sector)	---	---	33	3.23

[a]U.S. Bureau of the Census, *Statistical Abstract of the United States, 1971* (Washington, D.C.: Government Printing Office, 1971), pp. 219-21.

Table 4-6
Manufacturing Employment Change by Sector in Turnaround-Reversal Counties, Ranked by Absolute Employment Change

Sector	Absolute Change	Percent Change	National Employment Change (Percent)[a]	National Average Hourly Earnings, 1970[a]
1959-1969				
Apparel and other textile products	28,885	81	12	2.39
Electrical equipment and supplies	20,480	406	30	3.29
Rubber and plastic products, NEC	18,586	1,273	51	3.20
Transportation equipment	16,632	158	16	4.07
Machinery, except electrical	9,476	197	33	3.77
Food and kindred products	7,629	47	00	3.16
Textile mill products	6,914	34	04	2.45
Furniture and fixtures	6,888	298	20	2.77
MANUFACTURING	136,594	80	15	3.36
1964-1969				
Electrical equipment and supplies	18,594	177	30	3.29
Rubber and plastic products, NEC	16,775	444	51	3.20
Apparel and other textile products	15,083	28	12	2.39
Transportation equipment	14,686	118	16	4.07
Food and kindred products	7,370	41	00	3.16
Machinery, except electrical	6,960	93	33	3.77
Chemicals and allied products	5,780	192	28	3.69
Fabricated metal products	5,777	110	22	3.53
MANUFACTURING	107,934	49	15	3.36
Nonagricultural industries (private sector)	---	---	33	3.23

[a]U.S. Bureau of the Census, *Statistical Abstract of the United States, 1971* (Washington, D.C.: Government Printing Office, 1971), pp. 219-21.

group. When manufacturing employment change is examined at the two-digit level, it appears that growth from this source in the Turnaround-Reversal group is based more on the attraction of nationally slow-growing sectors than is the case for the Turnaround-Acceleration group, although the difference is not marked. The data thus are consistent with Thompson's trickle-down hypothesis concerning manufacturing decentralization, especially inasmuch as the Turnaround-Reversal counties tend to be more distant from SMSAs than are those in the Turnaround-Acceleration group. However, the evidence is sufficiently mixed that qualifications would have to be made concerning differences between regions and even within regions.

Employment Change: Two-Digit SIC Code Level for Services

Between 1960 and 1970 service employment in the nation grew by 56 percent.[4] The one-digit SIC estimates indicate that service employment grew by 87 percent in the Turnaround-Acceleration group and by 84 percent in the Turnaround-Reversal group from 1959 to 1969. (The corresponding 1964-69 rates for the two groups were 46 and 49 percent, respectively.) The two-digit estimates give approximately the same results (see table 4-4).

Before considering the nature of this evolution it is first necessary to note the large employment changes in medical and health and nonprofit membership organization employment, particularly those in the Turnaround-Reversal group. For this last group, these two sectors account for 72 percent of the total absolute change in service employment from 1959 to 1969 and for 78 percent of the total absolute change from 1964 to 1969. I made inquiries among persons familiar with *County Business Patterns* data to determine if such large changes might have been the result of new Social Security coverage rather than actual employment increases. On the basis of these investigations it appears that the increase in medical and health employment is actual employment growth resulting from the rapid growth of rural hospitals and health facilities made possible by the Hill-Burton Act. The increase in the nonprofit organizations is somewhat more difficult to pinpoint. During the 1960s there was considerable growth of cooperatives and similar organizations in rural areas. In some cases farmers who were not covered may have become covered upon joining such organizations. The amount of true employment increase reflected in the nonprofit organization figures can thus be only conjectural.

In any case, the data shown in table 4-7 reveal important differences in the two categories of turnaround counties. The more rural Turnaround-Reversal counties had greater absolute growth in the medical and health sector for both periods, even though the percentage change figures indicate that they began from a lower base than did the more "urban" Turnaround-Acceleration counties. The growth in nonprofit membership employment in the Turnaround-Reversal

Table 4-7

Service Employment Change by Sector in Turnaround Counties, Ranked by Absolute Employment Change

	Turnaround-Reversal			Turnaround-Acceleration	
Sector	Absolute Change	Percent Change	Sector	Absolute Change	Percent Change
1964-1969					
Medical and other health services	13,107	77	Medical and other health services	9,023	41
Nonprofit membership organizations	9,400	248	Educational services	6,739	81
Hotels and other lodging places	1,687	24	Nonprofit membership organizations	5,155	105
Educational services	1,397	54	Hotels and other lodging places	3,357	54
Amusement and recreation services, NEC	1,044	68	Amusement and recreation services, NEC	1,339	59
1959-1969					
Medical and other health services	16,964	147	Medical and other health services	14,257	89
Nonprofit membership organizations	9,686	348	Educational services	9,340	176
Hotels and other lodging places	3,535	75	Hotels and other lodging places	5,854	164
Personal services	2,173	29	Nonprofit membership organizations	4,396	100
Educational services	1,828	100	Amusement and recreation services, NEC	2,474	216

counties is considerably greater in absolute numbers and still greater in terms of rate of increase. This remarkable increase is consistent with the educated guess that it is related to the formation of agriculturally related organizations in the more rural Turnaround-Reversal group.

Examination of the other leading sectors with respect to absolute growth also indicates that Turnaround-Acceleration counties benefited more from participation in urban fields. Educational services employment ranks second in growth for these counties during both periods. It grew by 81 percent from 1964 to 1969 (compared with 54 percent in the Turnaround-Reversal counties, which also had a much lower base) and by 176 percent from 1959 to 1969 (compared with 100 percent in the Turnaround-Reversal counties).

Both groups of counties did well in employment growth in the hotel and other lodging places sector, which grew by 33 percent nationally from 1960 to 1970.[5] From 1959 to 1969 this sector ranked third in absolute increase in the Turnaround-Acceleration group, increasing by 164 percent, compared with a 75 percent increase in the Turnaround-Reversal group, where it also ranked third. For the 1964-69 period, the rates of growth were 54 and 24 percent, respectively.

Employment related to recreation ranked fifth in the Turnaround-Acceleration counties during both periods but had a high 216 percent rate of growth for 1959-69. This sector ranked fifth for the Turnaround-Reversal group for 1964-69 but only sixth for 1959, despite growth of 138 percent.

Summary and Conclusions

In chapter 2 it was argued that urban and rural America are becoming increasingly integrated, and that the future distribution of population and economic activity will be determined largely by the evolution of the national system of metropolitan areas. While many nonmetropolitan areas will continue to decline or stagnate, others will be in a position to grow by taking advantage of the emergence of urban fields, a geographically, socially, and economically wider community of interests than that represented by the older distinctions between "rural" and "urban," or even SMSA and non-SMSA. It also was pointed out that many nonmetropolitan areas lacking proximity to SMSAs might be able to capture a significant amount of employment in those sectors, primarily in manufacturing, which are decentralizing from SMSAs.

This chapter has examined recent employment change in nonmetropolitan counties in the light of these general propositions, with particular emphasis on counties that have reversed population stagnation or decline. Employment changes, based on *County Business Patterns* data, were investigated for the period from 1959 to 1969 and that from 1964 to 1969, because of unavailability of data by county in many cases for 1959. Changes in all five categories of counties being studied were analyzed at the one-digit SIC code level. Changes in manufacturing and service employment were analyzed at the two-digit level for the Turnaround-Reversal and Turnaround-Acceleration groups of counties.

In general, the results indicate that counties in the Consistent Fast Gainer category, those with the greatest proximity to SMSAs, not only have the highest rates of employment gain but rank especially high in sectors that are the most "urban" in nature. The turnaround counties have the next highest total employment growth rates, although the reasons differ between the two groups. The Turnaround-Acceleration counties, which tend to be closer to SMSAs than any other group except the Consistent Fast Gainers, have done relatively well in the growth of non-goods-producing jobs, whereas the major source of expansion in the Turnaround-Reversal counties has been manufacturing. When manufacturing employment growth is examined at the two-digit SIC level, it appears that growth from this source in the Turnaround-Reversal group is based more on the attraction of nationally slow-growing sectors than is the case for the Turnaround-Acceleration group, although the difference in this regard is not marked. Although the rate of expansion of the service sector did not differ greatly between the two groups of turnaround counties, examination of service employment change at the two-digit level shows that Turnaround-Acceleration counties benefited more from participation in urban fields. Finally, counties in the Stagnant Gainer and Loser categories had low total employment growth, and they rank low in most sectors. Thus the results presented in this chapter are quite consistent with the general arguments developed in chapter 2.

5

Minnesota and Wisconsin

With the exception of one county the Turnaround-Reversal counties in Wisconsin fall into two widely separated groups of contiguous counties. One group lies north and northwest of Madison (Sauk, Waushara, Marquette, Adams, Juneau, Monroe, and Jackson); the other stretches across the northern part of the state from Green Bay all the way to the Minnesota border (Oconto, Marinette, Forest, Vilas, Price, Sawyer, Washburn, and Burnett). The one exception, Dunn County, is separated by one county from the Minneapolis-St. Paul SMSA. Minnesota has two contiguous groups of Turnaround-Reversal counties. The first consists of Mille Lacs and Kanabec counties, about sixty miles north of Minneapolis. The other clusters around the large lakes of north central Minnesota (Wadena, Cass, Hubbard, Becker, Beltrami, and Pennington).

The Turnaround-Acceleration counties are more scattered but tend to be concentrated around the Minneapolis-St. Paul SMSA and, to a lesser extent, Milwaukee and Madison. There are thirteen in Wisconsin and eleven in Minnesota.

The Stagnant Gainer Counties (five in Wisconsin and nine in Minnesota) and Loser Counties (fourteen in Wisconsin and twenty-four in Minnesota) are widely dispersed. On the other hand, the two Consistent Fast Gainer counties in Wisconsin (Jefferson and Walworth) border the Milwaukee SMSA; the four in Minnesota (Scott, Carver, Sherburne, and Isanti) border the Minneapolis-St. Paul SMSA.

Employment Change

As the data in table 5-1 indicate, the Turnaround-Reversal counties had the highest rate of growth in total employment for the 1964-69 period and were second only to the Consistent Fast Gainers for the 1959-69 period. In both periods they had the highest rate of growth in manufacturing. They also ranked relatively high in most of the non-goods-producing sectors, where the rate of growth in the services sector was particularly high. Manufacturing and services together accounted for 17,536 of the 26,248 absolute increase in total employment between 1964 and 1969 and for 19,770 of the 30,947 comparable increase for the 1959-69 period.

The Turnaround-Acceleration counties grew considerably more slowly in total employment, ranking fourth during both time intervals. With the exception

Table 5-1

Absolute and Percentage Employment Change by Sector (One-digit SIC Code) in Selected Minnesota and Wisconsin Counties by Population Change Category, 1964-69 and 1959-69

	Total	Agricultural Services, Forestry, Fisheries	Mining	Contract Construction	Manufacturing
Absolute Change, 1964-69					
Loser	18,138	−207	−93	1,283	5,021
Stagnant Gainer	31,198	44	108	2,076	11,779
Turnaround-Reversal	26,248	122	152	1,488	11,733
Turnaround-Acceleration	44,066	265	−116	3,788	14,831
Consistent Fast Gainer	10,852	33	−64	593	2,911
Percentage Change, 1964-69					
Loser	24.0	−17.9	−22.0	39.2	22.3
Stagnant Gainer	29.5	10.9	47.4	48.7	23.0
Turnaround-Reversal	42.8	51.5	45.1	56.8	54.2
Turnaround-Acceleration	29.4	50.5	−16.1	58.3	23.7
Consistent Fast Gainer	32.9	13.6	−36.4	53.5	18.4
Absolute Change, 1959-69					
Loser	14,654	123	−193	873	5,981
Stagnant Gainer	40,404	111	91	1,786	17,063
Turnaround-Reversal	30,947	27	−113	1,346	12,465
Turnaround-Acceleration	56,450	336	−423	4,375	19,709
Consistent Fast Gainer	17,937	100	−6	674	6,919
Percentage Change, 1959-69					
Loser	18.5	14.9	−37.0	23.7	27.8
Stagnant Gainer	41.9	33.0	37.1	39.2	37.1
Turnaround-Reversal	54.6	8.1	−18.8	48.7	59.6
Turnaround-Acceleration	41.0	74.0	−41.1	74.0	34.2
Consistent Fast Gainer	69.1	57.1	−5.1	65.6	58.5

Table 5-1 (Continued)
Minnesota and Wisconsin

	Transportation and Other Public Utilities	Wholesale Trade	Retail Trade	Finance, Insurance, and Real Estate (FIRE)	Services	Unclassified Establishments
Absolute Change, 1964-69						
Loser	581	1,103	4,430	1,208	4,683	97
Stagnant Gainer	1,166	918	6,651	1,326	7,142	-6
Turnaround-Reversal	635	728	4,810	723	5,803	94
Turnaround-Acceleration	1,661	1,222	11,090	1,917	10,061	39
Consistent Fast Gainer	528	456	2,695	439	3,125	97
Percentage Change, 1964-69						
Loser	11.1	20.8	19.0	30.0	45.2	47.5
Stagnant Gainer	23.8	17.3	32.1	28.6	52.3	-2.8
Turnaround-Reversal	15.0	20.7	27.3	30.6	66.8	66.7
Turnaround-Acceleration	20.0	14.8	32.4	27.7	48.1	13.8
Consistent Fast Gainer	26.8	36.5	37.8	47.2	71.3	293.9
Absolute Change, 1959-69						
Loser	516	393	4,878	1,580	6,176	-360
Stagnant Gainer	1,147	945	7,943	1,849	9,650	-192
Turnaround-Reversal	983	959	7,054	1,091	7,305	-145
Turnaround-Acceleration	2,590	540	13,155	3,197	13,221	-365
Consistent Fast Gainer	780	500	3,854	596	4,464	43
Percentage Change, 1959-69						
Loser	9.8	6.5	21.4	43.3	69.7	-54.5
Stagnant Gainer	23.3	17.9	40.9	45.0	86.5	-47.5
Turnaround-Reversal	25.2	29.2	45.9	54.6	101.6	-38.2
Turnaround-Acceleration	35.2	6.0	40.9	56.6	74.4	-53.2
Consistent Fast Gainer	45.4	41.5	64.6	77.0	146.6	49.4

of agricultural employment, for which only spotty data were available, their highest rates of growth were in construction and services. Although they ranked second in rate of manufacturing employment growth from 1964 to 1969, their rate was only slightly ahead of that of the other groups and still well under half that of the Turnaround-Reversal group. During both periods manufacturing, retail trade, and services together accounted for the great bulk of total growth in absolute employment.

The Consistent Fast Gainer counties had the highest rate of total employment increase between 1959 and 1969, although they were second to the Turn-around-Reversal group between 1964 and 1969. In both periods they had the highest rate of growth in the transportation sector and clearly dominated the non-goods-producing wholesale trade, retail trade, FIRE, and services sectors in terms of rate of growth. They were a close second to the Turnaround-Reversal group in manufacturing growth between 1959 and 1969, but had the lowest rate of growth in this sector from 1964 to 1969. The overall performance of the Consistent Fast Gainers, especially with respect to the more "urban-oriented" sectors, clearly reflects their proximity to large SMSAs.

In contrast, counties in the Loser category had the lowest rate of total employment growth during both periods, and they ranked last in most individual sectors. The Stagnant Gainers ranked relatively low in employment growth in most sectors for both periods. Only in mining did they rank first, but the absolute gains involved were negligible.

When manufacturing is considered at the two-digit SIC level the biggest gains in employment in the Turnaround-Reversal counties between 1964 and 1969 were made in the instruments, apparel, chemicals, miscellaneous, machinery, and electrical equipment sectors. For the 1959-69 period the biggest gains were in the instruments, fabricated metals, apparel, chemicals, and machinery sectors. During both periods there were employment declines in the textile, leather, stone-clay-glass, and transportation equipment sectors, and employment in the lumber and wood products sector declined between 1959 and 1969.

The Turnaround-Acceleration counties experienced their greatest manu-facturing growth in the ordnance, electrical equipment, instruments, fabricated metals, and machinery sectors between 1964 and 1969, and in the ordnance, machinery, electrical equipment, fabricated metals, instruments, primary metals, and paper sectors between 1959 and 1969. Losses were sustained in both periods in textiles, lumber and wood products, furniture, and transportation equipment; and during the 1964-69 period there were losses in the food, apparel, and chemicals sectors. A particularly severe decline in transportation equipment employment between 1964 and 1969 was largely responsible for making the rate of manufacturing employment increase less than half that in the Turnaround-Reversal counties.

The high rates of service employment growth in both turnaround groups were caused for the most part by increases in the medical and nonprofit membership organization sectors. In the Turnaround-Reversal group they accounted for 77 percent of the increase from 1964 to 1969 and for 53 percent of the increase between 1959 and 1969. In the Turnaround-Acceleration group they accounted for 58 percent of services growth during both periods. However, educational services also grew rapidly in both groups, particularly in the Turnaround-Acceleration counties. Hotel employment grew rapidly in the Turnaround-Acceleration group and also showed a substantial increase in the Turnaround-Reversal counties, but recreation employment growth was low, particularly in the Turnaround-Reversal counties.

Minnesota

Minnesota is the marketing, distribution, and financial center of the upper Midwest. Although agriculture remains important, factories replaced farming as the dominant source of income in 1952. Value added by Minnesota's more than 5200 manufacturing firms was $4.81 billion in 1969, almost double the corresponding figure at the beginning of the decade. Minnesota is the headquarters of thirteen of the nation's five hundred largest industrial corporations, and over half of the hundred largest operate manufacturing, warehousing, and research and development facilities in the state. Minneapolis and St. Paul constitute the primary marketplace of the upper Midwest, but rapid growth of diverse industrial, commercial, and technical activities has extended the influence of the Twin Cities to the national level. Population in the Twin Cities and their forty-five surrounding suburban communities has more than doubled in the past five years, making this the third-fastest-growing metropolitan area in the country.

In 1960 Minnesota's gross state product was $8.30 billion, but by 1969 it had nearly doubled to $16.43 billion. Agricultural production and net worth per farm have been rising as the number of farms has decreased and the average size of farms has increased. In 1970 the state's 122,000 farms generated more than $2 billion in cash farm income, and $275 million worth of agricultural commodities — mostly soy beans and dairy products — were shipped to world markets. Minnesota supplies more oats, turkeys, creamery butter, and sweet corn for processing than any other state. It ranks second in production of sunflower and sweet clover seeds, dry milk, hay, and honey, and third in production of American cheese and in total meat output. The food and kindred products sector heads manufacturing rankings with respect to employment, payrolls, and value added. More than 264,000 are employed in this sector. The machinery sector ranks second, and not surprisingly farm equipment plays a major role.

Although Minnesota's heritage as a breadbasket state is still much in evidence, a burgeoning rural renaissance has turned many small farm communities into sophisticated small cities capable of supporting a unique way of life.

Throughout the state there are 205 Chambers of Commerce and 252 local development groups whose function is to assist industrial expansion. Many groups have directed their efforts toward building and marketing speculative industrial facilities. As of January 1971 there were 1.3 million square feet of new speculative buildings, and developers were marketing over a hundred industrial, office, and research parks throughout the state.[1]

In 1970 construction was started on 470 new and expanded industrial facilities in Minnesota, representing an investment of over $372 million. This was the largest annual expenditure for new and expanded facilities ever recorded in the state and compares with investments of $309 million in 1969 and $302 million in 1968 (see table 5-2). Rural areas outside of the seven-county Twin City SMSA and Duluth accounted for almost 70 percent of the new investment in 1970. In the manufacturing sector the rural areas accounted for 4271 new jobs, or over twice the number created in the metropolitan areas.[2]

One example of the many small towns that recognize the value of industrial expansion and are using ingenious methods to bring it about is Brainerd, in Crow Wing, a Turnaround-Acceleration county 125 miles northwest of Minneapolis. With some five hundred lakes in the immediate area, the town became a resort center, but employment was seasonal and during the winter months some four thousand persons were out of work. Moreover, Brainerd had early become a rail head, but technological advances drastically reduced employment in the town's railroad car repair shops. To rebuild the local economy a community development corporation was organized and $30,000 was raised by selling shares of stock and an equal amount of debentures to more than a hundred groups and individuals in the community. With supplemental funds from the Small Business Administration the city was able to attract several small manufacturing firms and to establish a 133-acre industrial park to attract new industry. Brainerd's most recent speculative industrial building is the product of a concerted effort by many persons. Seven building trades unions donated their skills to erect the building, local merchants furnished building materials at net cost, local financial institutions offered low-interest funds, and the Chamber of Commerce fed the workers daily on the job. Brainerd's $5-million-a-year resort business has picked up added profits by remaining open later in the fall to handle conventions. Two ski areas and the 20,000 snowmobiles in the area have enabled seven resorts to remain open all winter. A new hundred-room motel has given a further boost to the tourist trade. Meanwhile, local developers are continuing to seek new sources of growth.[3] It is also noteworthy that the town of Crosby, fifteen miles from Brainerd, has added a large snowmobile manufacturing firm; it employs 350 persons in a community of 2241 persons. The unemployment rate in Crosby was recently down to 3 percent, compared with 7 percent in Brainerd.[4]

The rise of the snowmobile in the upper Midwest probably has been a phenomenon unparalleled since the advent of the Model T. At the end of the 1970-71 season Minnesota had an estimated 247,076 machines, while Wisconsin

Table 5-2

Minnesota's Industrial Growth by Area, 1968-1969-1970

	Number	Investment	Square Feet	New Jobs
New Rural Industry				
1968	83	$121,153,360	1,760,645	2,967
1969	139	136,107,445	2,376,425	4,104
1970	140	94,228,080	2,071,082	2,411
Expanded Rural Industry				
1968	132	48,607,494	3,339,011	4,742
1969	147	47,214,479	2,922,675	3,179
1970	132	161,687,000	1,676,030	2,234
Total New and Expanded Rural Industry				
1968	215	169,760,854	5,099,656	7,709
1969	286	183,321,924	5,299,100	7,283
1970	272	255,915,080	3,747,112	4,645
New Metropolitan Industry				
1968	130	66,532,520	4,880,625	2,604
1969	172	54,491,152	4,179,752	3,711
1970	111	78,702,900	4,595,534	1,749
Expanded Metropolitan Industry				
1968	161	66,626,179	4,679,641	3,466
1969	154	47,214,479	2,922,675	4,347
1970	87	35,590,500	1,752,284	1,018
Total New and Expanded Metropolitan Industry				
1968	291	133,158,699	9,560,266	6,070
1969	326	125,780,636	8,749,261	8,058
1970	198	116,293,400	6,347,818	2,767

Source: *Minnesota's New and Expanded Industries* (St. Paul: Minnesota Department of Economic Development, 1971), p. 12.

and Michigan had 175,000 and 207,000, respectively. This amounted to one machine for every six families in Minnesota, about one for every eight in Wisconsin, and about one for every eleven in Michigan.[5] Minnesota is already the major producer of snowmobiles, which have brought not only winter pleasure but also economic growth. In addition to the output of the Crosby plant, snowmobiles are manufactured in Roseau County, and Arctic Enterprises, the world's second largest producer of snowmobiles, has added 90,000 square feet a year for the last three years at its Thief River Falls plant in Pennington County, a Turnaround-Reversal county 330 miles northwest of Minneapolis.[6] At the latest count Arctic employed 1700 persons in a town of 8618 persons; the county's next largest manufacturing firm, which processes turkeys, employs 170.[7]

Minnesota is richly endowed with surface water: there are five big rivers and hundreds of smaller ones, in addition to over 15,000 lakes. Recreation demand has no doubt been partly responsible for the growth of most of the state's Turnaround-Reversal counties, which tend either to contain or to be near the largest central and northcentral lakes. Some small towns are also becoming major boat manufacturing centers. Little Falls, Pipestone, and Moorhead, in the western part of Minnesota, all support boat manufacturing firms that supply national markets. The major employer in Kanabec County, a Turnaround-Reversal county sixty miles north of Minneapolis, produces both houseboats and snowmobiles.

Another type of enterprise that seems well suited to Minnesota's rural areas is the mobile and modular home manufacturing industry. Between 1969 and 1971 the number of mobile home manufacturers in the state jumped from two to sixteen (a phenomenon which is of course not reflected in our employment data). One reason for this rapid expansion was the institution of a policy permitting fourteen-foot-wide loads to be transported over state and federal roads in Minnesota. The labor skills required, the building and equipment requirements, the sources of supplies and services, and the locational relationship of the product to its market favor location in rural areas. Almost all of the sixteen manufacturers have located their plants in small cities and towns and draw their employees from the towns and rural areas surrounding them. Total investment in plant facilities is $5.8 million, and total employment in the plants is over 1300, with a payroll of more than $7 million.[8]

Nonfarm growth will probably continue over all areas of Minnesota. Although total population has been declining for a decade and usually longer in over 60 percent of the state's counties, nonfarm population has increased in the past decade in over 90 percent of the counties. Nonfarm population growth has been highest in the most urbanized areas and lowest where the nonfarm economy is most directly dependent on farm trade and services. The only exception has been the central cities of Minneapolis and St. Paul, where growth has occurred rapidly around the edges while core areas have been partly vacated. The four

Consistent Fast Gainer counties, which had immigration rates ranging from 15.8 to 27.5 percent from 1960 to 1970, all border the Twin City SMSA. Moreover, with the exception of Crow Wing, all of the Turnaround-Acceleration counties (including three in Wisconsin) either border the Twin City SMSA or a Consistent Fast Gainer county, or else are contiguous with these other Turnaround-Acceleration counties.

The growth of most medium-size cities and small towns has tended to follow the same decentralized pattern as that in the Twin Cities. Net movement has been and will continue to be toward the principal service and industrial centers but not into their older existing areas. The new pattern of nonfarm population distribution is oriented much less toward railroads and flatlands and much more toward highways, lakes, woods, and rolling land. It also is more open and lower in overall density; this applies not only to all classes of residential development but even to commercial and industrial development. In some large contiguous areas of Minnesota all minor civil divisions have grown recently; over 99 percent of the state's total population increase has occurred within these growth regions. Most of the "complete shopping" and "wholesale-retail" centers are within the growth regions. Size of city, however, provides no assurance of growth. Of the 36 "complete shopping" and "wholesale-retail" centers outside of the Twin Cities, 14 declined in the past decade. Most of those that declined had grown in the previous decade, and most that had declined in the 1950s grew during the 1960s. Instability of local growth rates is likely to increase as many small and medium-size places shift their economic base from farm trade to manufacturing, since most will be dependent upon the shifting fortunes of one or two plants. The majority of rural communities will continue to be bypassed by industrial employment because there simply are not enough plants to go around, but they may experience indirect effects through the growth of commuter populations. In any case, stability of growth rate in smaller places will increasingly depend upon their ability to be part of a growth region and to reach multiple diverse centers of employment opportunity from any given residential location. Major factors will be proximity of small urban areas to one another and the quality of their transportation linkages. The growth regions will generally be in or near established growth centers but will continue to spread out. Moreover, the dependability of their growth rates is likely to be greater, the nearer they are to the Twin Cities.[9]

Although many parts of Minnesota, particularly in the north and the west, will continue to decline in population, this is not necessarily incompatible with efficient resource allocation from a statewide or national viewpoint. Outmigrants from Minnesota's rural areas are well prepared, in relation to those from many other rural areas, for life and work in an urban-industrial environment. And the people left behind in Minnesota counties that are losing population are not generally suffering in terms of either quality of life style or economic status. For example, per capita income in 1969 in the eleven westernmost Loser counties had remarkably low variation, ranging from $2245 in Grant County to $2787 in Renville County. These figures may seem low in comparison with the state average of $3599, but then there is no nonmetropolitan county in Minnesota with per capita income above the state average. (It is evident that state averages obscure rural conditions, but cost-of-living adjustments — and in some cases psychic income — would make the advantages of metropolitan areas less than they appear in crude per capita income comparisons.) On the other hand, these Loser counties compare favorably with the Turnaround-Reversal counties. With the exception of Pennington County, whose per capita income in 1969 was $2879, the six northern Turnaround-Reversal counties had per capita incomes ranging from $1809 in Cass County to $2130 in Wadena County, a value below that of the lowest county of the eleven westernmost Loser counties. The other two Turnaround-Reversal counties are closer to the Twin Cities. Nevertheless, Mille Lacs's per capita income of $2070 was below that of any of the relevant Loser counties, and Kanabec's $2345 was below the comparable average for nine of the eleven westernmost counties.[10]

The relatively healthy condition of nonmetropolitan Minnesota is primarily attributable to the state's investment in human resources. Of the forty-eight contiguous states, Minnesota ranked fourth in 1971 in average current expenditures per pupil in average daily school attendance.[11] Minnesota consistently places among the lowest states in percentage of draftees rejected for failure to pass mental tests. Rejection rates are only one fifth the national average, and for the past five years the state has ranked lowest three times. Moreover, over 93 percent of ninth-graders entering high school in Minnesota complete their education. Twenty-eight area vocational-technical schools annually turn out several thousand skilled workers, many of whom have been trained in programs designed to meet the specific requirements of industry. The state operates six four-year colleges and eighteen public junior colleges; there are also nine private junior colleges and twenty-seven private liberal arts colleges and universities.[12] The University of Minnesota, whose graduate school ranks among the top ten in number of Ph.D.'s conferred, is without question one of the most distinguished institutions of higher learning in the nation.

Even if many of the better-educated young people in nonmetropolitan Minnesota leave for larger cities, it is nonetheless true that the quality of the labor force is a very significant factor in both the prosperity of agriculture and the substantial growth of nonfarm employment in nonmetropolitan areas. In this respect, the state has much to teach the rest of the nation.

Central Wisconsin

The data in table 5-3 show that all of the Turnaround-Acceleration counties in central Wisconsin experienced considerable net inmigration during the 1960s after having high net outmigration during the 1950s. Four of the counties —

Table 5-3

Net Migration of Population in Central Wisconsin Turnaround Counties, 1950-60 and 1960-70

County	1950-60	1960-70	County	1950-60	1960-70
Turnaround-Reversal			Turnaround-Acceleration		
Sauk	−7,361	−900	Sheboygan	−4,914	2,664
Marquette	−926	262	Fond du Lac	−2,845	1,717
Waushara	−1,273	956	Green Lake	−736	548
Adams	−1,019	1510	Columbia	−1,378	914
Juneau	−3,440	19	Portage	−3,169	5,589
Monroe	−5,009	−2,327	Waupaca	−3,124	790
Jackson	−2,553	−461			

Source: *A Map Story of Wisconsin's Economy* (Madison: Wisconsin Division of Economic Development, 1972), maps 4 and 7.

Sheboygan, Fond du Lac, Green Lake, and Columbia — form a continuous arch linking the Milwaukee and Madison SMSAs via the Fox River Valley. As can be seen on map 5-1, Sheboygan County had a large increase in absolute manufacturing employment. Fond du Lac County also is one of Wisconsin's strong industrial counties, having long been a center for foods, knit goods, leather tanning, and machinery. Recent industrial growth has been largely responsible for the population increase in Green Lake County, although it is also an important farming and recreation center. Columbia County has had moderate manufacturing growth, but its population growth is perhaps more attributable to the tourist industries in the Wisconsin Dells and Lodi areas, as well as to opportunities for employment in services at the state capital, in neighboring Dane County. The relative importance of recreation to Columbia County is clearly indicated by map 5-2, which shows nonresident usage of Wisconsin recreational facilities on the peak day of an average summer weekend in 1970. The data were derived from thirty-seven sampling stations on the state boundary. The stations were selected so that they accounted for 90 percent of the traffic crossing the state line on nonurban highways. The other two Turnaround-Acceleration counties in central Wisconsin, Portage and Waupaca, benefited respectively from university growth and extensive inmigration and from expansion of the dynamic mobile home and travel trailer industry.[13]

The seven contiguous Turnaround-Reversal counties in central Wisconsin have benefited in part from the construction of Interstate Highway 94, which links the Milwaukee-Chicago industrial complex with the Twin Cities; four are traversed by the route. A number of new man-made lakes, extensive irrigation, and the growth of the food processing industry also have been instrumental in reversing population decline in this area.

Sauk County, which is on Interstate 94, had both one of the highest absolute gains and one of the highest rates of gain in manufacturing jobs of any county in

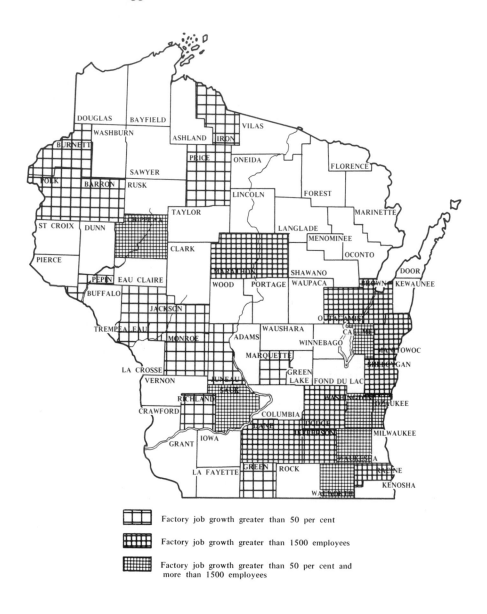

Factory job growth greater than 50 per cent

Factory job growth greater than 1500 employees

Factory job growth greater than 50 per cent and
more than 1500 employees

Source: Wisconsin Division of Economic Development. Employment Gains are based on the
average of 1969 and 1970 compared to the average of 1956 and 1959. Data were derived
from *County Business Patterns.*

Map 5-1. Gain in Wisconsin Manufacturing Jobs, Average of 1970 and 1969
Against Average of 1959 and 1956

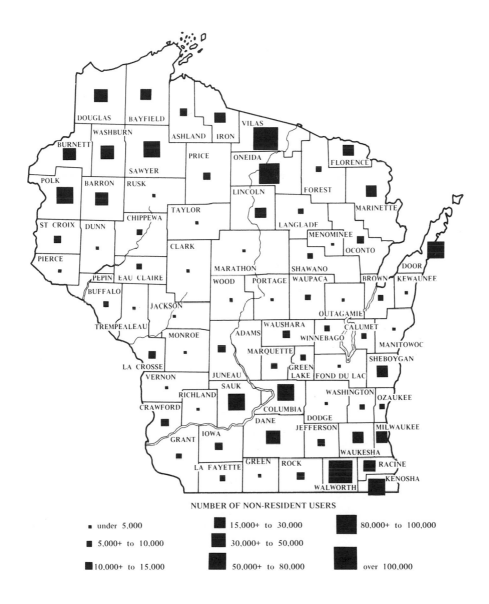

NUMBER OF NON-RESIDENT USERS

- ▪ under 5,000
- ◾ 5,000+ to 10,000
- ◼ 10,000+ to 15,000

- ◼ 15,000+ to 30,000
- ◼ 30,000+ to 50,000
- ◼ 50,000+ to 80,000

- ◼ 80,000+ to 100,000
- ◼ over 100,000

Source: Wisconsin Department of Transportation

Map 5-2. Nonresident Usage of Wisconsin Recreational Facilities on the Peak Day of an Average Summer Weekend, 1970

Wisconsin (see map 5-1). A large ordnance facility in Sauk County provides employment not only for the local population but also for commuters from Columbia County. Sauk also shares the Dells of the Wisconsin River with Columbia, and the access provided by Interstate 94 no doubt helps explain its attractiveness as a recreation area (see map 5-2). Juneau, Monroe, and Jackson counties, the Turnaround-Reversal counties up the pike from Sauk, have each experienced relatively high growth of factory jobs (see map 5-1).

Juneau County, which experienced a 5.5 percent rate of population increase between 1960 and 1970 (and net inmigration of nineteen persons!), is particularly interesting as a case study because trends in population change there have been common to much of Wisconsin. The county's present population of 18,455 is about the same as it was in 1890. The peak population was reached in 1900, when there were 20,629 persons. There was a back-to-the-land tendency during the Depression years, then a decline in the 1950s. The growth of population in the 1960s came as a surprise to many observers, as was the case for numerous Wisconsin counties. Dairying is the largest source of farm income. Since 1950 the number of farms has declined rapidly, although more recently losses have slowed. The decline in Juneau County farms, 13.8 percent, was slightly less than the corresponding state decline of 16.7 percent. Now an estimated one third of all county land is in farms, but over 380 farmers reported a hundred or more days of off-farm work in 1969. At one time Juneau County produced considerable quantities of potatoes and other vegetables; although much of this land has reverted to forests, irrigation and fertilizers are bringing back this type of agriculture. However, it is manufacturing that has accounted for much of the county's recent growth. There were noticeable increases from 1958 to 1963, then quite significant growth from 1963 to 1968. The older food and lumber industries have been supplemented with new firms. The largest employers produce a wide variety of products, including dry cell batteries, gaskets, stainless steel vessels, refrigeration equipment, refrigerated trucks, and vacuum-metalized metals. Because of the Interstate Highway and available labor it is anticipated that manufacturing growth will continue. Retail sales in Juneau county are relatively high for rural areas and approximated the state average of $1577 per capita in 1967. Substantial growth in recreational facilities largely accounts for recent retail trade increases.

If Interstate Highway 94 has played a part in stimulating the growth of Juneau and other turnaround counties, this was less apparent for turnaround counties near but not on the highway. Indeed, such factors as irrigation and retirement homes seem more important in Adams, Waushara, and Marquette counties, to the north of Madison. Irrigation has become a way of life on many Wisconsin potato and vegetable farms. Of the 105,000 acres of irrigated land in Wisconsin in 1969, Adams and Waushara counties accounted for 32,300 acres. (Neighboring Portage County, in the Turnaround-Acceleration group, had 25,000 acres of irrigated land in 1969.) In the five-year period from 1964 to

1969 alone, 43,000 acres of irrigated land were added to the state total; Adams and Waushara counties added about 16,000 acres during this time, while irrigated acreage in Portage county increased by about another 8000 acres. There can be little doubt that the "golden sands" area comprising these three counties represents a major success story in the transformation of marginal land to high productivity. Despite manufacturing employment increases, particularly in Marquette County (see map 5-1 p. 68), many residents of the counties not on the Interstate Highway commute to jobs in other counties. Retail sales figures indicate considerable income from tourism and summer cottage owners, although population age distribution data indicate that recent population gains are related to an influx of retired persons.

In general, then, the turnaround counties in central Wisconsin have benefited from a variety of favorable circumstances, but it is clear that manufacturing decentralization and amenities favorable to leisure-recreation-retirement growth have been particularly important. Proximity to Madison and the Milwaukee-Chicago lakefront industrial complex has placed the area in a relatively favorable position, and the Interstate Highway System has particularly affected some of the counties by tying them closer to the urban fields of the large SMSAs. Although agriculture is viable, and in some cases increasingly so because of irrigation, many farm families earn a high proportion of their total income from nonfarm sources. It is likely that recent population growth will continue and that distinctions between rural and urban life styles will be increasingly blurred.

Northern Wisconsin

Wisconsin's four northernmost counties, which peaked in population in 1920 when mining, agriculture, and lumbering activities reached their zenith, all continue to lose population. However, a tier of counties to the south of this area, stretching all the way from Green Bay on the east to the Minnesota border on the west, all grew after previously losing population. To be sure, the gains were usually quite modest and net outmigration still characterized most of these Turnaround-Reversal counties. With the exception of Vilas County, which grew by 17.4 percent from 1960 to 1970 and had a net inmigration rate of 15.5 percent, the rate of growth in the eight counties ranged between 0.7 and 3.3 percent. Only one other county, Washburn, experienced net inmigration, and then it amounted to a net gain of only eighty-eight persons. Still, the improvement in these counties and two adjacent Turnaround-Acceleration counties is noteworthy, especially in view of the continuing erosion of the agricultural base. The area has been characterized by dramatic declines in number of farms. The statewide decline of 16.7 percent between 1964 and 1969 was in itself remarkable, but the rates of decline in the northern counties were all greatly in excess of this figure, ranging to as high as 46.1 percent in Oneida

County. The fact that this is prime lake country is largely responsible for its turnaround status. A growing number of people from Chicago, Milwaukee, and other metropolitan centers who vacationed in the area for years are now retiring to live there on a permanent basis. Although large numbers of young people still leave for the big cities, there is now significant return migration of persons in this group who find that the psychic income of nonmetropolitan living more than compensates for lower monetary rewards.

Map 5-2 (p. 69) shows the importance of recreation to the northern counties and especially to Vilas County, the fastest growing. Map 5-1 (p. 68) shows that the rate of growth of manufacturing has been relatively high in Price and Burnett counties, but this is of course related to a low base. In Burnett County, for example, the agricultural work force decreased faster than manufacturing jobs increased between 1960 and 1970. In 1969 it still had only 52 manufacturing jobs per 1000 population, compared with the state average of 118. For most of the northern turnaround area it is possible that small manufacturing enterprises can operate successfully if they do not require location near large cities or if they do not require raw materials that are expensive to fabricate and ship. However, the future of the area still depends more on the degree to which people value elbow room, clean air, and lack of congestion, and the degree to which they prefer hunting and fishing to urban amenities.

In western Wisconsin, but to the south of the tier of Turnaround-Reversal counties, are five Turnaround-Acceleration counties. Three of these border the Twin Cities SMSA. Another, Chippewa County, had a labor force in 1960 that included more agricultural workers than factory workers. However, in 1970, 14 percent of the residents reported agricultural employment whereas 29 percent reported manufacturing employment, a figure just short of the state average of 31 percent. The exceptional degree of industrial expansion was largely a result of the reactivation of a shell-making plant, which employed over 2500 workers in 1970. This ordnance facility also has given employment to many commuters from the remaining Turnaround-Acceleration county, Eau Claire, whose principal city lies near Chippewa County. The growth of Eau Claire State University has also more than balanced migration losses. The impetus to growth in Chippewa and Eau Claire counties may well decline as university enrollments taper off and the war in Southeast Asia winds down.

The one "isolated" Turnaround-Reversal county is sandwiched between the five Turnaround-Acceleration counties in western Wisconsin. Dunn County, which is traversed by Interstate Highway 94, had net outmigration of 4348 persons in the 1950s but gained 1182 persons from net inmigration during the 1960s. Agricultural employment declined from 5660 in 1930 to 1918 in 1970, but this still left 18 percent of the county labor force in agriculture, compared with 6.5 percent for Wisconsin as a whole. Although the industrial base of Dunn County is still comparatively small, many residents commute to jobs in neighboring counties and even to the Twin Cities. A study of the influence of

Interstate Highway 94 on Dunn County and St. Croix County, which lies between it and the Twin Cities, concludes:

> . . . the spreading of direct benefits of lower vehicle operating costs to other aspects of the economy is a slower process than the creation of lower transportation costs. Local residents can take advantage of lower operating costs for highway travel. However, it appears that the influence of low transport costs is not manifested in higher farm real estate values. Also, there have been no drastic changes in trade centers and trade areas in the two counties. If the improved highway is to cause material changes in these aspects of the local economy, it will evidently take a longer time than the three to five years considered in this study.[14]

Thus, although the Interstate Highway System certainly has contributed to the growth of population and economic activity in some of Wisconsin's turnaround counties, its presence does not guarantee growth. (Of course, population retention may be enhanced by improved opportunity for long-distance commuting.) And, as the northern turnaround counties demonstrate, growth certainly can take place over large areas without the benefit of the Interstate System.

Summary and Conclusions

The presence of a relatively large number of turnaround counties in Minnesota and Wisconsin is explained by a number of frequently interrelated factors. With a few exceptions the spread of major urban fields has been a principal cause of the expansion of the Turnaround-Acceleration counties. The construction of the Interstate Highway System has in some instances been a major contributor to this process, as well as to similar growth in some of the central Wisconsin Turnaround-Reversal counties. However, it has not been responsible for growth in most of the Turnaround-Reversal counties or in many of the Turnaround-Acceleration counties. Here one has to look to amenities conducive to tourism, recreation, and retirement, or to manufacturing decentralization, or to some combination of these phenomena. A relatively well-educated labor force is also an asset to both states. This point was discussed in some detail with respect to Minnesota, but it also should be pointed out that of the contiguous states, Wisconsin ranks seventh in average current expenditures per pupil in average daily attendance,[15] and has well-developed university and vocational-technical education systems.

It is appropriate to conclude this chapter with a summary of the results of a recent study covering thirty-nine branch plants established in Minnesota, Wisconsin, Upper Michigan, northern Illinois, and northern Iowa.[16] The plants were located in thirty-four nonmetropolitan communities between 1964 and

1971 by thirty-one metropolitan companies. The study is of particular interest because all but seven of the plants were located in Minnesota and Wisconsin. Fourteen of the home offices were in Minneapolis-St. Paul and nine were in the Chicago-Milwaukee area. Eleven of the branch plants produced electrical equipment and eight were in the shoes and garments sectors. Eighteen of the branch plants were located from one to two hundred miles from corporate headquarters and another six were at a distance of from two to five hundred miles. The purpose of the study, which was carried out under contract with the U.S. Department of Agriculture, was to determine what motivates metropolitan companies to establish branch plants in rural areas and what communities have done to successfully attract these new branch plants. Personal conferences were held with nearly two hundred top management people in headquarters and branch plants and with leaders of the respective nonmetropolitan communities.

Executives of the metropolitan-based companies were unanimous in the opinion that movement of manufacturing facilities to nonmetropolitan areas not only will continue but will probably accelerate. Without using the term, some industry leaders saw manufacturing decentralizing within the context of urban fields. They see large cities of the future functioning as centers of government, education, service, and culture, furnishing administrative, technological, and financial support to manufacturing facilities in nonmetropolitan areas. A few even stated that they would never again establish production facilities in metropolitan areas.

All company spokesmen felt that both the supply and the productivity of nonmetropolitan labor were good. Nonmetropolitan workers were said to be more appreciative of jobs and to bring a better work attitude to the plant. Farmers and farm wives especially were praised for good work habits. Most of the companies experienced less turnover and less absenteeism in their nonmetropolitan branch plants. A number, however, noted a reluctance to work overtime because of a need to join car pools or to perform evening chores on farms. Only one company executive ranked metropolitan workers generally higher than nonmetropolitan workers. A few executives admitted that lower wages were a reason for moving, adding that this was the only way they could compete with the South or foreign producers. They also pointed out that living costs tend to be lower away from big cities. Many plant operations required women, whose role was described in a variety of ways. Some respondents held that farm women are accustomed to hard work or that middle-aged women are more stable employees. It also was maintained that women are more dexterous than men and that they maintain a positive work attitude even when performing monotonous tasks. On the other hand, some housewives worked only long enough to earn a new television set or automobile. Half of the plants were union, half nonunion. The pattern was to establish nonunion plants in communities where this fitted the local tradition but union plants where other plants were organized.

Branch plant managers generally were brought in from outside; the number of management and technical personnel transferred to a branch plant seemed to vary directly with the degree of sophistication of the manufacturing operation. In all, however, fewer than 150 families were transferred into the thirty-four communities. Eleven companies established branches in communities where similar firms had operated and a pool of trained workers was available. Four were attracted by the presence of vocational schools and two by colleges as a source of part-time workers and technical people. Nevertheless, whatever the preliminary training nearly every company depended upon on-the-job training, and as plants became established they relied less upon outside help in recruiting and training workers. Every community covered had a Chamber of Commerce and most had an industrial development group. With but few exceptions the communities sought out companies that they thought might be interested in establishing branches in their areas. The real selling job was done in face-to-face presentations by local groups to company officials. The latter generally praised the efforts of communities in selling themselves to industry. Nevertheless, there was no established pattern for companies seeking branch locations – every experience was different. Once the branch plants were established community leaders praised the efforts of branch personnel in local affairs. Whatever their initial reluctance may have been, branch managers liked life in nonmetropolitan communities and commended the friendliness and ready assistance of the local communities when the plants had problems. Even if immediate population growth did not follow the plants' establishment, the economic impact was soon felt in increased area income. This in turn usually resulted in improved civic facilities. Finally, it is noteworthy that physical and social improvements usually followed rather than preceded the establishment of branch plants.

6 The Ozarks

The largest block of contiguous Turnaround-Reversal counties in the country is located in the Ozarks region. Most of these counties are in Arkansas and lie northwest of a diagonal line running from the southeast to the northeast corner of the state. In addition, there are a large number of Turnaround-Reversal counties in adjacent parts of Missouri, Oklahoma, and Texas. Arkansas accounts for thirty-four counties in this category, Oklahoma for fourteen, Missouri for eighteen, and Texas for eleven. Curiously, in the entire area there are only six Turnaround-Acceleration counties, seven Stagnant Gainers, and five Consistent Fast Gainers (all near the St. Louis SMSA). Losers are more numerous, with eight counties in Kansas, fourteen in Missouri, twelve in Arkansas, and thirteen in Texas.

Employment Change

The data in table 6-1 show that for the 1964-69 period the rate of total employment change was about the same for all population change categories except Losers, which lagged well behind the others. The rankings of the various groups vary a great deal among one-digit SIC sectors with respect to rate of change; however, the base year values for all but the Turnaround-Reversal and Loser counties are relatively small. Although the Turnaround-Reversal group ranked only third in manufacturing employment increase, this sector was still of primary importance to these counties. It accounted for over half of the Turnaround-Reversal total change in employment, a higher proportion than for any other group. This group also had absolute growth in services and retail trade. The Turnaround-Acceleration counties had the highest growth rates in the non-goods-producing retail trade, wholesale trade, and FIRE sectors; these counties also had fairly rapid service employment growth.

For the 1959-69 period the Turnaround-Acceleration and Consistent Fast Gainer counties generally had the highest growth rates in the non-goods-producing sectors. In manufacturing, however, the Turnaround-Reversal group had the highest growth rate. Manufacturing accounted for almost half of the total absolute employment increase within these counties, although relatively large absolute gains were registered also in the services and retail trade sectors.

Manufacturing gains in the Turnaround-Reversal counties were spread over a variety of sectors at the two-digit SIC level. The largest absolute gains were in

77

Table 6-1

Absolute and Percentage Employment Change by Sector (One-digit SIC Code) in Selected Ozarks Counties, by Population Change Category, 1964-69 and 1959-69

	Total	Agricultural Services, Forestry, Fisheries	Mining	Contract Construction	Manufacturing
Absolute Change, 1964-69					
Loser	30,700	133	-432	2,463	12,232
Stagnant Gainer	8,224	25	-246	791	3,626
Turnaround-Reversal	61,447	428	1,169	2,439	31,824
Turnaround-Acceleration	8,401	-8	65	1,199	2,245
Consistent Fast Gainer	3,444	-20	-10	204	1,571
Percentage Change, 1964-69					
Loser	20.1	11.7	-7.1	30.8	20.1
Stagnant Gainer	33.5	71.4	-6.9	49.7	61.3
Turnaround-Reversal	33.7	25.8	25.4	24.4	45.5
Turnaround-Acceleration	38.1	-1.9	32.8	93.1	28.8
Consistent Fast Gainer	35.2	-45.5	-7.4	45.0	63.5
Absolute Change, 1959-69					
Loser	25,530	177	1,577	237	11,579
Stagnant Gainer	196	7	-1,155	-21	295
Turnaround-Reversal	75,011	1,033	1,336	4,275	36,730
Turnaround-Acceleration	11,314	113	70	1,323	3,390
Consistent Fast Gainer	2,317	-1	67	-456	257
Percentage Change, 1959-69					
Loser	25.2	29.6	76.5	3.6	30.8
Stagnant Gainer	2.2	350.0	-47.2	-5.4	11.9
Turnaround-Reversal	52.8	111.9	49.0	64.3	67.6
Turnaround-Acceleration	66.2	40.1	36.6	124.6	53.5
Consistent Fast Gainer	21.2	-4.0	115.5	-41.0	6.8

Table 6-1 (Continued)
Employment Change

	Transportation and Other Public Utilities	Wholesale Trade	Retail Trade	Finance, Insurance, and Real Estate (FIRE)	Services	Unclassified Establishments
Absolute Change, 1964-69						
Loser	824	1,010	5,359	1,106	7,917	79
Stagnant Gainer	415	537	1,643	355	1,066	13
Turnaround-Reversal	1,598	968	9,391	2,565	10,756	249
Turnaround-Acceleration	531	304	2,110	603	1,399	-48
Consistent Fast Gainer	249	128	1,125	-340	563	-38
Percentage Change, 1964-69						
Loser	8.2	13.0	15.7	16.2	45.2	12.4
Stagnant Gainer	26.7	33.0	30.1	33.5	29.5	12.3
Turnaround-Reversal	15.3	9.4	22.1	35.1	43.5	23.1
Turnaround-Acceleration	28.4	33.5	40.1	75.4	42.2	-28.6
Consistent Fast Gainer	29.0	28.2	38.4	-38.0	38.1	-44.7
Absolute Change, 1959-69						
Loser	98	882	3,719	1,242	6,411	-394
Stagnant Gainer	-4	51	327	173	542	-20
Turnaround-Reversal	2,211	1,781	11,231	3,509	13,272	-602
Turnaround-Acceleration	731	298	2,608	715	2,152	-95
Consistent Fast Gainer	444	187	777	301	881	-134
Percentage Change, 1959-69						
Loser	1.2	17.3	15.2	26.6	57.7	-45.4
Stagnant Gainer	-.7	14.2	20.1	61.1	74.9	-37.7
Turnaround-Reversal	25.5	20.7	32.3	64.5	71.5	-33.8
Turnaround-Acceleration	48.1	35.0	63.2	122.4	110.4	-46.6
Consistent Fast Gainer	66.8	47.3	23.7	119.0	76.1	-74.0

the food, electrical equipment, apparel, fabricated metals, and transportation equipment sectors during the period from 1964 to 1969. These sectors, together with machinery (except electrical), also were the most prominent gainers during the 1959-69 period.

Net employment growth in the Turnaround-Acceleration counties was held down by losses in the apparel, lumber and wood products, petroleum, clay-stone-glass, and especially the transportation equipment sectors. Highest absolute increases were in the food, miscellaneous, and fabricated metals sectors.

Services growth in the Turnaround-Reversal counties was accounted for primarily by the medical and health and nonprofit membership organization sectors, which together were responsible for about three quarters of the absolute increase during both periods. Educational services ranked third in absolute growth for the 1964-69 period; hotel employment ranked third for the 1959-69 period. Medical and health and nonprofit membership organizations also accounted for most of the service employment growth in the Turnaround-Acceleration group, with the balance spread among a number of other sectors.

Arkansas

Between 1950 and 1960 the population of Arkansas declined by 6.5 percent, to 1,786,272 persons. During that decade there was net outmigration of 433,000 persons, at a strikingly high rate of 23 percent. The net outmigration for whites was 20 percent; that for blacks was 37 percent. In distinct contrast, the state's population grew by 7.7 percent between 1960 and 1970. It is estimated that there was net outmigration of 51,000 persons, one eighth the number of the previous decade. However, this gross figure masks a significant difference in the racial composition of net migration. During the 1960s there was actually a net immigration of an estimated 43,069 whites; blacks, however, had net outmigration of 94,058. In other words, the respective net migration rates of 3 percent and 25 percent indicate a reversal of the white outmigration trend of the 1950s but a continuation of the black outmigration pattern.[1] Moreover, practically all of the forty-one counties that experienced net outmigration during the 1960s are located in southern and eastern Arkansas, where the black population is very heavily concentrated.

The areas of heavy black concentration are where the majority of the hard social problems of this group and of the state are found. In these counties the symptoms which lead to despair and hopelessness and finally to the venting of frustration through violence are present. These counties lead the state in poverty, poor schools, poor social services, poor relationships between the two races and lack of political representation of blacks on any sort of meaningful level. The age distribution of blacks in these counties is not a favorable one in that there are many young people and many old ones with few middle ages people in between. And all but a few are locked in desperate poverty.[2]

It is imperative, therefore, to note that the remarkable turnaround that has taken place "in Arkansas" is really a phenomenon affecting that part of the state which is overwhelmingly white in racial composition. Whether or not employers have deliberately sought out white areas, as the prima facie evidence suggests, it does seem clear that they have been attracted by the prospect of low wages. This evidence will be examined below.

The Employment Security Division of the Arkansas Department of Labor points out that, in keeping with the employment change data presented above,

from 1960 to 1968, manufacturing employment increased 54 percent in Arkansas as compared with only 17.5 percent for the nation. From 1950 to 1968, *industrial expansion has probably been the most outstanding factor in Arkansas' economic growth.* Manufacturing jobs doubled during this time by gaining a total of almost 82,000 workers. Between 1965 and 1968, Arkansas' factory employment increased almost 6 percent each year while the national increase was only 3 percent.[3]

The structure of manufacturing employment and average hourly earnings by major industry groups for Arkansas and the United States in 1969 are presented in table 6-2. Of the major groups shown, only the paper and the rubber and plastics sectors have higher average hourly earnings in Arkansas compared with the nation's. However, they account for only 8.2 percent of total manufacturing employment in Arkansas. With the exception of the chemicals sector, which employs only 3.3 percent of the Arkansas industrial labor force, no other Arkansas sector has average hourly earnings over 84 percent of the national average. For all manufacturing, the Arkansas average is 73 percent of that for the nation. Employment projections from 1968 to 1975 indicate that jobs in durable goods will increase by 23.2 percent whereas those in nondurable goods will increase by only 21.1 percent.[4] In other words, future growth is expected to be relatively concentrated in those sectors where average hourly earnings are even less than the state manufacturing average.

Turning more specifically to the thirty-four Turnaround-Reversal counties, it is instructive that only eight were below the 164 percent state average increase in total wages paid to manufacturing workers between 1960 and 1970.[5] In 1970, twenty-one of these counties ranked in the lower half of all Arkansas counties with respect to size of average weekly wages in employment covered by the Arkansas Employment Security Law.[6]

Of course, low wages are not the sole reason for the industrial expansion of Arkansas. Some of the factors that influence plant relocations to the state are exemplified by the case of the Wolverine Toy Division of Sprang Industries. Because of conditions that limited Wolverine's ability to expand and modernize its Pittsburgh plant, the firm decided to move its operations to Logan County, a Turnaround-Reversal county in northwest Arkansas. One reason for this choice was the more central location of the Arkansas site. The center of gravity of the nation's population has of course shifted westward, and it is important for a firm

Table 6-2

Average Hourly Earnings and Percent of Total Manufacturing Employment by Major Industry Groups, United States and Arkansas, 1969

	Average Hourly Earnings, 1969			Percent of Total Manufacturing Employment—1969	
	Arkansas	United States	Arkansas as Percent of United States	Arkansas	United States
All Manufacturing	$2.33	$3.19	73	100.0	100.0
Durable Goods	2.27	3.38	67	52.3	59.0
Lumber and wood products, except furniture	2.09	2.73	77	13.3	3.0
Furniture and fixtures	2.15	2.62	82	7.4	2.4
Primary metal industries	2.85	3.79	75	2.8	6.7
Fabricated metal products	2.46	3.34	74	4.2	7.2
Machinery, except electrical	2.42	3.58	68	3.3	10.0
Electrical machinery	2.35	3.09	76	9.2	10.1
Nondurable Goods	2.40	2.91	82	47.7	41.0
Food and kindred products	2.03	2.95	69	14.8	8.9
Apparel and finished products	1.93	2.31	84	9.0	7.0
Paper and allied products	3.38	3.24	104	5.1	3.6
Printing, publishing, and allied products	2.78	3.69	75	3.9	5.4
Chemicals and allied products	3.18	3.47	92	3.3	5.2
Rubber and miscellaneous plastics	3.13	3.07	102	3.1	2.9

Source: Statement of Dr. Barton A. Westerlund, Director, Industrial Research and Extension Center, University of Arkansas (Little Rock) before the Commission on Population Growth and the American Future, June 7, 1971, unpublished paper, Appendix E.

that distributes its products nationwide to consider a relatively central location. Arkansas's "good labor supply from the standpoint of quality and quantity" also was a factor, although Wolverine "has a very limited need for skilled labor." In addition to the availability of relatively inexpensive and spacious industrial sites, construction costs are lower, not only because of labor costs but also because of "the beneficial effect that warmer weather has on building designs and related costs." Natural gas and power costs also are substantially lower than in much of the nation and there is an abundant supply of water at "reasonable rates to industry." Good opportunities for hunting, fishing, boating, and other recreational activities were considered increasingly important in attracting a growing labor supply to support future plant expansion. Finally, "from the Government down to our courts, law making bodies and community leadership are doing their best to make industry welcome." The principal disadvantages experienced in the Arkansas location were lack of low-cost housing and inadequate medical services.[7]

Wolverine found that many job applicants "desire to live in this area but cannot. They would move back if work were available. All seem to want to get out of urban areas such as Dallas, Los Angeles, St. Paul, etc. In addition, about 40% of our work force are people who have moved into this area from urban areas."[8] This experience is consistent with a more general analysis of industrial development in the Ozarks, which found that "migrants tended to intervene between jobs and the rural poor who would be targets for an industrialization program."[9]

The Ozarks: A Summary View

Despite the remarkably high proportion of Turnaround-Reversal counties in the Ozarks the data in table 6-3 clearly reveal that the region still lags behind the nation in many respects. Since 1959 per capita income in the Ozarks has been virtually steady at two thirds of the national average. In 1967, for example, the Ozarks figure was $2082, while that for the nation was $3159. One reason for this income gap is that the proportion of the population employed is smaller in the Ozarks than in the country as a whole. If the national average rate of 38 percent had prevailed in the region in 1967, instead of the actual rate of 31 percent, it is estimated that there would have been an additional 200,000 jobs. Moreover, those persons who are in the Ozarks labor force generally earn lower wages than do their counterparts in the same industries in other parts of the nation, and they are concentrated in low-wage industries. If in 1967 each of the region's full-time equivalent wage and salary workers had received the national annual average *for his particular industry,* regional wages and salaries would have averaged an estimated $6002, or about 95.6 percent of the United States average per worker. The remaining $180 million of the Ozarks's $940 million wage and salary gap can be attributed to an unfavorable industry mix. A relatively high

Table 6-3
Selected Comparison Indicators, United States and Ozarks Region

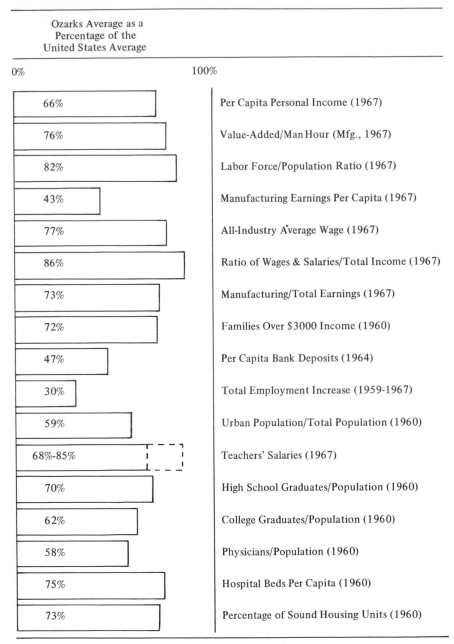

Ozarks Average as a
Percentage of the
United States Average

| 0% | | 100% |

66%	Per Capita Personal Income (1967)
76%	Value-Added/Man Hour (Mfg., 1967)
82%	Labor Force/Population Ratio (1967)
43%	Manufacturing Earnings Per Capita (1967)
77%	All-Industry Average Wage (1967)
86%	Ratio of Wages & Salaries/Total Income (1967)
73%	Manufacturing/Total Earnings (1967)
72%	Families Over $3000 Income (1960)
47%	Per Capita Bank Deposits (1964)
30%	Total Employment Increase (1959-1967)
59%	Urban Population/Total Population (1960)
68%-85%	Teachers' Salaries (1967)
70%	High School Graduates/Population (1960)
62%	College Graduates/Population (1960)
58%	Physicians/Population (1960)
75%	Hospital Beds Per Capita (1960)
73%	Percentage of Sound Housing Units (1960)

Source: *1971 Annual Report* (Little Rock and Washington, D.C.: Ozarks Regional Commission, 1972), Part II, p. IV.

proportion of agricultural employment in the region also was a significant element affecting average earnings. In 1967, 15.4 percent of total regional employment was in the agricultural sector, a proportion over three times the national average of 4.9 percent. In that year the average American agricultural worker received $4870 compared with $6698 for all workers. In the Ozarks, however, the average agricultural worker received only $1744.[10]

Shortly after serving as governor of Arkansas, Winthrop Rockefeller, in testimony to the Commission on Population Growth and the American Future, maintained that the key to the future progress of such regions as the Ozarks lies in a shift of investment away from manufacturing toward services and research, and he stressed the need for development of leisure and recreational activities, high-technology industries with emphasis on research, medical and health centers, and new forms of educational institutions.[11] Although he did not not use the term, he also argued that the development of such activities depends on the extension of urban fields: "There must be excellent access to the urban centers so that a mutually-supportive relationship can be cultivated -- and a psychological identification and dependency between city and countryside established."[12] Up to the present, however, the experience of the turnaround counties in the Ozarks conforms more to Wilbur Thompson's trickle-down hypothesis, discussed in chapter 2. Thus a study of rural industrialization and population growth in the area concludes that "the occurrence of low wage, labor intensive manufacturing in these rural counties raises the possibility that a 'filtering down' process suggested by Thompson may be occurring. That is, manufacturers who rely on the existence of pools of low wage, surplus labor are having to move on out of areas as the surplus disappears through competition with other, higher wage employees."[13]

The Ozarks Regional Commission has suggested some of the problems to be overcome: educational levels are below those of the nation as a whole; assimilation of urban, technological attitudes has been slow and resistance to change great; local financial resources may be deficient; and *skilled* labor is in short supply.[14] The commission and the relevant states are addressing themselves to the solution of these and related problems, but it is debatable whether the resources being committed are commensurate with the magnitude of the needs.

A Note on the McClellan-Kerr Waterway and Nonmetropolitan Development

The McClellan-Kerr Waterway is the largest and most expensive ($1.2 billion) project ever undertaken by the U.S. Army Corps of Engineers. It provides a navigation route from the Mississippi River through Arkansas to Catoosa, Oklahoma, near Tulsa. The navigation channel, which has a minimum depth of nine feet, has been provided with a series of locks and dams, twelve in Arkansas and five in Oklahoma. Congress approved the concept of the Arkansas River navigation system in 1949 and initial work on bank stabilization along critical portions of the river began the same year. However, the necessary appropriations for large-scale construction were not made until 1957. From 1959 on, construction proceeded smoothly until the system was finally finished in 1971.[15]

Although work on the McClellan-Kerr Waterway was not completed during the 1960s, (the decade that is the focus of this volume,) its potential role in attracting economic activity should have borne some results during that period, either on the basis of the work completed then or on the basis of the anticipated completion of the entire project in the early 1970s. The Corps of Engineers, in a document released in 1968, asserted that "one of the accepted axioms of history is that civilizations flourish on the banks of great rivers," and that "economists say elements for industrial development are present in the [Arkansas River] valley." Moreover, "Evidence that new industries will be attracted to the area and that existing industries will expand is already being demonstrated."[16]

In contrast to that authorizing the Tennessee Valley Authority, the legislation authorizing the McClellan-Kerr Waterway seemed to favor a series of public works projects rather than a coordinated effort in economic development. The effect of the federal government in the planning and operation of the system was to be minimized. In speaking of the need for the waterway, Senator Kerr stated:

Well, I'll tell you how necessary it is. If we don't promote this on a basis that we want, fifteen years from now the national necessity for its increased production through development will be so great that the Federal Government will move in here, and take this, and make it a Federal authority project, just as they did in the Tennessee Valley, and they will do it not primarily for our benefit, but for the benefit of the nation.[17]

Although the vast majority of the nation's taxpayers may have seen little harm in federal tax money benefiting the nation, overall economic planning nonetheless played little part in physical planning for the waterway. Of course, this would not necessarily preclude development in the area.

The final verdict on the degree of development resulting from the creation of the waterway must be made in the future, but it is nevertheless instructive to consider empirically the employment changes the Arkansas-Verdigris Basin from 1959 to 1971.

Variation in manufacturing and total employment was examined in eighty-five counties of Arkansas and Oklahoma: the forty-four counties of the Arkansas portion of the Ozarks Regional Commission, four counties of Arkansas not in the commission area but on the Arkansas River, and the thirty-seven counties of the Oklahoma portion of the commission area. Employment statistics were obtained from *County Business Patterns.* The period of the study is from 1959 to 1971, i.e., from the beginning of construction on the waterway to the latest year for which data were available. In situations where manufacturing employment information was not disclosed, in accordance with Department of Commerce policy, estimates were derived by the method discussed in chapter 4.

To determine whether counties along the waterway grew faster than those off the waterway during the years examined, t-tests at the .05 level of significance were used for both manufacturing and total employment. The computation process was as follows:

1. Average employment for each county during the period 1959 to 1966 inclusive was computed.

2. Average employment for each county from 1967 to 1971 inclusive was computed.

3. The ratios of the 1967-71 average to the pre-1967 average was obtained for each county. (A county ratio greater than one denotes employment growth in the 1967-71 period compared with the pre-1967 period.)

4. Weighted ratios of employment change for each county were derived by multiplying the simple ratio of step 3 by the county's proportion of the entire sample's total employment for 1971.

5. The significance of difference in the means of the weighted ratios for the waterway counties and non-waterway counties was then tested.

These calculations were made first using manufacturing data and then using total employment data. There were two reasons for bifurcating the data into the pre-1967 and 1967-71 periods. One was to reduce the effect of Vietnam War expenditures within the area; a dividing point should have two years of high expenditures (1965 and 1966) on one side and two years (1967 and 1968) on the other. The second reason, however, was more fundamental. In late 1966 the Arkansas River project was half completed; such a temporal separation would show whether, as the waterway neared completion, the waterway counties had more rapid employment growth than the non-waterway counties.

The purpose of weighting the ratio of each county was to deliberately prejudice the results in favor of counties with large labor forces. If the waterway counties had more employment growth (in manufacturing and in total employment) than the nonwaterway counties, as the project neared completion, this differential would be intensified.

The t-tests for the data in tables 6-4 through 6-7 indicate that both manufacturing and total employment grew significantly faster in the twenty-one counties along the waterway than they did in the sixty-four counties not on the waterway. However, if SMSA counties are removed, thereby lessening the possibility of employment growth due to economies of agglomeration, there is no significant differential between waterway and nonwaterway counties, although waterway counties had somewhat higher rates of growth in both

Table 6-4

Mean Weighted Employment Ratios (1967-71 to 1959-66), Arkansas and Oklahoma

	Waterway (n=21)	Nonwaterway (n=64)	
Manufacturing Employment	.0308	.0126	t = 2.28
Total Employment	.0304	.0102	t = 2.29

Table 6-5

Mean Weighted Employment Ratios (1967-71 to 1959-66), Arkansas and Oklahoma, SMSA Counties Excluded

	Waterway (n=15)	Nonwaterway (n=62)	
Manufacturing Employment	.0225	.0197	t = .38
Total Employment	.0185	.0168	t = .30

Table 6-6

Mean Weighted Employment Ratios (1967-71 to 1959-66), Arkansas, SMSA Counties Excluded

	Waterway (n=11)	Nonwaterway (n=32)	
Manufacturing Employment	.0376	.0371	t = .03
Total Employment	.0298	.0332	t = −.24

Table 6-7

Mean Weighted Employment Ratios (1967-71 to 1959-66), Oklahoma, SMSA Counties Included

	Waterway (n=6)	Nonwaterway (n=31)	
Manufacturing Employment	.0298	.0405	t = −.58
Total Employment	.0376	.0316	t = .48

manufacturing and total employment. If just the counties of Arkansas are analyzed, with the SMSA counties removed, there is no significant difference between the waterway and nonwaterway counties. In waterway counties the manufacturing growth rate is higher but the total employment growth rate is lower.

Comparable results were found for Oklahoma, although in this case the two SMSA counties were not removed because there were only six counties on the waterway. In Oklahoma the nonwaterway counties grew faster in manufacturing employment but not in total employment. In neither case was there a significant difference between waterway and nonwaterway counties.

Taken together, these results indicate that if the waterway has had a beneficial effect on employment, because of either the navigation facilities or the presence of fresh water and inexpensive hydroelectricity, this has occurred in the SMSA counties that already experienced economies of agglomeration. Field studies probably are needed to determine to what extent employment growth in the Fort Smith, Little Rock, and Pine Bluff SMSAs may have resulted from a wider range of governmental investments, external economies generated by general development, the presence of the McClellan-Kerr Waterway, and other factors. In any case, the nonmetropolitan counties on the waterway do not appear to have gained any significant advantage over those elsewhere.

Moreover, if the waterway's potential for initiating development is realized to a greater extent in the future, it may indeed owe little to present planning efforts. One study in this regard points out:

Coordinated development policies are urgently needed. No adequate coordinated effort has been made to determine the optimum and orderly development of the Arkansas-Verdigris River System in either Arkansas or Oklahoma by local, state or Federal governments, or by the private sector. As of July, 1970, economic research on the development of the waterway had been done on an ad hoc basis by various governmental agencies and private firms to satisfy specific and limited objectives. Adjustments to secure rational economic development are difficult to make once suboptimal activities are well underway.[18]

In 1969 the Ozarks Regional Commission reached an agreement with the Little Rock District of the Corps of Engineers to study economic development possibilities in the Arkansas River Valley. However, even this effort has faltered. Three years later the initial information stage of the plan was not yet started; the commission has at this writing not even asked the Corps of Engineers to begin collecting data relevant to development.[19] Moreover, even the states' role in the planning process has been very limited.[20]

Thus neither the federal government nor the states of Arkansas and Oklahoma have any agencies to coordinate effectively the use of a $1.2 billion federal investment in an area that has a pressing need for improved economic conditions. Had the federal government established in the Arkansas Basin a river authority similar to the Tennessee Valley Authority, at the initial time of planning and construction of the waterway, a framework for interstate and intrastate integration and coordination of activities between various governmental agencies and representatives of the private sector would exist today. Instead, there is only a patchwork of fragmented and ineffective ex post facto proposals. And no doubt nonmetropolitan areas will pay the greatest price in terms of forgone opportunities.

7 The Tennessee Valley

Of Tennessee's ninety-five counties, fifty-six are in the turnaround categories. In addition to being numerous, the turnaround counties are sufficiently dispersed so that their BEA (Bureau of Economic Analysis) regions cover not only all of Tennessee but also overlap those of neighboring states. Given the state's variety of people and its physical geography—ranging from the highest peaks in the Great Smoky Mountains in the east to flat cotton lands far to the west—it is particularly noteworthy that, with the exception of Vermont, Tennessee is the only state that has all of its counties included in this study.

Although Tennessee will be the main focus of this chapter, consideration will also be given to a broader area, corresponding approximately to the region covered by the Tennessee Valley Authority. The parts of Kentucky, North Carolina, Georgia, Alabama, and Mississippi which lie in this broader area contain a relatively large number of turnaround counties. Tennessee had thirty-eight Turnaround-Reversal and eighteen Turnaround-Acceleration counties; the other five states together had thirty-five Turnaround-Reversal and six Turnaround-Acceleration counties in the region considered. Although there were still many counties in the broader region which declined in population from 1960 to 1970, there were only seven in the Consistent Fast Gainer category (three of which bordered the Chattanooga SMSA) and only eleven widely dispersed Stagnant Gainer counties.

Employment Change

The data in table 7-1 refer to the whole area approximating that covered by the Tennessee Valley Authority. Between 1964 and 1969 the Turnaround-Reversal counties had the highest absolute and percentage increase in total employment. Between 1959 and 1964 they ranked second to the Consistent Fast Gainers in rate of total employment growth. Although this group had relatively rapid growth in the construction, wholesale trade, retail trade, FIRE, and service sectors between 1964 and 1969, the sector that clearly was primarily responsible for the high rate of total employment growth was manufacturing. A similar pattern exists for the period from 1959 to 1969. During both periods the Turnaround-Reversal counties had the highest growth rates in manufacturing. From 1964 to 1969 manufacturing employment increase accounted for about two thirds of the total employment increase in this group; from 1959 to 1969 the comparable proportion was 70 percent.

91

Table 7-1
Absolute and Percentage Employment Change by Sector (One-digit SIC Code) in Selected Tennessee Valley Counties, by Population Change Category, 1964-69 and 1959-69

	Total	Agricultural Services, Forestry, Fisheries	Mining	Contract Construction	Manufacturing
Absolute Change, 1964-69					
Loser	33,225	166	-1,901	1,216	16,160
Stagnant Gainer	61,430	27	57	6,632	34,381
Turnaround-Reversal	76,022	189	392	4,928	49,578
Turnaround-Acceleration	56,394	69	182	4,108	33,439
Consistent Fast Gainer	36,141	310	-9	2,059	19,503
Percentage Change, 1964-69					
Loser	23.4	30.1	-26.1	22.6	20.9
Stagnant Gainer	30.3	5.7	10.7	61.4	29.3
Turnaround-Reversal	39.3	18.1	12.7	56.0	43.9
Turnaround-Acceleration	34.7	11.6	10.5	41.4	40.5
Consistent Fast Gainer	35.1	54.3	-2.8	38.0	34.8
Absolute Change, 1959-69					
Loser	43,040	220	-5,427	1,615	27,699
Stagnant Gainer	70,674	152	34	6,124	36,797
Turnaround-Reversal	105,518	617	263	4,748	72,740
Turnaround-Acceleration	84,728	231	-261	7,026	47,917
Consistent Fast Gainer	56,268	137	78	3,500	30,719
Percentage Change, 1959-69					
Loser	36.2	53.4	-51.5	35.8	47.9
Stagnant Gainer	43.3	45.2	8.6	70.4	37.8
Turnaround-Reversal	70.8	112.4	9.0	64.8	89.6
Turnaround-Acceleration	63.1	53.2	-12.0	100.2	70.3
Consistent Fast Gainer	73.1	18.7	35.3	102.8	74.3

Table 7-1 (Continued)
Tennessee Valley

	Transportation and Other Public Utilities	Wholesale Trade	Retail Trade	Finance Insurance, and Real Estate (FIRE)	Services	Unclassified Establishments
Absolute Change, 1964-69						
Loser	149	1,007	4,325	936	10,929	142
Stagnant Gainer	1,754	2,208	6,822	1,536	7,900	123
Turnaround-Reversal	1,456	1,988	7,050	2,390	7,531	441
Turnaround-Acceleration	1,578	904	8,248	1,650	6,005	231
Consistent Fast Gainer	1,457	1,720	5,220	790	4,808	276
Percentage Change, 1964-69						
Loser	2.7	22.0	17.2	22.9	91.6	22.7
Stagnant Gainer	21.7	28.4	21.4	20.4	43.8	20.3
Turnaround-Reversal	23.2	30.9	21.6	48.3	46.0	49.2
Turnaround-Acceleration	29.3	10.5	28.9	25.7	33.1	40.1
Consistent Fast Gainer	36.1	35.5	34.3	22.5	38.0	84.9
Absolute Change, 1959-69						
Loser	772	708	5,119	1,384	11,311	−563
Stagnant Gainer	3,033	2,599	9,130	2,916	10,076	−189
Turnaround-Reversal	1,386	2,600	9,504	3,316	10,649	−157
Turnaround-Acceleration	1,855	2,888	11,534	3,181	10,521	−137
Consistent Fast Gainer	2,237	2,698	7,204	1,776	7,896	−4
Percentage Change, 1959-69						
Loser	17.6	16.9	23.6	42.5	105.8	−45.0
Stagnant Gainer	52.4	41.4	35.8	55.9	77.8	−21.8
Turnaround-Reversal	22.7	50.1	33.7	89.4	86.5	−10.6
Turnaround-Acceleration	36.3	43.4	45.6	65.0	77.2	−14.5
Consistent Fast Gainer	75.5	72.2	58.5	72.8	85.3	−.7

The Turnaround-Acceleration counties ranked third in rate of total employment increase during both periods. Here, too, the role of the manufacturing sector was particularly significant. It accounted for 59 percent of the total employment increase between 1964 and 1969 and for 57 percent of such increase between 1959 and 1969.

The Consistent Fast Gainer counties had considerable manufacturing employment growth, but, as is typically the case, they also had high growth rates in the non-goods-producing sectors. Manufacturing growth was important too in the Stagnant Gainer and Loser categories, but the rates of manufacturing change and total employment change in these groups were well behind those in the other groups. The Loser counties had the lowest rates of total employment growth in both periods, as well as in most individual sectors.

When manufacturing and service employment change for the turnaround counties are examined at the two-digit SIC level, it is evident that manufacturing gains are broadly based. For the Turnaround-Reversal counties the biggest absolute gains from 1964 to 1969 were in the rubber and plastics, electrical equipment, transportation equipment, and apparel sectors. The greatest percentage gains were in the chemicals, rubber and plastics, primary metals, machinery, electrical equipment, and transportation equipment sectors. The pattern was much the same for the 1959-69 period. For the Turnaround-Acceleration counties the biggest absolute gains from 1964 to 1969 were in the textiles, primary metals, electrical equipment, and transportation equipment sectors; from 1959 to 1964 the largest absolute gains were in the apparel, primary metals, electrical equipment, chemicals, machinery, and transportation equipment sectors. Rate of employment growth from 1964 to 1969 was highest in the rubber and plastics, transportation equipment, primary metals, fabricated metals, electrical equipment, and printing sectors. A similar pattern prevailed from 1959 to 1969.

For both groups of turnaround counties, the medical and health, educational services, and nonprofit membership organization sectors accounted for the overwhelming preponderance of total absolute growth in the services sector, although a few other sectors had high rates of growth.

Tennessee

There is widespread feeling in Tennessee that its population and employment trends make it not only part of but a leader in Southern renaissance. Tennessee's rural population declined by almost 5 percent from 1960 to 1970, but its urban population grew by almost 24 percent. (This still left the state 59 percent urban in 1970, compared with the national average of 74 percent.[1] Tennessee had net outmigration of 52,624 persons between 1960 and 1970, yet this was less than one fifth of the 272,500 net loss during the previous decade.[2] Moreover, only twenty-six of the state's ninety-five counties lost population between 1960 and 1970, compared with fifty-nine during the previous decade.[3]

Although Tennessee still ranks only forty-third among the states in per capita income, its growth in this regard was greater than that of the nation between 1960 and 1970. During this period the national value increased from $2216 to $3190; the Tennessee value almost doubled, moving from $1544 to $3051.[4] Behind this growth in per capita income is a large-scale shift of workers from farms to factories. The numbers of both farms and farmworkers have decreased, but average farm size is rising, and for every two jobs lost in the agricultural sector, five were gained in manufacturing between 1963 and 1969.[5] The manufacturing sector is not only growing but becoming more diverse. Although low-wage industries predominate in rural counties, the rates of increase of the primary metals, chemicals, and rubber and plastics groups—all high-wage sectors[6]—are high in Tennessee's turnaround counties.

The textile mills that moved south in the 1940s to be near cotton sources gave Tennessee its first real industrial impetus. They supplanted earlier coal, timber, and limestone extraction activities. Local coal was inferior to that mined elsewhere; whole forests were destroyed by the "cut, slash, and slay" techniques used to fell large trees for railroad ties; and the limestone of the Cumberland Plateau was, although handsome, difficult to transport.

Textile and garment plants are still important sources of employment, particularly in the more recently developed western portion of the state. Small apparel plants continue to locate, and relocate, in eastern mountain areas because they are not hampered by lack of level ground and adequate transportation facilities. However, new plants of these kinds are less eagerly sought in Tennessee. They pay low wages and because their skill requirements are minimal they do little to upgrade labor force capabilities. In the rugged rural areas favored by the smallest textile plants male unemployment is a serious problem, yet these firms consistently hire work forces that are 85 percent or more female. Furthermore, employment in the textile industry lacks security. Layoffs are frequent and plants often relocate when threatened with unionization. It is also noteworthy that a significant part of the population decline experienced by rural Tennessee counties after World War II was a result of the closing or cutting back of production in textile plants that made war-related fabrics. Since a number of present-day textile firms in Tennessee produce uniforms and material for military uses, the tapering off of the war in Southeast Asia may once again seriously reduce employment in areas dependent on the mills.

Some of the newer, growing industries in the state share the drawbacks of textile and garment manufacturing. Furniture plants pay low wages and hire largely female labor. Food processors, often branches of such large national companies as Pepsi Cola, Procter and Gamble, and Quaker Oats, are attracted to low-wage, heavily female, nonunionized labor markets. But some others do pay higher wages, upgrade worker skills, and emphasize male employment. The chemicals and primary metals groups consist of large, water-using firms, attracted to the area as much by its water resources and cheap power as by low wages. Producers of mobile homes, rubber and plastics, electrical machinery, and auto and metal parts often consider low wages less of an inducement to movement into Tennessee than the state's large labor supply, available land, and low-cost power. Even the textile industry may refurbish its tarnished image. Particularly in the central part of the state, home-owned garment and textile plants are beginning to branch into neighboring counties, grow larger, and become less transient. With increased use of synthetic fibers, required job skills may broaden, dependence on untrained labor may lessen, and employment opportunities may improve for males.

As its manufacturing base broadens, new plants in Tennessee are increasingly branches of existing firms or expansions of existing plants. Relocations are increasingly rare, partly because they are less sought after and partly because they are forbidden when assistance from the Economic Development Administration is involved. New plants and expansions grew from 332 in 1959 to 427 in 1969, and employment in them increased from 17,250 to 32,923.[7] Firms are still recruited from the Northeast and Middle West but special tax concessions are no longer granted to them. (Interviews indicated that Tennessee feels itself ten years ahead of such states as Arkansas and Mississippi with respect to taxation and bond incentives, which have been abandoned in Tennessee. An abundant supply of labor, cheap power, manufacturing wage rates 85 percent of the national average[8]—Tennessee is a "right to work" state—and the "amenities of southern life" are felt to be sufficient inducements to locate in Tennessee.) Another indication of the state's confidence in its ability to grow is criticism of continued recruitment of out-of-state firms. A number of officials even fear that encouraging northern-owned branch plants to enter the state will weaken Tennessee's development. According to this argument, firms owned in New York, Chicago, Pittsburgh, and other northern metropolitan centers are not hiring local engineers and architects, and home-grown middle-management is not being developed. Moreover, marketing and advertising services are imported, profits are exported, and local resource employment is generally neglected.

Local initiative is given much credit for increased manufacturing employment in Tennessee, although this has been especially instrumental with respect to lumber, furniture, and textile firms, the three lowest-paying manufacturing groups. Enthusiastic Chambers of Commerce and increased banking competition have spurred industrial development in rural areas, but union organization has been discouraged. Lack of union power is often cited as an incentive to location in the state; however, the evidence is mixed. (The Tennessee Manpower Council claims that about 1 million of the state's 1.6 million nonagricultural workers belong to unions, although other agencies cited somewhat lower figures.) Metropolitan areas and the trucking industry particularly are unionized, although some nonmetropolitan branches of large national companies also are in this category. An Eastman Kodak plant in Sullivan County, a Goodyear plant in Obion County, and a Union Carbide branch in Maury County are examples. However, many other major employers are not unionized. ITT in Gibson County, with 2000 employees; Harvey Aluminum, also in Gibson, with 2610 workers; DuPont in Humphreys County; and such major food processors as Coca-Cola, Royal Crown Cola, Pepsi Cola, Quaker Oats, and Procter and Gamble are examples. Even the largest garment plants, the HIS branches in Carroll County, which employ 2175 workers (90 percent of whom are female), have successfully resisted union organization.[9]

Turning more specifically to the geographic distribution of turnaround counties in Tennessee, it is curious that in the quarter of the state that lies west of the Tennessee River there are twelve Turnaround-Reversal counties and two Turnaround-Acceleration counties. The remaining nonmetropolitan counties in the area, five Loser counties, lie between the Memphis SMSA and the turnaround counties.

Both the Loser counties and the turnaround counties in this western area have fertile croplands that produce cotton, corn, and soy beans; both groups also lagged behind the rest of the state in rate of industrialization, particularly the Loser counties. One of the latter, Fayette County, has the lowest per capita income in the state and a school dropout rate of over 66 percent.[10] Its labor force is largely female, and its few garment, furniture, and metal parts firms are not unionized. Tipton County, like Fayette, is adjacent to the Memphis SMSA and near a large and growing naval base that is just within the metropolitan area. Yet base workers are not moving into Tipton, which has a school dropout rate of over 55 percent.[11] In this part of Tennessee cotton farms are still large enough to be called plantations. Cotton crop farming is highly mechanized, and, because it is subject to acreage restrictions, some land is held idle in soil banks. Mechanization and untilled land have accelerated the decline in farm employment opportunities in the area. Unlike the regions to the north and east, however, it has experienced little growth in manufacturing employment to offset lessened agricultural opportunities. An important element in explaining the Loser group's decline is its racial composition. Fifty-five percent of the blacks in Tennessee live west of the Tennessee River,[12] and most live in the southwestern corner. Displaced from the land, and with little alternative factory employment, they have been leaving in large numbers, some for Memphis but most for Chicago, Detroit, and other northern cities.

Labor market information for the Loser counties in the southwest is difficult to obtain because the few firms there often are reluctant to give information that might be used to accelerate federal integration efforts. Manufacturing plants have been loathe to move into the area not only because it is heavily agricultural or because its labor force is relatively unskilled but also because it is largely black. (Little effort is made, moreover, at the state level to encourage firms to locate there.) Firms producing for sale to the federal government are particularly reticent because of the government's equal-opportunity employment provisions.

(Some state officials responsible for economic development regard it as a "proven scientific fact" that "those people" cannot learn as rapidly as "we" can, and they regard efforts to improve equality of employment opportunity as a clear imposition. Some also disapproved of TVA, maintaining that it impedes industrial development by paying wages that are "too high." Although many state officials cited low skill levels and insufficient education as possible constraints on Tennessee's economic development, racial discrimination was rarely noted as a factor. The Tennessee Manpower Council was a notable exception to these remarks.)

The plight of the Loser counties surrounding Memphis is accentuated by the fact that most of the counties west and south of Nashville, some two hundred miles from Memphis, are in the turnaround category. The growth of the turnaround counties is largely attributable to a large available labor force (much of it female), relatively low wages, available land, lack of unions, and a good transportation system. In addition, most of the Turnaround-Acceleration counties in the area border the Nashville SMSA or are relatively close to it. Two of these Turnaround-Acceleration counties, both of which border the Nashville SMSA, had the region's highest proportion of persons not working in their home counties in 1960.[13]

The hub of the western Tennessee area between Nashville and Memphis is Jackson, in Madison County. Between 1960 and 1970 Jackson grew by 18.2 percent, to almost 40,000 residents, making it the largest non-SMSA city in Tennessee.

Jackson lies on Interstate 40, between Memphis and Nashville, and is traversed by two other U.S. highways. Like the rest of the Southwest, its major crops are cotton, corn, and soybeans, but only 14 percent of its labor force is in agriculture.[14] Textile and garment manufacturing, lumber and furniture production, an Owens-Corning fiberglass plant, food processing (mostly in branch plants of major national firms), a Rockwell Manufacturing Company power tools factory, and metal parts and small machine production employ the bulk of its labor force. The largest textile plant in the area, that of the Bemis Company, with 906 employees, has a 64 percent male labor force; the employees are affiliated primarily with the Textile Workers Union, but the Garment Workers, Teamsters, and International Association of Machinists unions also are represented. Male employment is generally relatively high in the area; in Jackson, only a furniture company and a garment firm have a labor force that is over 50 percent female.

New Johnsonville, on the Tennessee River in Humphreys County, also in the Turnaround-Acceleration group, is the site of a large TVA, steam-generated electricity plant. The county as a whole has moved from predominantly low-wage apparel manufacturing employment to higher-paying heavy industry, and over 90 percent of the area's employees are male. The TVA facility is itself a large employer; the Consolidated Aluminum Corporation and a DuPont titanium dioxide plant together provide over 1000 jobs. Another 422 jobs are provided by a manganese firm attracted by relatively inexpensive electrical power. (Many workers commute to the power complex from Benton County, a Turnaround-Reversal county west of the river.)

Most of the Turnaround-Reversal counties in the west are dependent on textile and garment plants (some of which are very large—an HIS sportswear plant in Gibson County employs 1800 people, 90 percent whom are female), furniture manufacturers, small metal parts firms, and footwear plants. There is a sprinkling of very large branches of national firms. A Goodyear tire plant in Obion County employs 1635 people; Gibson County contains an ITT telecommunications plant with 2000 employees and a Harvey Aluminum plant with 2610—neither of them unionized.

Montgomery County, the sole Consistent Fast Gainer in the west, is a transportation center. Two rivers, two U.S. highways, and two railroads span the county. Interstate 24, when completed, will pass through it. The county derives much employment from three large rubber and leather shoe manufacturing firms, a heating and cooling equipment plant with 1500 employees, and several small metal parts companies; however, Fort Campbell, a sprawling army reservation that straddles the Tennessee-Kentucky border, also has been important to its growth. (Christian and Trigg counties, in Kentucky, have been losing population for the last twenty years, although they, too, contain parts of Fort Campbell.)

East of Nashville the terrain rises gently to the Cumberland Plateau. Strip mines nibbling at the green hills are visible even from Interstate Highway 40; the trees themselves are scrub oak, second-growth leftovers of once rich forests. Some of this wood is used to produce charcoal, an area export, but it also contributes to an even more important regional industry—furniture. About 1950, several pieces of "promotional" furniture were produced in Cookeville, in Putnam County. Furniture stores often display such furniture as loss leaders. A promotional sofa and chair set made of poor quality rough lumber may sell for $50 or $60. Its role is to induce customers to buy more and higher priced pieces. The idea caught on, and promotional furniture plants sprang up in Macon, Jackson, and Overton counties. More recently, several companies in the area have begun to produce better quality medium-priced furniture. Other major wood-using industries in the region are pallet makers and coffin manufacturers.

Another innovation for the Upper Cumberland region was the development of a powdered metals industry. Metals reduced to dust are mixed in desired proportions, and the powder is then pressed into small machine parts. This process produces parts more cheaply than the more common methods of pressing them out of metal sheets or molding them in cores. Two of the three powdered metals plants in the south are located in the Upper Cumberland region. The market for their products is growing; Oster and Oneida, manufacturers of household appliances, are among the major buyers. Production of rubber and plastic products, mobile homes, auto parts, and small metal machines and parts has broadened the employment base of the area, but not rapidly enough to absorb all of the unemployed and underemployed.

There is still considerable migration to Indiana and Michigan, although the desire to return, given employment opportunities, is evidently strong. An advertisement in a Tennessee newspaper some years ago for forty job openings in Clay County brought several hundred responses from former residents in Gary, Muncie, and Detroit. Most of the migrants have high-school diplomas, although the median educational level of the area is only 8.1 years.[15] There is also a great deal of internal migration within the region. Cookeville in Putnam County, Crossville in Cumberland County, and McMinnville in Warren County all import labor from Van Buren, White, DeKalb, and Overton counties. A number of Cumberland County residents work in Oak Ridge. DeKalb workers commute to Rutherford and Wilson counties, and many Macon and Smith county residents travel to the Nashville area.

Of the thirteen contiguous turnaround counties that stretch from the Nashville SMSA to the Knoxville SMSA, Putnam county seems to have the greatest potential for sustained high growth. Cookeville, located about midway between Nashville and Knoxville on Interstate Highway 40, is the home of Tennessee Technological University and a center of attraction for workers commuting from surrounding counties to jobs in its garment, auto parts, heating and air conditioning, ballbearing, and charcoal plants. Neighboring Cumberland county produces mobile homes, synthetic yarns, rubber and plastic products, heaters, and garments, and in addition has several food processing plants. However, its sustained growth may be most influenced by second-home developments. As in other parts of the country, the natural beauty of the area is threatened by poor planning and even shoddy construction. (In Tennessee, zoning and building codes are determined by the counties, and there seems to be little concern at the state level for the damage being done to the environment.) As one observer remarked, these new residential areas are evidence of development, but not progress.

Important characteristics of turnaround counties in central Tennessee appear to be individual entrepreneurship, aggressive Chambers of Commerce, and community enthusiasm for growth. On the other hand, a high proportion of the industry that has grown in the region — textiles, apparel, furniture, food processing — has been of the low-wage variety. Public housing is severely pressed, a problem not helped by an increasing influx of persons who migrated from the region during and after World War II; these return migrants usually come home to retire, but often on inadequate incomes. The northern counties of central Tennessee will probably continue to experience population decline. They have accessibility difficulties because of the rugged terrain, but they also lack the entrepreneurship and Chamber of Commerce zeal found in the turnaround counties to the south. A lack of competitive banking also has been cited as a restraint on growth; Overton County, a northern Turnaround-Reversal county bordered by four of the Loser Counties, began to grow when a second bank moved in and created a more competitive atmosphere, which led in turn to the creation of a vigorous Chamber of Commerce.

The rich lands east of Knoxville were first settled by Pennsylvania Dutch farmers. The Turnaround-Acceleration counties of Greene, Jefferson, Cocke, and Sevier have prospered as agricultural communities since their settlement. (Of the four, only Cocke County suffered some depression before its modern growth period.) Tobacco is the main cash crop of the region, followed by dairy farming and beef cattle. More recent growth can be attributed to manufacturing development and, in Sevier County, to recreation and tourism. Textiles, garments, furniture, and food processing dominate the area's manufacturing sector. The area was industrialized before the western counties began to attract manufacturing firms, and its plants tend to be older and larger than similar ones in the west.

Sevier County contains large textile and garment plants, and a number of small handicraft shops, producing pottery, handmade furniture, and dulcimers. But its greatest growth is due to the expansion of its tourism and recreational facilities. The area around Gatlinburg, the gateway to the Great Smokey Mountains, teems with high-priced hotels, "Swiss villages," and quickly and shoddily constructed resort communities. Sevier County is just becoming aware of the violence being done its land and is forming a planning council. However, without state supervision of subdivision ordinances, Sevier, like Cumberland County, will find land use regulation difficult. Many Sevier residents still oppose any regulations that restrict an individual's right to do as he wishes with privately held property. Exploitation of the land will surely increase, for summer tourism in Sevier is being supplemented by a growing ski industry. Snow machines are used to extend the season, and recreational facilities are now being used almost year round. In addition, the area is becoming popular for fall conventions and fairs.

The Turnaround-Reversal counties of Claiborne, Union, Grainger, and Hawkins, which lie northeast of Knoxville, created their own industrial jobs. Readily available electrical power and a large labor force enabled these counties to recruit branch plants of out-of-state firms. Hawkins County has a fairly diverse industrial sector. Textiles, furniture, glass, and plastics firms are its major employers, and female employment is high. Textiles are also important to Claiborne County, though it has a locally owned mobile home plant which produces campers. Union and Grainger counties are less industrialized. They serve as residence communities for commuters to the Knox and Hamblen county employment centers. Grainger does contain a mobile home plant, but most of its residents work outside the county.

The extreme northeastern portion of Tennessee consists of a rugged and variable mountainous region, as well as the Great Valley, whose level terrain invites large manufacturing and warehousing facilities. Manufacturing is the largest single sector in the area; it grew by 43 percent between 1964 and 1971, while the agricultural sector declined from 11 percent of the work force to 7 percent.[16] A number of very large manufacturing firms are found in the area, most clustering around Kingsport and Bristol in Sullivan County. These, and the cities of Elizabethton in Carter County and Johnson City in Washington County, account for over half the entire region's industrial growth. The largest firms are found in chemicals (which employs 32 percent of the region's manufacturing workers but is hampered by a lack of sufficient water resources,[17]) electronics, and paper and printing. Electrical machinery parts manufactured elsewhere are assembled in the area, and glass products, textile, and apparel plants add to employment opportunities.

Industry first developed around the Kingsport-Bristol-Johnson City area because of available utility services, but firms then began to move toward rural areas for labor. More recently, Appalachian Regional Commission funds have been an important element in sustaining the area's growth. Efficient use of local resources also has been promoted by increasing intercounty cooperation. The Tri-Cities, for example, share a regional airport and an industrial park. Nearby Elizabethton is joining the three larger cities in other cooperative ventures, while Monroe and Lowdon counties are planning a joint water facility.

Finally, it is instructive to note some policy implications of labor mobility in the Tennessee Valley region.[18] Between 1960 and 1965, the Tennessee Valley region (defined here to include 201 counties) had a net loss of 8600 workers as a result of migration. Although there was net inmigration of 2700 white males, there was net outmigration of 2200 white females, 8300 black males, and 800 black females. The southeast accounted for more than 60 percent of all inmigrants and the Great Lakes states for another 15 percent. During the 1960-65 period employment in manufacturing represented the largest proportion of the increase in total employment, accounting for slightly over 40 percent of the increase. It is low-wage manufacturing industries;[19] male employment in these sectors rose by 24,800, female by 41,800. New entrants were the most important source of new manufacturing workers. Net entry (entrants minus retirees) represented about 60 percent of the increase. Within the region's high-wage manufacturing sector[20] there was net inmigration of 6000 experienced manufacturing workers, even though the region lost a net 1600 manufacturing workers to other regions. In other words, a net importation of experienced workers into high-wage industries was more than offset by losses from the medium- and low-wage sectors. The importance of experience in high-wage manufacturing is seen in the fact that retirees outnumbered new entrants. In contrast, 81 percent of the net growth in low-wage manufacturing and 73 percent of that in medium-wage manufacturing was accounted for by new entrants. Thus, the Tennessee Valley has been importing skilled workers from the North and West into high-wage sectors, whereas low- and medium-wage sectors draw more directly on local new entrants to the labor force. It is evident that:

either the market mechanism for the transfer of workers between medium- and high-wage manufacturing is inadequate or that the skills required in high-wage manufacturing are different from those possessed by resident medium-wage manufacturing workers. The apparent inability of the region to meet the needs of high-wage industry for skilled workers suggests the need for training and placement programs which will provide the skilled workers the region now imports in sizable numbers and to replace imported workers who retire. This replacement market for workers may in the long run be one of the major impacts of the current industrial development. Fortunately, the need for such replacements can be anticipated and appropriate training programmed well in advance.[21]

The importation of skilled workers may thus be viewed as a first step in a process that permits more rapid development, and which will lead, in time, to improved opportunities for the resident labor force.

Northern Alabama

In the entire part of Alabama lying north of Birmingham — approximately one third of the state — only one county (Cherokee, on the Georgia border) lost population between 1960 and 1970. There were ten Turnaround-Reversal counties and two Turnaround-Acceleration counties in the area.

Growth in the five-county Top of Alabama Regional Council of Governments (TARCOG) area, in the northeast corner of the state, was particularly rapid. While the entire state of Alabama grew by 177,000 persons from 1960 to 1970, the population of the TARCOG region grew by over 80,000. The region was transformed from an agricultural to a manufacturing and service-based economy. About 45,000 new jobs were created, outmigration slowed to a trickle, and incomes rose rapidly. The growth of Huntsville during this period tends to obscure the fact that during the last part of the 1960s there was unprecedented industrial employment expansion in each of the four outlying counties. For example, Jackson County, in the Turnaround-Reversal category, had only 1980 manufacturing jobs in 1960 for its population of nearly 40,000. By 1965 manufacturing employment had risen to 2720; during the next five years Revere Copper and Brass and Goodyear built plants in the Scottsboro area, bringing the manufacturing total to over 5000 jobs. Marshall County, in the Turnaround-Acceleration category, had a similar, if less dramatic, increase, from 3490 in 1965 to over 6000 in 1971.[22]

The rapid expansion of the TARCOG region began about twenty years ago when the federal government decided to move the core of the nation's missile and rocket development team to Huntsville. Many of the billions of dollars that have been invested in research and development related to the aerospace industry have passed through the economy of Huntsville and adjacent areas. Huntsville grew from a population of a little over 15,000 in 1950 to a metropolitan area of 137,000 persons in 1970. During its peak growth years in the 1960s it was one of the four fastest-growing cities in the nation. Although cutbacks in the aerospace field in the later 1960s affected the Huntsville area, the slack was largely taken up by rapid industrial growth.

The role of TVA has also been significant in this area. According to one report, TVA

constitutes possibly the TARCOG region's most valuable resource. The 201 counties in the Tennessee Valley region have been one of the South's greatest growth areas outside the sub-tropical regions. Within that 201-county area those counties with direct access to the river have, as a group, shown greater gains than those counties not on the river. This observation is most important for the TARCOG counties as four of the five counties in the region have considerable developable land on the Tennessee River. Only DeKalb County has no access to the river and has predictably grown at the slowest rate during the past 10 years.[23]

While it is expected that the 1970s will extend the expansion of the 1965-70 period, the TARCOG region nevertheless faces area development problems. The industry mix is dominated by slowly, or at best moderately, growing industries that pay low wages and employ relatively unskilled workers. The rural counties are overly dependent on the textile, apparel, and food processing sectors, which pay even lower wages per employee than the statewide averages for these sectors. The instability of the aerospace economy is also a problem; employment may well decline in this sector over the next decade. Per capita incomes in the region's rural counties are only two thirds of that of Madison County (Huntsville), and housing quality for rural residents is on average far below that in urban areas.[24] According to 1970 census estimates, 22 percent of the families in Limestone County live below the poverty level; the corresponding figures for DeKalb and Jackson counties were 29 and 22 percent, respectively. The Alabama total was 31 percent for all families and 26 percent for rural families.[25] Lack of sufficient food, inadequate housing, and poor health complicate the poverty problem by handicapping the poor with respect to the training and employment opportunities that would break the poverty cycle. Nevertheless, an improved system of manpower planning and manpower training is critical.

Today in many parts of the region vocational and technical training and education programs are offered in skill areas that are not in heavy demand. Agricultural education programs still dominate the vocational programs of some schools in an era when more jobs are lost in agriculture than gained. Furthermore, the industrial development efforts of the region's cities and counties are often handicapped by the lack of adequate training programs for the skills needed by prospective industries.[26]

Despite these problems the region at least has the advantage of being able to work toward their resolution within a context of growth, a prospect not often open to those parts of the state that are more heavily black in racial composition. A little over a quarter of Alabama's population in 1970 was black; the corresponding proportion in the TARCOG region was only 11 percent. Here, as in other growing areas of the South, a marked predominance of whites appears to be an advantage in the quest for new economic activity.

The Turnaround-Reversal counties outside of the TARCOG region also are heavily white. Whereas blacks make up a little over 11 percent of the national population, they represent only 1 percent of the population of Cullman County; 2 percent of Blount County; 3 percent of Marion County; and 5 percent of Franklin County. They account for 14 percent of the population in Fayette, Lamar, and St. Clair counties. In Lawrence County blacks make up 19 percent of the population.[27] (Data were not given for Winston County, which apparently was omitted by mistake from the third count census volume for Alabama.)

Lawrence County, with a relatively high proportion of blacks, appears to be growing largely as a result of residents who actually work in neighboring counties, in cities such as Florence, Muscle Shoals, Sheffield, Tuscumbia, and Decatur. Most of the land in Lawrence County is held by very conservative large landowners; one informed observer described it as "still in the nineteenth century." In contrast, Cullman County, with only 521 blacks in a population of 52,445, was largely settled by Germans and has no history of slave ownership. Cullman, one of six Turnaround-Reversal counties bordering the Birmingham SMSA, has been more closely linked to the latter by the construction of Interstate Highway 65. It contains the largest poultry processing facility in Alabama and has attracted a number of other small industries.

St. Clair County is a residential suburb of Birmingham and may well become part of the SMSA by 1980. Much of its growth can be attributed to a dam and lake complex built by the Alabama Power Company. Power and recreational facilities have particularly contributed to the growth of Pell City, which has become a favored residential area for persons working in Birmingham. Neighboring Blount County has benefited even more from "spillovers" from Birmingham.

Marion, Franklin, and Winston counties, in the northwestern part of Alabama, have shifted from primarily agricultural pursuits to industry, primarily the manufacturing of mobile homes. (Even within the agricultural sector there has been a shift from cotton to cattle and soybeans.) Manufacturing activities linked to mobile home production (bedding, furniture, trussed roofs) have also appeared. Although the major mobile home plants in this area were relocated from northern Indiana, a number of the smaller ones have been developed locally. Finally, Franklin County has gained a considerable number of residents who commute to Florence for employment.

Northeastern Mississippi

In the northeastern corner of Mississippi there are seven Turnaround-Reversal counties and one Turnaround-Acceleration county. This block is contiguous with large blocks of turnaround counties in Tennessee to the north and Alabama to the east. The Mississippi turnaround counties have experienced rapid manufacturing employment growth. Again, as in much of the growing South, population composition is heavily white. Whereas 37 percent of the population of Mississippi as a whole was black in 1970, in the northeastern turnaround counties only 17 percent of the population was black. Excluding the southernmost county, Monroe, which has about one third of all the blacks in the area, the proportion of blacks is less than 14 percent.[28]

A recent study[29] by Thomas Till comparing two of these turnaround counties to two counties in the southwestern part of the state sheds a great deal of light on the reasons for growth in the former and stagnation in the latter. The northeastern counties, Tippah and Alcorn, are oriented toward the city of Corinth. Their combined total nonfarm employment grew twice as fast of that in the nation during the 1960s, and their rate of manufacturing employment growth was four times as great. In contrast, the two southwestern counties, Adams and Jefferson, which are oriented toward Natchez, lost population, stagnated in manufacturing, and had total nonfarm employment growth below that of the nation. It may be noted that all four counties were more than fifty miles from an SMSA.

The southwestern counties, among the first settled in Mississippi, were originally cotton country; the stately antebellum mansions of Natchez attest to the wealth of the early plantation owners. Today, however, cotton has been largely displaced by corn, sorghum, and cattle. Lumbering also is important; most of the large pine forests are owned by large paper companies. Fayette, the county seat of Jefferson County, gained a measure of fame from the election of Charles Evers and an all-black city council in 1969.

The northeastern counties are in hill country extending from the Appalachians. The uneven terrain made it an area of small farmers, and populism flourished in opposition to the planter aristocracy, though not on racial matters. These counties are close to the Tennessee River and have benefitted from favorable power rates. In many ways, they are more a part of the border south areas in Tennessee than they are of the traditional Mississippi of Natchez.

Till's interviews with local and state officials, as well as local industry executives, indicated that companies moving to rural southern counties wish to avoid unions. This hurts Natchez, where over half of the manufacturing employees work in two unionized plants that pay relatively high wages. Lower-wage industries are reluctant to locate there out of fear of unionization and upward pressure on wage rates. In Corinth, only three out of sixteen manufacturing firms are unionized. Such large firms as ITT (1197 employees), Wurlitzer (650), Corinth Manufacturing (500), and Century Electric (612) are nonunion.

A second factor behind the growth disparities was the quality of the labor force. It was generally agreed that two decades of rapid industrialization have given workers in the northeastern counties greater factory experience and skills than in the southwestern counties, where, outside of Natchez, there has been little but agricultural and lumbering work. Citing the factory discipline in his Corinth plant, an executive indicated that the efficiency of his labor force was 85 percent of norms based on time and motion studies, whereas similar plants elsewhere had difficulty reaching 75 percent.

It also was generally agreed that it is difficult to get industry to go to heavily black areas. The two northeastern counties are only 14 percent black, while the two southwestern counties are 54 percent black. Many manufacturers feel that blacks tend to unionize more readily than rural whites. Blacks tend to have fewer factory skills and less experience (which would be related to past discrimination against black applicants), and hence lower productivity. There were differences in opinion over the relative productivity of blacks once they acquired job skills. However, one official who did not seem otherwise sympathethic to blacks admitted that manufacturers in southern Mississippi have been generally satisfied with the productivity of black workers once the transition period had passed.

There was considerable disagreement over the importance of community leadership, but none over the fact that relative nearness to midwestern and eastern markets (as well as southern SMSA markets) favored the northeastern counties. It also was agreed that access to lower TVA power rates was instrumental in bringing some capital intensive firms to the northeast.

To the extent that these observations are correct, it would seem that lack of unionization, heavily white racial composition, labor quality, lower power rates, and relative nearness to national markets will continue to favor the growth of the northeast and handicap those areas most in need of more and better employment opportunities.

The Role of the Tennessee Valley Authority

Controversy has surrounded the Tennessee Valley Authority since its establishment as a federal corporation in 1933. In a summary review of published materials and recent interviews concerning the TVA's activities, Ray Marshall concludes:

In contrast to its active and aggressive approach to the physical development of the area, TVA has taken a very passive approach to human resource development. It is probably not surprising, therefore, that TVA has achieved a worldwide reputation as a successful multi-unit, multi-purpose river management system but has had less impact on social and economic development. In other words, TVA clearly has had an impact as a power-producing, flood control, and reclamation agency and undoubtedly has caused per capita incomes in the area to be higher than they would have been without TVA's programs, but we know

Table 7-2

New Industrial Plants and Expansions in the TVA Area: Establishments Added or Expanded, Electric Energy Required, Employment and Payrolls Created, and Investment, Manufacturing Groups Ranked by 1963-68 Average Weekly Earnings for the United States, 1959-68

Average weekly earnings and manufacturing group[a]	Establishments	Electrical energy (KWs)	Employment	Annual payrolls	Investment Total	Investment Per establishment	Investment Per worker
	number	thousand	thousand	million dollars	million dollars	thousand dollars	thousand dollars
$125 or higher							
29–Petroleum, coal products	42	10	0.7	4.9	6	146	9.1
37–Transportation equipment	188	58	16.0	113.0	80	426	5.0
33–Primary metals	164	1,222	9.6	66.6	597	3,642	61.9
35–Nonelectrical machinery	297	96	15.7	103.4	143	481	9.1
Total	691	1,386	42.0	287.9	826	1,196	19.7
$110-124							
28–Chemicals	384	999	21.5	135.1	1,024	2,667	47.7
27–Printing, publishing	111	13	3.1	19.2	27	243	8.6
34–Fabricated metals	356	93	17.5	105.8.	166	467	9.5
26–Paper, allied	125	177	10.4	61.6	387	3,095	37.4
Total	976	1,282	52.5	321.7	1,604	1,644	30.6
$100-109							
32–Stone, clay, glass	296	147	8.3	47.4	162	547	19.5
38–Instruments	48	16	4.5	25.9	40	828	8.7
30–Rubber, miscellaneous plastics	179	102	14.3	80.4	188	1,048	13.1
36–Electrical machinery	254	183	34.2	187.8	246	969	7.2
20–Food, kindred products	431	90	10.8	56.5	109	254	10.2
Total	1,208	538	72.1	398.0	745	617	10.3

$80-99						
24–Lumber, wood products	297	56	8.8	40.6	49	166	5.6
25–Furniture, fixtures	336	66	26.5	121.2	82	242	3.1
Total	633	122	35.3	161.8	131	207	3.7
Less than $80						
22–Textiles	393	181	27.8	112.1	187	475	6.7
31–Leathers	92	25	9.8	36.6	24	264	2.5
23–Apparel	635	95	87.7	305.9	115	181	1.3
Total	1,120	301	125.3	454.6	326	291	2.6
All other						
39–Miscellaneous[b]	163	24	7.7	34.7	29	180	3.8
Total	4,791	3,653	334.9	1,658.7	3,661	764	10.9

[a]Average weekly earning represent those for production workers as listed in *Handbook of Labor Statistics 1968* (39).

[b]Includes 10 establishments in groups 19 (ordnance) and 21 (tobacco).

Source: Claude C. Haren, "Rural Industrial Growth in the 1960's," *American Journal of Agricultural Economics*, Vol. 53, No. 3 (August, 1970), p. 435.

very little about the distribution of TVA program benefits among various income and racial groups or the extent to which various groups influenced TVA's program content. We do know that the TVA has given very little attention to influencing these socioeconomic relations and apparently elected to ally itself primarily with the controlling political and economic interests in the valley.[30]

Having reviewed the materials upon which Marshall's assessment is based, I agree with its basic points. Nevertheless, the fact that the area covered by the TVA corresponds closely to the cluster of counties selected quite independently for study in this chapter implies some possible association.

In the ten-year period from 1959 through 1968 nearly 5000 new plants and expansions were constructed in the Tennessee Valley region, at a cost of about $3.5 billion. At the same time, TVA invested three quarters of a billion dollars in additional electrical energy generation capacity. Table 7-2 presents data on industrial expansion and electrical energy required in the TVA area from 1959 to 1968, by manufacturing groups ranked by 1963-68 average weekly earnings for the United States. Investment in new and improved facilities per worker was only about one half the average for the whole country, a phenomenon that might be expected in a rural area where plentiful and relatively cheap labor is a major attraction for industry. Almost half of the new manufacturing jobs in the Tennessee Valley region were in lumber and wood products, furniture, textiles, leather, and apparel — industries whose weekly earnings averaged less than $100. On the other hand, the primary metals, chemicals, and paper and allied products sectors attracted over half of the investment funds flowing into the region during the ten-year period. These three sectors also were responsible for an even greater proportion of the increased demand for electrical energy, accounting for nearly two thirds of the kilowatt-hours required over the decade. Yet they provided only 14 percent of the plant additions and only 12 percent of the employment increase.

The lesson to be drawn is clear. Although there is some correlation between TVA's relatively cheap electrical power and economic development, it is difficult to assert a causal relationship between employment growth in the Tennessee Valley and TVA power. Claude Haren is essentially correct in maintaining that "recent developments point to a continuation of the role of the Tennessee Valley area in setting the pace for increased industrial diversification and decentralization in the South. The region, too, could well move to the forefront in broadening area economic bases and adding to the community amenities needed throughout so much of today's rural America."[31] Although cheap power and cheap labor do not mean that the Tennessee Valley has the overall amenities of the northern regions examined in this volume, its attractiveness is nonetheless real. Greater understanding of these advantages nevertheless requires more detailed investigation than permitted by the resources available here.

8 Colorado and New Mexico

With the exception of one fifteen-mile break, a continuous chain of turnaround counties runs through central Colorado and New Mexico from the Wyoming border well down into New Mexico. In this area there are nine Turnaround-Reversal counties in Colorado and two in New Mexico; there are four Turnaround-Acceleration counties in Colorado and two in New Mexico. The two states together also have, within the areas being considered, five Stagnant Gainers (all in the western parts of the states), twenty-three widely scattered Losers, and five Consistent Fast Gainers.

Two of the Consistent Fast Gainer counties, Douglas and Larimer, border the Denver SMSA. Douglas County has become in many respects a dormitory community for Denver workers. It has acquired a considerable amount of suburban sprawl because of the demand for large lots by people moving out of the metropolitan area. Larimer County, on Interstate Highway 25 linking Denver and Cheyenne, Wyoming, has grown not only because of its strategic position from a transportation standpoint, but also because of the expansion of Colorado State University at Fort Collins. Moreover, a large number of persons who work in a recently established major Kodak plant in Weld County, to the east, live in Larimer County. The other three Consistent Fast Gainers — Fremont, Chaffee, and Pitkin (which contains Aspen) — lie on the route linking Colorado Springs with the Aspen winter sports area. Canon City, in Fremont County, is itself a major tourism and retirement center, but the county also has diversified manufacturing and is a major producer of the carnations sold on many an American streetcorner. Chaffee County provides services to a large number of tourists and is home for a considerable number of miners who work in Lake County, to the north.

Employment Change

The Consistent Fast Gainer counties had the highest absolute total employment gains, as well as the highest rates of growth, for both the 1964-69 and 1959-69 periods (see table 8-1). Between 1964 and 1969 they had the highest growth rates in construction, manufacturing, transportation, retail trade, and FIRE. Between 1959 and 1969 they had the highest growth rates in manufacturing, transportation, retail trade, FIRE, and services. The Loser and Stagnant Gainer groups had by far the lowest rates of total employment growth in both periods, though they did have relatively high rates of manufacturing employment growth in both periods.

111

Table 8-1
Absolute and Percentage Employment Change by Sector (One-digit SIC Code) in Selected Colorado and New Mexico Counties, by Population Change Category, 1964-69 and 1959-69

	Total	Agricultural Services, Forestry, Fisheries	Mining	Contract Construction	Manufacturing
Absolute Change, 1964-69					
Loser	5,193	111	454	478	1,635
Stagnant Gainer	6,058	44	846	98	1,478
Turnaround-Reversal	3,273	0	656	180	88
Turnaround-Acceleration	5,235	34	-600	380	314
Consistent Fast Gainer	9,979	24	-113	926	2,941
Percentage Change, 1964-69					
Loser	20.4	205.6	12.4	26.3	72.5
Stagnant Gainer	25.0	122.2	18.9	7.5	83.9
Turnaround-Reversal	48.2	0	69.6	31.3	12.6
Turnaround-Acceleration	36.3	77.3	-18.3	37.0	28.4
Consistent Fast Gainer	64.6	53.3	-23.0	75.1	92.1
Absolute Change, 1959-69					
Loser	5,234	122	330	601	1,855
Stagnant Gainer	6,471	41	470	-499	1,490
Turnaround-Reversal	4,830	3	848	474	169
Turnaround-Acceleration	6,516	63	457	-9	14
Consistent Fast Gainer	13,634	34	-163	1,322	3,224
Percentage Change, 1959-69					
Loser	20.6	283.7	8.8	35.4	91.2
Stagnant Gainer	29.6	110.8	9.7	-28.2	86.6
Turnaround-Reversal	92.3	33.3	113.1	168.1	27.3
Turnaround-Acceleration	55.1	484.6	20.6	-.8	1.3
Consistent Fast Gainer	115.6	97.1	-30.1	157.9	110.7

Table 8-1 (Continued)
Colorado and New Mexico

	Transportation and Other Public Utilities	Wholesale Trade	Retail Trade	Finance, Insurance, and Real Estate (FIRE)	Services	Unclassified Establishments
Absolute Change, 1964-69						
Loser	-576	145	1,155	173	1,476	117
Stagnant Gainer	121	273	1,529	261	1,438	-29
Turnaround-Reversal	65	54	742	149	1,313	33
Turnaround-Acceleration	65	77	1,590	24	2,843	75
Consistent Fast Gainer	301	-76	2,801	626	2,592	-28
Percentage Change, 1964-69						
Loser	-19.1	-.7	-.9	14.8	34.5	82.4
Stagnant	5.2	7.5	16.0	25.3	28.1	-18.4
Turnaround-Reversal	11.7	40.9	36.1	55.8	89.7	36.3
Turnaround-Acceleration	7.5	16.1	47.0	2.4	91.5	64.1
Consistent Fast Gainer	37.0	-12.2	60.1	86.2	74.0	-18.5
Absolute Change, 1959-69						
Loser	-785	131	1,088	217	1,577	87
Stagnant Gainer	447	478	1,591	345	2,211	-101
Turnaround-Reversal	168	73	1,133	224	1,696	57
Turnaround-Acceleration	108	159	1,747	112	3,395	37
Consistent Fast Gainer	323	58	4,063	783	3,948	49
Percentage Change, 1959-69						
Loser	-24.3	6.7	14.9	19.4	37.7	50.6
Stagnant Gainer	22.4	34.7	27.4	39.4	68.8	-44.3
Turnaround-Reversal	37.0	64.6	68.0	116.7	157.0	85.1
Turnaround-Acceleration	13.9	42.4	57.4	13.0	153.8	36.6
Consistent Fast Gainer	40.8	11.8	119.6	137.6	183.9	66.2

Of the turnaround counties, the Turnaround-Reversal group had the highest rates of growth in total employment between both 1964 and 1969 and 1959 and 1969. Between 1964 and 1969 the growth rates for this group were particularly high in the service sector, followed by mining. In absolute terms, these two sectors accounted for 60 percent of total employment growth. These two sectors and the retail trade sector accounted for 83 percent of the absolute increase. From 1959 to 1969 the construction sector had a remarkably high rate of growth, but it was followed closely by services. FIRE and mining also registered relatively rapid gains. Absolute growth was greatest in services, which accounted for over a third of the total employment increase, followed by retail trade, mining, and construction.

The services and retail trade sectors were even more important in the growth of the Turnaround-Acceleration counties, with the former having particularly high rates of growth and absolute increases during both time periods. Between 1964 and 1969 they accounted for 85 percent of the absolute increase in total employment; between 1959 and 1969 the comparable figure was 79 percent. As in the case of the Turnaround-Reversal group, manufacturing gains were practically negligible. From 1964 to 1969, the greatest gains in service employment in the Turnaround-Reversal counties were in the recreation and hotel sectors; for the 1959-69 period the greatest gains were in the hotel, nonprofit membership organization, and recreation sectors. In both time periods the greatest service employment increases in the Turnaround-Acceleration counties were in the nonprofit membership organization, medical and health, educational services, and hotel sectors. Because *County Business Patterns* data refer only to employment in mid-March in each year, employment in the recreation sector is no doubt understated; summer recreation employment is of course omitted altogether and the winter recreation season would have passed its peak.

New Mexico

From 1930 to 1940 the population of New Mexico grew over three times as rapidly as that of the United States. In the next two decades the state's rate of growth was almost twice that of the nation as a whole. However, from 1960 to 1970 the growth rate was only 6.8 percent (down from 39.6 percent the previous decade), or about half the rate of increase for the rest of the nation. This phenomenon is even more striking when one considers that neighboring states grew relatively rapidly: Arizona by 36 percent; Colorado, 25.8 percent; Utah, 18.9 percent; and Texas, 16.9 percent.

The reasons for New Mexico's relatively slow growth — and a net outmigration rate of 12.8 percent between 1960 and 1970, or some 120,000 persons — are still conjectural. Declines in the potash and oil industries have led to movement away from areas where these industries were important; and the closing of some military installations, especially Walker Air Force Base in the southeast part of the state, has had a depressing effect on the places concerned.[1] Undoubtedly declines in agricultural employment were not offset by increases in other sectors in many parts of the state.

The region which is the principal concern of this section contrasts rather notably with the rest of the state. North central New Mexico, for present purposes, includes Bernalillo County (the Albuquerque SMSA), Santa Fe County (Santa Fe city), and the five counties between them and the Colorado border. Of the four New Mexico counties that grew by 20 percent or more between 1960 and 1970, three are in this relatively small area. (This allows for an upward rounding of Santa Fe's 19.5 percent growth rate.) Sandoval County grew by 23 percent; Bernalillo and Santa Fe grew by 20 percent each. (Curry County, one of only two counties in the eastern part of the state to grow in population, registered a 21 percent increase.) In absolute terms the two fastest-growing counties in New Mexico were Bernalillo, which grew by 53,575 persons, and Santa Fe, which added 8786 persons to its population. Santa Fe was classified as a nonmetropolitan Turnaround-Acceleration county because its population was just short of that needed for SMSA status. The other Turnaround-Acceleration county, Sandoval, undoubtedly owes its top ranking in population growth to the fact that it is adjacent to both Bernalillo and Santa Fe counties and is traversed by Interstate Highway 25, which links Albuquerque and Sante Fe. In 1970 Sandoval County was still over 75 percent rural according to Bureau of the Census criteria, but many of its residents commute to Santa Fe, and more especially Albuquerque, to work, and others shop and otherwise participate in "urban" life on a fairly regular basis.

The two Turnaround-Reversal counties also are over 75 percent rural. The very modest 4 percent growth of population in Rio Arriba County is solely attributable to the expansion of population in the Espanola area, which overlaps Rio Arriba and Santa Fe counties. Many persons working in nearby Los Alamos[2] live in Espanola, and others who work in the city of Santa Fe, only twenty-three miles away, take advantage of cheaper housing costs in the smaller city. The truly rural areas of this vast county have experienced a diminishing agricultural base and contracting population. Between 1940 and 1960 Taos County declined in population because of shrinking agricultural activity and consequent outmigration of redundant workers. However, the county grew by about 10 percent between 1960 and 1970 as a result of expanded mining activity near Questa and growth of the town of Taos, which contains the best known of all the Pueblo communities.[3]

In general, then, rural areas in north central New Mexico have declined in population, or at best remained constant. The dominant trend is one of rural decline accompanied by intensive urban growth primarily limited to the vicinity of the Rio Grande Valley. The centers of growth in the region are the Santa Fe-Espanola-Los Alamos triangle and the Santa Fe-Albuquerque axis.

Nevertheless, the attractiveness of the growth areas cannot be divorced from the attributes of the whole region. Browsing through a propaganda document published by the New Mexico Department of Development's Tourist Division I was struck by the almost exact geographic coincidence of its section on the "historic area" and the turnaround counties being studied here. Despite its promotional flavor the terse description of the region rings true:

History pervades all of New Mexico, but this region was from the late 16th Century the center of Spanish settlement, the capital of the province of New Spain, and eventually the terminal point for the 19th Century trade route called the Santa Fe Trail. The city of Santa Fe, capital of New Mexico since 1609, still reflects the Indian-Spanish architecture and way of life, as do Taos, the famous art colony, and many small mountain villages in the Sangre de Cristo Range. Much of this area is high mountain country, cool and green, watered by mountain streams, a lure to campers, hikers, hunters, fishermen and in recent years, skiers. More than a dozen Indian pueblos nestle in the valleys of the Rio Grande and its tributaries, and the fascinating ruins of hundreds of earlier Indian settlements attract both tourists and archaeologists. Science is important here, too. The new city of Los Alamos, a nuclear research center, symbolizes the modern energy which complements the historic atmosphere of this region.[4]

Despite the attractiveness of north central New Mexico and its turnaround status, the concentration of growth in a relatively few areas has still left considerable poverty, especially in the declining rural areas. For example, at the end of 1970 New Mexico had a 6.5 percent rate of unemployment. The two Turnaround-Reversal counties, Rio Arriba and Taos, had corresponding rates of 18.6 and 10.6 percent, respectively. Even Santa Fe County had a relatively high 6.8 percent unemployment rate. All of the turnaround counties had a higher proportion of the population receiving welfare payments than did the state as a whole; whereas the state had 7.7 percent of the population in this status, the proportion in the turnaround counties ranged from 8.2 percent in Santa Fe County to 17.8 percent in Taos County. A similar pattern prevailed with respect to the percentage of the total population in food stamp or commodity programs. The relevant state average in 1971 was 14.8 percent; in the north central turnaround counties it ranged from 18.4 percent in Santa Fe County to 35.1 percent in Taos County, with Sandoval County not far behind at 35.0 percent.[5] In 1959, 24.4 percent of the families in New Mexico had incomes under $3000, but in the north central turnaround counties the comparable proportions were 26.3 percent in Santa Fe County; 50.2 percent in Rio Arriba County; 58.3 percent in Sandoval County; and 64.9 percent in Taos County.[6]

The relatively high levels of poverty in the turnaround counties no doubt weigh most heavily on the Spanish Americans and Indians who are relatively concentrated in the rural areas. In 1960, over half of the population of Santa Fe County was in the Spanish surname group, and in each of the other turnaround counties the proportion was about 70 percent.[7] The following Pueblo Indian tribes, with 1968 population estimates, are located in the turnaround counties:

Cochiti (490); Jemez (1380); Laguna, in part (2880); Nambe (200); Picuris (80); Pojoaque (40); Sandia, in part (180); San Felipe (1340); San Ildefonso (420); San Juan (790); Santa Ana (400); Santa Clara (710); Santo Domingo (1940); Taos (1190); Tesuque (300); and Zia (380). In addition, there are an estimated 1500 Jicarilla Apaches and the area contains part of the Canoncito Navajo tribe, with an estimated 740 members.[8]

Expanded industrial and tourism-recreation activities frequently are advocated as means to extend greater opportunity to the economically less fortunate groups in central New Mexico, as elsewhere. However, such policies may conflict with the objectives of those who are primarily concerned with protection of the environment. One regional organization has put the question in the following terms:

The issue of regional growth versus regional stability is increasingly emerging as a subject of concern in the local public dialogue. One side points to northcentral New Mexico's "cultural uniqueness" and "natural beauty" in arguing for a curb to continued population growth. The other side speaks of "economic betterment" and "sharing of the region's benefits" as reasons for encouraging expansion.[9]

While visiting the area under study I passed a large billboard in Sandoval County advocating the "undevelopment" of New Mexico. The self-proclaimed sponsor of the simple, direct message was a group calling itself the "New Mexico Undevelopment Commission." (Unfortunately, the billboard partially blocked a magnificent panoramic view of the desert and mountains.) As a relatively affluent outsider, my immediate reaction was one of wholehearted sympathy. It is interesting, after all, to visit areas where large numbers of people are still poor enough to be quaint. Moreover, the melting pot may be more destructive than a certain amount of economic deprivation, at least insofar as the distinct southwestern subcultures are concerned. In any event, the training of an economist certainly confers no authority in these matters. It is a simple matter to write that economic development should proceed at the maximum possible rate consistent with the preservation of valuable subcultures whose loss would be irreparable. However, I am not sure what this really means in practice.

Colorado

Denver has long been a primary distribution point for the Rocky Mountain region. Economic, social, and cultural development has tended to be concentrated along the Front Range, running north and south from Denver; over 90 percent of Colorado's population growth during the past fifty years has occurred within a narrow band extending from Fort Collins in the north to Pueblo in the south. Currently, more than 70 percent of the state's total population resides within this area.[10] In 1970, the Denver SMSA had 56 percent of the total state population. The Colorado Springs SMSA, to the south, accounted for another 11 percent, while the Pueblo SMSA had 5 percent.[11] In terms of absolute growth between 1960 and 1970, eight counties accounted for 93 percent of the total gain among the thirty-one counties that gained population, and for 98 percent of the net population gain for Colorado. Seven of these eight counties were either in or adjacent to the Denver SMSA; the eighth represented the Colorado Springs SMSA.[12]

Despite the fact that most nonmetropolitan Colorado counties lost population between 1960 and 1970, there were ten Turnaround-Reversal counties and three Turnaround-Acceleration counties in the mountainous west-central area. The single most important factor contributing to the growth of these counties is recreation.

The western mountain region has a number of advantages that have favored the development of recreation activities. There are large areas of federal land accessible to the public at low fees, and high elevations provide cool summer weather. The road network also is fairly well developed for a mountainous region. Surveys of summer tourists have indicated that "driving for pleasure" is their principal outdoor recreation activity, followed by walking and sightseeing. The mountains also offer excellent opportunities for hunting, fishing, river float trips, and camping.[13]

The ski industry is an important contributor to the mountain economy during the winter months when other outdoor recreation activities are experiencing their off season. Skiing has been the most rapidly growing part of the tourism sector during the past decade; the number of visits to national forest winter recreation areas has increased from less than 800,000 in 1962 to an estimated 3,731,000 in 1972.[14] A recent study of the characteristics of skiers at Colorado ski areas is especially instructive in view of chapter 2's discussion of the extension of urban fields to nonmetropolitan areas. Survey data compiled in 1968 by the Denver Research Institute indicated that 60 percent of the Colorado resident skiers lived in the Denver metropolitan area. Moreover, the probability of finding a skier in a Colorado family earning more than $15,000 a year was about three times greater than the probability of finding one in a family with an annual income of less than $10,000. Half of all skiers in Colorado in 1968 lived within an hour and a half of a ski area, but 60 percent of even the out-of-state skiers lived within 100 miles of a Colorado ski area. Thus, a large number of the out-of-state skiers in Colorado were not there simply because of a lack of facilities near their homes. About 10 percent of the skiers owned property near a ski area. Among Coloradans the probability of owning such property increased directly with distance between the owner's home and the nearest ski area. This relationship did not hold for out-of-state skiers. (On a regional basis the states bordering the Great Lakes provided the greatest number of out-of-state skiers to Colorado areas. Illinois, Minnesota and California were the principal sources of out-of-state skiers.) Property ownership was also directly related to annual income, especially at the higher levels; nearly one fourth of

Colorado skiers with annual incomes exceeding $25,000 owned ski area property.[15]

During the 1968-69 season, skiers in Colorado spent an estimated $55,894,000 in the state, of which $38,598,000 was spent in ski areas. Out-of-state skiers spent $33,981,000 in Colorado and $27,185,000 in ski areas.[16]

The role of expanding recreation activities in reversing population decline is clearly seen in Routt County, which experienced a 35 percent population decrease during the 1950s but grew by 12 percent during the 1960s. Steamboat Springs, the county seat, has had a rapidly growing winter sports industry since the early 1960s. Between 1966 and 1970 alone, receipts of restaurants, lodging places and service stations grew from $2.94 million to $4.53 million.[17] At present the accelerated growth of Routt County seems assured. In 1970 Ling-Temco-Vought began developing the Mount Werner area as a ski resort. This activity has induced large flows of capital from Denver banks and insurance companies into the area. One Denver company has purchased 12,000 acres south of Steamboat Springs for the construction of condominiums, and another company is similarly developing a 7200-acre tract north of the county seat.

Grand County, which is adjacent to Routt County, experienced a 16 percent population increase in the 1960s after an 11 percent decline during the 1950s. Grand County contains a part of Rocky Mountain National Park, and over half of its total area is comprised of national forests. While winter recreation is important to the local economy, the Shadow Mountain Reservoir has attracted increasing numbers of water sports enthusiasts. Jackson County, which is adjacent to both Routt and Grant Counties, grew by 3 percent in the 1960s after a 12 percent decline during the previous decade, but it still has net outmigration. This sparsely populated and largely agricultural county may expand further on the basis of recreation activities, but its growth seems less assured than that of its Turnaround-Reversal neighbors.

Further to the south, Gunnison County, which lies halfway between Colorado Springs and the Utah border, grew by a remarkable 38 percent during the 1960s, after declining by 5 percent the previous decade. The completion of Blue Mesa Reservoir has made this county a major water recreation area. The growth of Western State College added about 2000 persons to the county's population during the 1960s. While there is some skiing in the area, its future attractiveness is likely to be more enhanced by water recreation opportunities that will be afforded by the construction of two new dams.

Of the two contiguous southern Turnaround-Reversal counties, Mineral and Archuleta, the former had a rather spectacular change from a 40 percent loss in the 1950s — the second largest percentage loss in the state — to an 85 percent increase in the 1960s — the third highest percentage gain in the state. However, Mineral County's absolute population was only 786 in 1970. Archuleta County declined by 14 percent in the 1950s and registered a modest 4 percent gain in the 1960s. Its 1970 population (2733) also was relatively small, and it experienced net outmigration of 367 persons between 1960 and 1970. Both counties are having land developed for second homes and both rely fairly heavily on the tourist trade. However, their location in the depressed San Luis Valley makes future growth prospects less bright than those for Routt, Grand, and Gunnison counties.

The remaining Turnaround-Reversal counties all border the Denver SMSA, though one, Teller County, is contiguous with El Paso County (Colorado Springs) on the latter's western border. Gilpin County grew by 86 percent between 1960 and 1970 (the second highest rate in the state), Clear Creek County by 72 percent, and the other two by well over the national average. Nevertheless, their absolute populations in 1970 ranged from 1272 in Gilpin County to only 4819 in Clear Creek County. These counties share a rough mountain topography, with minimum elevation ranging from 6880 to 7600 feet and maximum elevation ranging from 12,500 to 14,284 feet. While cattle ranching and mining are significant in the area, its growth prospects are clearly related to tourism, recreation, second homes, and even some dormitory community development for people who work in the Denver SMSA.

The three Turnaround-Acceleration counties lie directly west of the Denver SMSA, but are separated from it by two small counties. Most of the world's molybdenum supply is produced in Lake County,[18] which is also popular as a year-round recreation area. Some residents of Lake County also commute to jobs in resorts in neighboring counties. Eagle and Garfield both share in the White River National Forest and Garfield contains part of Routt National Forest. Both counties offer many recreational opportunities. The Vail winter recreation area, which opened less than ten years ago in Eagle County, has already overtaken the Aspen area in popularity; during the 1970-71 season it had over half a million visitors. Garfield County contains the Glenwood Springs ski resort, and has further benefited from the recreational development of Roaring Fork Valley. Though some plants and a mine have recently been shut down, Garfield County contains large oil shale beds with potential production of 50,000 tons of ore per day.

Apart from those areas with recreational and scenic attractiveness or higher education facilities, most of western Colorado appears to be emptying out. (Most counties in the eastern and southern quarters of the state also have lost population for at least two decades.) While there are exceptional cases of firms locating major facilities in rural western counties, much of the area is hampered by lack of transportation, manpower, and little control over its water resources. (The Western Slope now provides water for Denver.)

On the other hand, there is considerable agitation for slowing population along the Front Range between Fort Collins and Colorado Springs. The vanguard of this movement is associated with the University of Colorado, the U.S. Bureau of Standards, and other groups in Boulder, which grew by 78 percent between 1960 and 1970. Boulder residents have twice passed referenda proposing rigid population growth restrictions. However, a recent moratorium on all building permits was declared illegal by the courts, and strict zoning ordinances and building permit limitations passed by the city council are being challenged by builders in the area. Denver, while less ardent, is now seeking only "clean" industries. Even so, the recent location of Johns Manville's headquarters there aroused some opposition on the grounds that it would produce more automobile congestion and air pollution, as well as tax the city's water supply. In November 1972, Denver citizens voted not to hold the 1976 Winter Olympics in their city. Despite these moves, Denver nevertheless seems more concerned with managing environmental problems associated with growth than with halting growth altogether, as is the case in Boulder.

Although Colorado Springs and Pueblo do not share the enthusiasm of Boulder and Denver for limiting growth, or at least do not hold it in the same degree, two bills have been proposed in the state legislature containing provisions that would have forbidden extension of water and sewer lines to new communities along the Front Range, and placed moratoria on building permits. These provisions were deleted before passage of the bills, but similar efforts will be made again. In keeping with pressures to decentralize population and economic activity, the Colorado Rural Development Commission was created in 1970 to promote dispersal of economic development to nonmetropolitan areas. An Interim Legislative Committee on Balanced Population Growth began hearings in September 1972, and the governor's current publicity campaign to "sell Colorado" has been revised, in comparison with similar earlier efforts, to play down the attractions of the Front Range in favor of the northeast, southeast, and western parts of the state. The prospects for the success of these attempts at decentralization are probably tenuous at best. Manpower, transportaion, and water supply problems are sufficiently severe in the west to preclude significant industrial or population growth. The plains counties of eastern Colorado are part of a general system of long-term population decline that extends from most of Montana, North Dakota, and western Minnesota in the northern plains all the way south to the Rio Grande River. To the extent that decentralization from the Front Range can be achieved, it will be in favor of the turnaround and Consistent Fast Gainer counties which are contiguous to the Denver, Colorado Springs, and Pueblo SMSAs — all on the Front Range — or to the west within approximately 150 air miles of Interstate Highway 25, which traverses and reinforces the north-south Front Range development axis.

However, even if future population growth could be diverted toward these relatively sparsely populated areas it is by no means certain that it would be welcome. As much as a quarter of the land now being "developed" for second homes, retirement homes, and similar uses has inadequate or no water resources. Apart from the disappointments that have been and will be experienced by "mail order" clients, there is also a threat of people pollution in more established mountain areas. (Low density average population values in mountain counties obviously conceal the fact that habitable areas may be very densely populated.) A resolution passed by the Aspen City Council in August 1972 deserves to be cited at length because it reflects widespread local sentiment in many such cases:

Whereas, the rapid growth rate of the City of Aspen and its environs has created ever increasing problems affecting the quality of living in the community.

And whereas, the City Council desires to preserve the community's historical-cultural heritage and broad social base, as well as preserving the community's natural resources including scenic views, natural rivers and wildlife.

And whereas, it is recognized that uncontrolled growth within the City of Aspen and the surrounding community will continue to cause irreversible damage to the life style of the community.

Now, therefore, be it resolved that the City of Aspen take the necessary steps to control and affect the rate of growth for Aspen and its vicinity which shall be in balance with public facilities (highways, transit, hospitals, sanitation, schools, etc.), insuring that the growth that does occur in Aspen and its vicinity preserves the natural resources, including scenic views, rivers and creeks, wildlife, and the open character of highway approaches to Aspen; and also preserves the community's historical-cultural heritage, quality recreational resources and broad social base; and improves the quality of life for its citizens.[19]

The issues that divide conservationists into opposing preservationist and developmentalist factions are clearly illustrated in the expanding Colorado mountain areas. Preservationists feel a strong commitment to protecting "the wilderness values of open air, rugged terrain, and primitive challenges to man's deepest individual resources."[20] The developmentalist position has tended to stress the philosophy that "our natural resources must be developed in the interest of our economic well-being; that governmental development or regulation ensures their use for the greatest interest of all the people; and that governmental action is needed not only for protection against monopolistic exploitation, but equally, if not more important, for wisest future use."[21]

Fortunately, the objectives of the preservationists and developmentalists need not be mutually exclusive in the present case. The growing mountain counties are extensive in area and their resources often permit multiple and compatible uses. With proper planning there can be further utilization of resources in the public domain along with the preservation of large tracts that can be passed unchanged to future generations. Moreover, some areas may serve one use today and be preserved for other uses later. For example, proper mining and timber production may be compatible with and even enhance recreation potentials for future needs. While preservationist objectives are appealing, properly controlled development need not necessarily be accompanied by air and water pollution or the devastation of natural beauty.[22]

123

Summary and Conclusions

The turnaround counties of New Mexico and Colorado contain some of the nation's most outstanding scenic, recreational and historical resources. Their growth is largely attributable to the demand for these resources by metropolitan populations, i.e., to the extension of urban fields. Manufacturing is of little consequence in these areas. There is a threat that unplanned growth may irreparably damage or destroy the resources that made the turnaround counties attractive in the first place. For many persons concerned about the environment the key problem "is how to bring about desirable development for the many rather than preservation of a natural endowment for the benefit of an elite few."[23]

While the growth of the past decade has improved living standards for many nonmetropolitan families, many others still live in poverty conditions. It was pointed out that this is particularly true for Spanish Americans and Indians in New Mexico. In Colorado, Where Spanish Americans account for 55,000 of the state's 471,000 rural population, 27.2 percent of rural nonfarm Spanish American families have incomes below the poverty level; 23.4 percent of the rural farm group fall in this category. The corresponding values for all rural nonfarm and rural farm families in Colorado are only 11.7 percent and 16.3 percent.[24] It may be hoped that in the future the benefits accruing from the unique resources of New Mexico and Colorado may be shared more evenly by all segments of the population.

9

Vermont and New Hampshire

Of the twenty-two counties in the Vermont-New Hampshire region, seventeen are in the turnaround categories, with eight in the Turnaround-Reversal group and nine in the Turnaround-Acceleration group. The only two Consistent Fast Gainers, Hillsborough and Rockingham, are the counties closest to the Boston SMSA. Windsor County, in east-central Vermont, is the only Stagnant Gainer county. There are two Loser counties, Coos, the northernmost county in New Hampshire, and Essex County, Vermont, which borders Coos County to the west.

Five Turnaround-Acceleration counties are in Vermont (Chittenden, Addison, Rutland, Windham, and Bennington) and four are in New Hampshire (Grafton, Belknap, Sullivan, and Merrimack). However, with the exception of Carroll County, all of the Turnaround-Reversal counties are in northern Vermont (Grande Isle, Franklin, Orleans, Lamoille, Washington, Caledonia, and Orange). For this reason the present chapter concentrates primarily on Vermont.

Employment Changes

The data in table 9-1 show employment change in the Vermont-New Hampshire region at the one-digit SIC code level, by population change category. Data were available for all counties for 1959, so the 1959-69 and 1964-69 periods both include the complete set of counties. With respect to total employment change over the decade, the Loser counties declined by about 9 percent despite significant growth in the retail trade and service sectors. The principal reason for this loss was steady decline in employment by the Brown Company (forest products), the largest employer in the Loser counties. The city of Berlin, in Coos County, was particularly affected. A recent annual report of the New Hampshire-Vermont Development Council, which serves the New Hampshire-Vermont Economic Development District (an Economic Development Administration district comprising approximately the northern halves of the two states) points out:

The unemployment rate in Berlin reached a peak of 6.1 percent, hardly excessive when compared with rates reported from other reporting centers. But, at almost the same time, 1970 census figures showed that Berlin's population had declined by almost 3,000, or 16 percent, since 1960. The conclusion has to be that Berlin's comparatively low unemployment rate does not reflect viability of the

125

Table 9-1
Absolute and Percentage Employment Change by Sector (One-digit SIC Code) in Selected Vermont and New Hampshire Counties, by Population Change Category, 1964-69 and 1959-69

	Total	Agricultural Services, Forestry, Fisheries	Mining	Contract Construction	Manufacturing
Absolute Change, 1964-69					
Loser	26	5	0	23	−770
Stagnant Gainer	1,843	0	0	369	133
Turnaround-Reversal	7,538	132	94	890	1,012
Turnaround-Acceleration	33,788	13	−98	2,851	12,290
Consistent Fast Gainer	6,726	16	7	903	1,303
Percentage Change, 1964-69					
Loser	.3	45.5	0	11.3	−13.8
Stagnant Gainer	16.6	0	0	98.7	2.0
Turnaround-Reversal	26.6	167.1	19.3	86.6	10.8
Turnaround-Acceleration	36.9	2.0	−21.4	71.5	35.0
Consistent Fast Gainer	36.1	11.6	100.0	90.8	19.5
Absolute Change, 1959-69					
Loser	−853	8	−2	56	−1,773
Stagnant Gainer	3,310	7	64	458	820
Turnaround-Reversal	8,492	152	119	857	−98
Turnaround-Acceleration	43,433	135	−367	3,809	12,685
Consistent Fast Gainer	10,406	11	14	965	2,039
Percentage Change, 1959-69					
Loser	−8.6	100.0	−14.3	32.7	−27.0
Stagnant Gainer	34.3	21.2	376.5	160.7	14.1
Turnaround-Reversal	31.0	257.6	25.8	80.8	−.9
Turnaround-Acceleration	53.0	26.0	−50.6	125.8	36.5
Consistent Fast Gainer	69.5	7.7		103.4	34.4

Table 9-1 (Continued)
Employment Change

	Transportation and Other Public Utilities	Wholesale Trade	Retail Trade	Finance, Insurance, and Real Estate (FIRE)	Services	Unclassified Establishments
Absolute Change, 1964-69						
Loser	11	4	230	58	440	17
Stagnant Gainer	171	47	484	37	563	39
Turnaround-Reversal	503	546	1,400	426	2,508	28
Turnaround-Acceleration	813	922	5,863	1,588	9,304	142
Consistent Fast Gainer	243	546	1,854	181	1,659	16
Percentage Change, 1964-69						
Loser	2.3	1.7	17.8	25.2	44.2	41.5
Stagnant Gainer	36.1	9.0	29.9	14.3	47.0	195.0
Turnaround-Reversal	34.2	46.8	21.8	23.8	39.5	19.7
Turnaround-Acceleration	15.6	23.1	35.5	36.6	43.7	67.6
Consistent Fast Gainer	24.7	70.9	38.8	24.4	47.1	32.0
Absolute Change, 1959-69						
Loser	-30	5	233	69	525	44
Stagnant Gainer	112	140	749	101	856	0
Turnaround-Reversal	499	507	1,900	618	3,998	-66
Turnaround-Acceleration	1,254	1,424	7,251	2,285	15,171	-206
Consistent Fast Gainer	456	622	3,000	464	2,820	20
Percentage Change, 1959-69						
Loser	-5.9	2.1	18.0	31.5	57.7	314.3
Stagnant Gainer	21.0	32.5	55.2	51.8	94.5	0
Turnaround-Reversal	33.8	42.0	32.0	38.7	82.3	-28.0
Turnaround-Acceleration	26.2	40.8	47.9	62.8	98.5	-36.9
Consistent Fast Gainer	59.1	89.6	82.7	101.1	119.5	43.5

local economy. Instead, it is the result of a mass outflow of people, almost certainly in search of employment elsewhere.[1]

Essex County also has suffered from the decline in soft-wood pulp utilization. The heaviest population losses in this county have been in the 0-14 and 25-44 age groups, indicating that persons in the prime working ages are moving away with their children. Nevertheless, the Vermont State Planning Office believes that increased recreational activity, based on the area's forests and lakes, will stabilize the population of Essex County and break the long decline that has occurred since 1890.[2] The increases in retail trade and service employment noted for the 1959-69 period indicate that this projection may be valid.

The single Stagnant Gainer county, Windsor, Vermont, is highly dependent on the machine tool industry for employment, and attempts to diversify its economy have not been very successful. If machine tool firms share in the recent upturn from the recession of 1970 and if second-home development continues there will probably be a modest increase in population. Hopes for second-home development are based on the fact that the Interstate Highway System has placed much of the county within two and a half hours' driving time from Boston.

The two Consistent Fast Gainer counties, those closest to Boston, had substantial growth in manufacturing employment, but their most impressive gains were in the non-goods-producing categories. The counties obviously continue to benefit from participation in the Boston urban field.

The Turnaround-Acceleration counties ranked second in rate of total employment increase to the Consistent Fast Gainers for the 1959-69 period, but had the highest rate for the more recent period. The rate of growth in manufacturing employment was particularly high, and absolute growth in this sector accounted for over one third of the total absolute employment increase for the 1964-69 period. Within the manufacturing sector there were substantial losses in the food, textiles, lumber and wood products, and stone, clay, and glass products sectors for both 1959-69 and 1964-69. The machinery (except electrical) and transportation equipment sectors also showed marked declines during the more recent period. However, the transportation equipment sector still ranked second in absolute gain for the 1959-69 period, led only by electrical equipment and supplies. These sectors gained by 3107 and 3299 employees, respectively. Other large gainers for the 1959-69 period were the printing and publishing and instruments sectors, which grew by 1907 and 1629 employees, respectively. Together electrical equipment, transportation equipment, printing and publishing, and instruments accounted for 9942 of the net absolute manufacturing increase of 12,685 employees. During the 1964-69 period the declines in the machinery and transportation equipment sectors were balanced by very rapid growth in the ordnance sector. Despite the instability of the ordnance sector, the general picture with respect to manufacturing in the

Turnaround-Acceleration counties is one of significant growth by trading off employment in nationally slow-growing industries for employment in more rapidly growing sectors.

The Turnaround-Acceleration counties ranked relatively high in absolute and percentage growth in construction, FIRE, and services for the 1959-69 period. They ranked in the middle of the five groups in wholesale trade, retail trade, and transportation. For the 1964-69 period, they ranked only fourth in construction and transportation growth, but vigorous growth in most of the non-goods producing sectors, as well as in manufacturing, gave the Turnaround-Acceleration group the highest growth in total employment from 1964 to 1969.

The importance of the service sector to the Turnaround-Acceleration counties is particularly noteworthy. Between 1964 and 1969 this sector trailed only manufacturing in absolute increase, and accounted for 28 percent of the total net employment increase. For the 1959-69 period, absolute growth in the service sector exceeded that in manufacturing by 15,171 to 12,685, and accounted for 35 percent of the total net increase in employment.

The most remarkable aspect of the growth of service employment in the Vermont-New Hampshire Turnaround-Acceleration counties has been rapid increases in the hotel and lodging, recreation, and educational services sectors. Between 1959 and 1969, hotel and lodging employment grew by 153 percent. The absolute increase of 2329 represented 40 percent of the absolute growth in this sector for Turnaround-Acceleration counties in all regions. Similarly, the absolute increase in recreation employment, 1794, accounted for nearly three fourths of the comparable growth in all regions. The 5314 increase in educational services employment represents over half of the comparable all-region increase of 9340. Clearly, recreational, cultural, and intellectual amenities have been quite instrumental in the growth of the Vermont-New Hampshire Turnaround-Acceleration counties. What Brian Berry has written about one of these counties may well be generalized to the whole group:

Gradients of distance-accretion will replace those of distance-decay. Persons of greater wealth and leisure will find homes and work among the more remote environments of hills, water and forest, while most will aspire to this as an ideal. This, of course, is another inversion; the environments historically least valued are rapidly becoming the most desired. The signs are already there to be noted. As I wrote this paper, for example, I read . . . about Windham county in south-eastern Vermont, a traditional Yankee area of woods, farms, and small towns, which is now being subdivided for second vacation homes − there will be more than 10,000 in only three or four years. And, following the vacation homes, will surely be the permanent residences and the industries.[3]

The Turnaround-Reversal counties, all but one of which are in northern Vermont, ranked fourth among the five population change categories in rate of total employment change from 1959 to 1969, but third for the 1964-69 period.

They differ markedly from the prevalent Turnaround-Reversal pattern in that manufacturing employment showed the lowest rate of increase of any one-digit sector for 1964-69. For the 1959-69 period manufacturing employment actually declined. Construction, wholesale trade, and service employment had the highest rates of growth from 1964 to 1969, while for the longer period services had the highest rate of growth, followed by construction.

At the two-digit level for manufacturing, the Turnaround-Reversal counties lost employment during both time periods in food, textiles, lumber and wood products, stone, clay, and glass products, and machinery (except electrical). The biggest employment increases were in electrical equipment and supplies and rubber and plastics products. As in the case of the Turnaround-Acceleration counties, nationally slow-growing sectors were being traded off for faster-growing sectors, but unlike the Turnaround-Acceleration group, the pace was not sufficient to increase total manufacturing employment substantially.

The rapid growth of service employment in the Turnaround-Reversal counties had a similar underlying pattern to that for the Turnaround-Acceleration group. Medical and health services had the greatest increase, but growth in the nonprofit organization membership sector, while rapid, was still less than that for comparable counties in the six regions studied. After medical and health services, the biggest absolute gains during the 1959-69 period were made in the hotel and lodging, recreation, and educational services sectors; a similar trend also was present for the 1964-69 period. The rates of growth in recreation and education services employment were even greater than those in the Turnaround-Acceleration counties. Thus, here too the interplay between traditional New England amenities and the extension of urban fields has served as a basis for growth.

Accessibility and Growth

Accessibility to Vermont and New Hampshire has been vastly improved in recent years, both because of the virtual completion of the Interstate Highway System and the construction of such limited-access highways as the Everett, Spaulding, and New Hampshire Turnpikes, which have greatly shortened travel time from the Boston SMSA to southeastern New Hampshire. In some cases travel times between New York City and the southern New England states of Massachusetts, Connecticut, and Rhode Island have been reduced by as much as 50 percent. For example, in 1950 it took about seven and a half hours to go from Boston to Burlington, Vermont (Chittenden County), but by 1970 the completion of Interstate 89 reduced the time to only four hours. The major centers of the White Mountains skiing complex in Grafton and Coos counties, New Hampshire, are now only four to four and a half hours from Boston, and Concord is less than a two-hour drive. The time required to get from New York City to Vermont and New Hampshire ranges from under four to six hours.[4]

In chapter 3 it was argued that while improved highway transportation facilities may certainly stimulate the growth of particular areas, more generally, differing population change patterns among the five county groups being investigated in this study are not explainable in terms of proximity to Interstate or other major highways, or in terms of number of major highways in a county. However, the northern Vermont-New Hampshire case is clearly exceptional. Whereas the average Turnaround-Reversal county in all of the regions studied is 2.21 counties away from Interstate Highways or limited-access divided highways, the comparable distance in northern Vermont-New Hampshire is only 1.75, the closest of any region. The comparable value for all Turnaround-Acceleration counties is 1.90, whereas in northern Vermont-New Hampshire it is 1.33. This is the lowest value of any region except central Texas, which has a value of 1.00; however, there are only two counties in this category in central Texas, compared with nine in northern Vermont-New Hampshire. Similarly, the Turnaround-Reversal counties have an average of 2.88 multilane highways, which is considerably above the average number in any other region or the overall average of 1.81. The same is true of the Turnaround-Acceleration counties, whose 4.11 average exceeds that of any other region and the overall average of 2.61.

Driving times to portions of Vermont and New Hampshire from New York, Boston, and Montreal are illustrated in map 9-1. The Boston SMSA is of course the closest to the areas in question. It is linked to Manchester, New Hampshire by U.S. Highway 3 and the Everett Turnpike by way of Lowell, Massachusetts and Nashua, New Hampshire, as well as by Interstate Highway 93. It also is linked to Portsmouth, New Hampshire, on the Maine border, by Interstate Highway 95 and the New Hampshire Turnpike. These highways have undoubtedly bound the two Consistent Fast Gainer counties — Hillsborough and Rockingham, New Hampshire — closer to the Boston SMSA and thereby reinforced their growth from participation in the Boston urban field. All of the Turnaround-Acceleration counties in New Hampshire are also traversed by new limited-access highways. Strafford County has no doubt benefited from the Spaulding Turnpike, which runs from Portsmouth, New Hampshire (Rockingham County) to Rochester. Every one of the other Turnaround-Acceleration counties in New Hampshire contains some part of Interstate Highway 89 or Interstate Highway 93, or both.

If people from Boston have been drawn more toward New Hampshire than Vermont because of its proximity, the converse holds for people from the New York City area, though of course the distance here is much greater. This may help to explain why New Hampshire is more densely settled than Vermont. New Hampshire has 82 persons per square mile, compared to the national value of 58, whereas in Vermont the density is only 48 persons per square mile. Moreover, in each of the past five decades the population growth rate in New Hampshire has exceeded that in Vermont. Yet Vermont had a remarkable acceleration in growth during the 1960s. While New Hampshire's population growth rate went

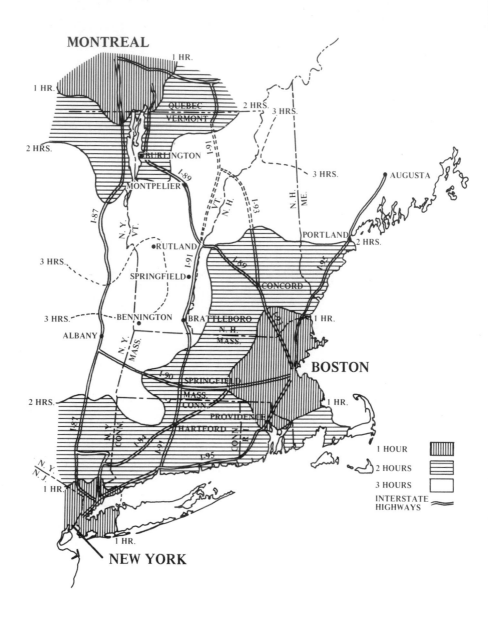

Source: *Vermont: Social and Economic Characteristics* (Montpelier: Vermont State Planning Office), p. vi.

Map 9-1. Driving Times to New England Locations — From Montreal, Boston, and New York City

from 13.8 in the 1950s to 21.5 in the 1960s, that in Vermont leaped from only 3.2 percent in the 1950s to 14.1 percent in the 1960s.[5] The fact that Vermont grew by more than the national average of 13.3 percent, and that all but two of its counties were in the turnaround categories is no doubt partly related to increased accessibility made possible by the Interstate Highway System. Interstate Highway 91, the principal link with the New York City area, though not entirely completed in the northern part of the state, traverses one Turnaround-Acceleration county (Windham, on the southern border) and three Turnaround-Reversal counties (Orange, Caledonia, and Orleans, in the northern part of the state). Interstate Highway 91 also intersects Interstate Highway 89, the main route from Boston, near White River Junction. Interstate Highway 89 traverses the Turnaround-Reversal counties of Orange, Washington, Franklin, and Grande Isle, as well as Chittenden County, in the Turnaround-Acceleration category. It is noteworthy that the single Loser county, Essex, is not served by the Interstate System. On the other hand, the Vermont county (Windsor) where Interstate Highways 89 and 91 intersect is the sole Stagnant Gainer, which indicates that potential advantages derived from highways do not necesssarily lead to rapid growth.

Chittenden County: A Special Case

The development stimulus that highways can provide to areas with existing growth potential is well illustrated in Chittenden County, which contains Vermont's largest city, Burlington. The extent to which this area has become a growth center in recent years is reflected in the following observations by the Vermont State Planning Office:

One policy alternative is to do nothing and allow existing market forces and institutional constraints to determine where economic activity will locate. To choose this alternative would mean that Chittenden County would continue to gain most of the new jobs. From 1960 to 1969, 69 percent of the new jobs in manufacturing and 37 percent of the new jobs in non-manufacturing were in Chittenden County. Industries will continue to locate there because of the large work force, the location on the interstate highway between Boston and Montreal and good rail connections. In addition, the location of a university, several colleges, and a medical center in Chittenden County make it an attractive area for management personnel. Trade and services will also locate near Burlington because of the large market area. They will locate near the interstate highway and where they are most visible in order to remind the customer of their presence.[6]

The rapid growth of Chittenden County is a recent phenomenon. Between 1960 and 1964 manufacturing employment in the county declined by 450 people, though this was offset by a large increase in service workers associated with a major medical center. Nevertheless, total employment grew by only 2200.

During this period, however, International Business Machines and General Electric built and began to operate branch plants in the Burlington area. Decisions to expand these plants in 1964 resulted in sharply increased manufacturing employment. They accounted for about two thirds of the 6350 job growth in durable manufacturing between 1964 and 1969. Their growth also induced expansion of other local firms providing services and parts, as well as a large increase in trade and service employment following the growth of residential areas where most of the labor force lived.

Burlington and its immediately adjacent built-up areas constitute the heart of a quasi-metropolitan area of nearly 100,000 people, or about 22 percent of all Vermonters. The area is quasi-metropolitan only in that its largest city does not by itself have a population of 50,000 or more and therefore does not meet the Bureau of the Census criterion for being "metropolitan." With its sister cities of South Burlington and Winooski, Greater Burlington has nearly 56,000 inhabitants, and there are over 43,000 persons living in the remainder of Chittenden County. Between 1960 and 1970 the whole area grew by 33.2 percent. The tri-partite core grew by 12 percent, but the Chittenden County hinterland grew by 76 percent. Chittenden County's total increase of 24,706 persons accounted for 45 percent of the total population growth of Vermont in an area with less than a quarter of the state's population.

The kinds of person moving into the Burlington area or Vermont in general are not readily identifiable from available statistical data. However, clues from age-distribution data suggest that young adults and families at or near retirement are coming into the state in considerable numbers. The latter phenomenon follows a long-established trend, whereas the former is quite recent. The influx of young adults is probably more relevant to Chittenden County than the movement of retired persons. Allied Van Lines, which handled 227,000 shipments nationally in 1969, reported that the number of families it had moved into Vermont in 1969 was four times greater than the number it moved out. This was the highest in-to-out movement ratio for any state. Since Allied's only Vermont telephone listing is in Burlington this ratio is no doubt more applicable to Chittenden County than the state as a whole. In any case, Vermont's Public Investment Plan points out that if the persons coming in "are predominantly 'family people,' with those leaving likely to be unattached young people, the implications for the state's economy, life style and public affairs are considerable. Families tend to bring resources, children, public service expectations, and a stake in the established order."[7]

The rapid growth of Chittenden County is by no means an unmixed blessing; communities around Burlington have experienced increasingly sharp growing pains. Places such as Colchester, Shelburne, and Charlotte have been taking on a "non-Vermont" aspect and life style characterized by commercial ribbons, shopping centers, and assembly-line residential developments. At the same time the core area is suffering from traffic congestion, residential deterioration, and downtown blight, while outer-ring communities are experiencing rising land values and problems of rural-to-urban change. Governmental costs in Chittenden County have increased more sharply than revenue growth as increased numbers of people demand new and larger public services in the form of schools, water, sewers, streets, libraries, police and fire protection, and so forth.[8] As a consequence many residents may welcome a slowing of development so that the supply of services can catch up with demand. Despite its potential for future growth, the county may not be as receptive to industrial expansion as it was in the early 1960s. Indeed, while Chittenden county is a relatively special case, there is increasing concern throughout the Vermont-New Hampshire region over the effects of growth on the environment.

Recreation, Second Homes, and the Environment

Only a decade ago Vermont had more cows than people. When, about 1963, the balance turned in favor of humans most Vermonters were gratified by the steadily swelling influx of tourists, second-home buyers, and other urban escapees.

Now, however, growing numbers of Vermonters are beginning to wish that all those non-Yankees would simply stay home. "Vermont ain't Vermont any more," complains Theron Boyd, a 70-year old farmer. "Folks used to come here because it was different. Now they're trying to make it look like every other state. That's the darn of it."[9]

The amenity base on which much of the population growth in Vermont and New Hampshire has been based is indeed a fragile thing, and people are its greatest threat. Each new permanent resident as well as each transient visitor represents an additional burden. Unfortunately, "Highway congestion, long ski lift lines, crowded shops, honky-tonk commercial highway strips, transistor radios, mobile home villages, sleazy subdivisions — in short, all the things one hoped one had left back in Boston or Bridgeport, Newark or Cleveland, are appearing in northern New England in greater and greater numbers."[10]

Throughout northern Vermont and New Hampshire there has been substantial rethinking in very recent years about the role of the recreation industry and related developments. The precipitant has been increasing awareness of three related phenomena. Recreational land, once regarded as an almost inexhaustible resource, has been eaten up at a worrisome rate, mostly by second-home developments, and many recreational developments also have been damaging from an ecological viewpoint. From the vantage point of both the states and local communities, there is recognition that there is a loss as well as a profit column on the recreation industry balance sheet.[11]

The importance of the recreation industry in northern New England is illustrated by the fact that up to 16 percent of Vermont's gross state product originates in this sector. In the summer of 1970 about four million persons visited Vermont. They spent approximately $84 million, of which $32.6 million went for food, $24.0 million for lodging, $10.0 million for entertainment, $7.5 million for gasoline, and $9.8 million for other expenses. The average visitor spent $8.75 per day and stayed in the state for 2.4 days. Estimates for the 1970-71 winter season indicate that skiers spent $52.6 million, of which $19.7 million went for skiing, $10.2 million for lodging, $8.6 million for food, $4.4 million for entertainment, $2.8 million for gasoline, and $6.8 million for other expenses. While the actual number of skiers was difficult to count, skier-days were estimated at 2.65 million for 1970-71. Vacation homeowners spend about $30 million a year in Vermont. Towns where vacation homes pay a relatively high proportion of the taxes generally are located in hilly areas and adjacent to lakes. Youth camps add another $5 million to the state's economy. In all, expenditures for recreation by out-of-state visitors amount to approximately $172 million annually.

Vermont's comparative advantage in providing skiing facilities has declined in recent years, for two reasons. Increased use of snow-making machines has enabled areas closer to population centers to provide reliable, good quality skiing for persons who can spend only a weekend skiing or who do not demand the long expert trails found in the Vermont mountains. At the same time, reduced group air fares have made it possible for many skiers to travel to the Rocky Mountains or even to the Alps at a cost not much different from that required to go to northern Vermont. On the other hand, if Vermont is losing its share of the ski market, increased affluence and leisure time have still brought about absolute expansion. In 1963 there were 72 skiing locations in the state, but by 1970 there were 77. During the same period the number of gondolas has grown from one to seven and the number of chairlifts from 34 to 70. The number of skier-days grew from 1.02 million to 2.65 million, and may be expected to increase further if the quality of the skiing compares favorably with competitive areas of Colorado and Europe.

The importance of the service sector varies widely from county to county and from season to season in Vermont, largely because of the importance of recreation. In absolute amounts, Chittenden County employers paid $12.6 million to service employees in 1969; Windham County was second with $7.9 million and Rutland third with $6.4 million. However, in measuring the relative importance of service employment to counties the ranking is different. By this standard, Lamoille County, in the Turnaround-Reversal group, ranked first, with 25 percent of all wages accounted for by the service sector. It was followed by Windham (13 percent) and Bennington (11 percent), the two southernmost counties, both in the Turnaround-Acceleration category. In general, however, the value of recreation-related jobs as a major contributor to family income was often severely limited by the great variation between months of high employment and low employment. Addison, Bennington, Essex, Franklin, Grande Isle, and Orange counties have been characterized by high summer employment, based for the most part on water amenities and summer camps. Lamoille and Windham counties have had relatively high winter employment based on the ski industry. Rutland, Washington, and Windsor counties have high summer and winter employment because the peaks in both seasons are similar, but this does not necessarily mean that the same persons work both seasons. Seasonally level service employment actually is characteristic of only three counties, Caledonia, Orleans, and Chittenden, whose absolutely large employment in this sector is stabilized by the large number of medical and educational service employees.

Thus, the primary benefit of the recreation sector in most counties may be provision of supplemental income through female and youth employment. If the principal male wage-earner relies on recreation-related employment he frequently must find alternative jobs in the slack season or else rely on state unemployment insurance or welfare. Here too there are problems because only 47 percent of service employment in Vermont was covered by unemployment insurance in 1969. It is quite clear that as the proportion of the labor force employed in recreation-related service activities increases it will be increasingly important to find supplementary sources of income, which may require added training programs and new hiring practices. Counties with high winter employment may wish to encourage the development of summer resorts, and counties which at present have only high summer employment may wish to do the opposite. If the workers were sufficiently mobile to move from county to county by season there would probably be social problems associated with a transient labor force, but in many instances distances are not too great to preclude increased commuting.

The population concentrations of southern New England and the New York City area have been the major source of second home buyers in northern New England. In 1968 there were 22,548 vacation homes in Vermont alone, of which 58 percent were owned by persons from outside the state. It is particularly significant that more and more families now use their "vacation home" as a year-round residence, a trend that no doubt will accelerate as completion of the Interstate Highway System brings more hinterland countryside area into marginal commuting range from major urban centers.[12] Growing concern with the actual and potential threat of the recreation boom to the environment also extends to new home developments.

"It's shocking to us to see professional people come up here without jobs," says Roland Loveless, head of [Vermont's] Development and Community Affairs agency. "We're not sure what's going to become of them." Even vacation homes may pose a threat. "What's going to happen to those so-called second homes?" asks state planning director Benjamin Partridge. "I'll tell you: Mom and the kids will stay in the country while Dad works in the city. You can imagine the expensive new services that will be demanded of small towns – new schools, sewage and utilities, more police and fire protection. And it's already happening".[13]

Such sentiments are by no means restricted to an isolated few. In a statewide poll taken in Vermont in 1971, 42 percent of the respondents favored closing the state to immigrants, and a white paper that recently circulated around the state office building in Montpelier proposed a future limit on the state's population. In the spring of 1972 the Vermont legislature cut back funds for the state's tourist offices in Montreal and New York. Some towns have adopted strict zoning laws to restrict developers.[14] However, the most significant step taken by the state is the development of new land-use guidelines.

Vermont has already adopted an Interim Land Capability Plan as a predecessor for a Capability and Development Plan and a Land Use Plan. The Interim Plan also is intended to serve as one measure by which proposals for development may be judged by District Environmental Commissions and the State Environmental Board.

The Interim Plan states that development should be reasonably related to existing land-use patterns and existing natural conditions, provided that such uses and patterns are not causing or contributing to environmental problems. In evaluating conformity with this policy consideration is to be given to an area's suitability and adequacy to support and accommodate development and related activities such as roads, transportation, governmental services, housing, water supply, and sewage disposal; and to the degree to which development may unreasonably or unnecessarily reduce the existing environmental quality of the area. Significant natural areas are to be protected from development that may cause irreparable damage, and places of outstanding esthetic, historical, or educational value are to be protected from development that unreasonably impairs their character and quality. Information concerning such sites shall be filed with the State Planning Office. The Interim Plan requires adequate sewage treatment and disposal, and states that development shall avoid areas of agricultural, forestry, recreational, or mineral extraction potential, if possible, when their preservation for such uses is of significant benefit to the public's health, safety and welfare. The impact of development on scenic quality, natural beauty, and esthetic values is to be considered in evaluating proposed projects, so that "the general atmosphere of Vermont" may be retained. Local communities are encouraged to adopt plans consistent with the Interim Plan and related state legislation. The state, towns, and other groups are encouraged to purchase or acquire rights in unique lands, scenic areas, and historic sites so as to provide them permanent protection. The Interim Plan calls for seeking ways to absorb the population growth expected by the year 2000 in the light of expected productive activities and environmental considerations; to reuse and recycle all types of waste products; and to eliminate strip development. Industrial development is encouraged, provided that industry adequately controls its wastes, satisfactorily relates to existing land uses and esthetic qualities, and accounts to the community for indirect costs to the community for essential services.[15]

The effectiveness with which these policies will be implemented remains to be seen, but they clearly seem to have the support of widespread public sentiment. It is unfortunate that New Hampshire has not made similar progress. As one Vermont citizen fighting the spread of an unwelcome condominium complex into her town put it: "We're not trying to stop progress. We simply want to slow it down so we can handle it."[16]

Summary and Conclusions

At least in the context of recent history, Vermont and New Hampshire for the first time have had inter-census population growth rates exceeding the rate of national growth. Between 1960 and 1970 New Hampshire grew by 21.5 percent while Vermont grew by 14.1 percent, compared to the national rate of 13.3 percent. In consequence, growth accelerated in many counties and long periods of decline were reversed in a relatively large number of northern Vermont counties. Several important factors have been instrumental in this process. Some 36 million people living in the megalopolitan strip extending from Washington, D.C. to Boston and some 2.5 million persons in the Montreal area have much easier access to Vermont and New Hampshire as a result of construction of the Interstate Highway System. Increasing affluence and shorter work weeks have increased demand for the exceptional recreation amenities of the area. In addition, there has been a significant influx of national firms. While the textile industry and other nationally slow-growing sectors have declined, they have been replaced by faster-growing sectors such as electronics and instruments.

While on the surface Vermont and New Hampshire, with their attractive blending of "rural" and "urban" life styles, represent one of nonmetropolitan America's major success stories, growth is no longer regarded as an unmixed blessing. There has been substantial rethinking about the ecologically damaging aspects of tourism, recreation, and second-home expansion, and even industrial development is no longer a sacred cow. To be sure, reservations about industrial growth are found for the most part in communities where unemployment is not regarded as a problem, but elsewhere there is some disposition to question the desirability of "just any old industry." Instead the objective tends to be attraction of firms that will improve the quality of the local economy, not simply make it larger. In general there is a new sophistication that is concerned more with the ends of development than the means. Particularly in Vermont, concrete plans are being formulated to deal with economic development in this context.

In Keith Warren Jennison's *Vermont Is Where You Find It,*[17] a classic little study of American regionalism of two and three decades ago, there appears a particularly striking photograph of a pastoral scene accompanied by the query "How are the crops this year?" The farmer replies, "Not so good for a good year, but not so bad for a bad year." In the contemporary world this has been sufficient to wipe out some northern New England yeomen. In many cases, however, the family farm has proven to be more successful than large corporation farming, particularly in the production of milk for the urban areas of southern New England. But use of land for farming will continue to decline rapidly unless there is curtailment of opportunities to use prime agricultural lands in other more profitable ways.

Although the 1970 Census indicates that Vermont is increasingly rural (the "urban" population actually declined by 4.7 percent while the "rural" population grew by 25.6 percent), this is misleading, because the growth of suburbs around the state's urban areas is not really an increase in rural living. Moreover, many farms are being acquired by Boston and New York families for second homes or places to retire. What then is to become of that peculiarly Yankee vision and life style that has enriched American culture from its beginnings? The fact that so many people are posing the question may help assure its preservation. In Jennison's book there is another picture, showing a hoary old Yankee seated pensively beside a very unimproved rural road. Down the road comes an outlander from the big city, who asks "How far is it to Fairfax?"

> "Dunno," replies the Yankee.
> "Does this road go to Fairfax?"
> "Dunno."
> "Say, you don't know much do you?"
> "Nope, but I ain't lost."

10 Northern Georgia and Central Texas

This chapter briefly studies growth in turnaround counties surrounding two rapidly growing southern SMSAs: Atlanta and Austin. In both cases employment growth at the one-digit SIC level is presented only for the 1964-69 period because of unavailability of data by county for 1959.

Northern Georgia

The BEA region whose center is Atlanta provides a striking example of the effects on nonmetropolitan counties of the extension of a major urban field. During the 1960s the Atlanta SMSA contained five counties. (Two more counties — Douglas and Rockdale — were added to the SMSA in 1972.) Of the remaining forty-four counties in the region, thirteen were in the Turnaround-Reversal category and another sixteen in the Turnaround-Acceleration category. Four counties were Stagnant Gainers, four were Consistent Fast Gainers, and seven were Losers.

The five-county Atlanta metropolitan area contains one third of Georgia's population; four of these counties had population growth greater than 50 percent between 1960 and 1970. Atlanta has long been the major southeastern regional distribution and service center, but now it also rapidly is becoming an international trade center. It has ten commercial consulates, and a number of foreign firms, most of them from Central and South America, have branches located in the metropolitan area. The state Department of Industry and Trade maintains an international division to recruit still more economic activity from abroad. Atlanta still derives the greatest part of its income from retail and wholesale trade, but employment in construction trades has been rising rapidly in response to increased demand for office, hotel, and residential buildings.

Between 1960 and 1970 Georgia's population grew by 16.4 percent, and the state experienced net inmigration for the first time since the Civil War. However, while 198,000 whites were added to the population through net migration, 154,000 blacks were lost. The rate of black net outmigration (14 percent) was twice that of net white inmigration.[1] In many respects, Georgia may be said to be growing by exchanging a rural black population for an even greater suburban white population.

Of the forty-four nonmetropolitan counties in the Atlanta BEA region, thirty-six experienced a net outmigration of blacks during the 1960s, but only fifteen had net outmigration of whites. Of the thirty-seven counties that grew in population, twenty-eight lost blacks through net migration; only nine of these counties had net outmigration of whites.[2]

Although the black population of the city of Atlanta grew by 35 percent during the 1960s, the movement of jobs to outlying areas and an inadequate transportation system have made it difficult for many central city residents to commute to the perimeter. (The black unemployment rate in the seven-county Atlanta Manpower Planning Area is over four times that for whites at this writing.[3]) On the other hand, the data in table 10-1 indicate that there is considerable commuting from nonmetropolitan counties to the metropolitan area. Over half of the workers living in Douglas county commuted to jobs in the SMSA. In another six counties from 33 to 48 percent of the workers commuted.

Table 10-1
Nonmetropolitan Counties from which at least 5 Percent of the Work Force Commutes to Work Places in the Atlanta SMSA, 1970

First Tier Around Atlanta SMSA	Percent Commuting
Douglas	58.50
Fayette	48.49
Henry	45.79
Paulding	45.63
Rockdale	42.29
Forsyth	33.63
Cherokee	32.66
Walton	15.83
Bartow	14.59
Spalding	13.44
Coweta	12.37
Barrow	11.50
Carroll	10.34
Hall	6.07
Second Tier Around Atlanta SMSA	
Newton	18.59
Butts	17.38
Dawson	7.25
Pike	6.58
Morgan	6.13

Source: "Commuter Patterns to the Atlanta Area from the 1970 Census." Atlanta Regional Commission Data Center, July 1972.

In all, there were nineteen counties in which 5 percent or more of the work force were employed in the SMSA.

The data in table 10-2 indicate that while manufacturing had the largest absolute increase in employment between 1964 and 1969 in each population change category, it did not have the highest rate of growth in any category. The contract construction and transportation sectors had higher growth rates in all five categories, and services grew more rapidly than manufacturing in all but the Loser category. Retail trade grew more rapidly than manufacturing in all categories except the Turnaround-Acceleration group. Although manufacturing employment remained high in absolute terms, the overall pattern of change is consistent with a growing resident population that commutes to work in the Atlanta SMSA.

Within the manufacturing sector, textiles and apparel are the leading employers in turnaround counties. However, in the Turnaround-Reversal group, food and kindred products is the most rapidly growing sector, while in Turnaround-Acceleration counties the higher paying chemicals, primary metals fabrication, transportation equipment, and stone, clay, and glass sectors are growing fastest. In both categories of counties the most rapidly growing service sectors are medical and other health services, and nonprofit membership organizations.

It is noteworthy that the relatively rapid expansion of population and economic activity in northern Georgia has, as in a number of similar areas elsewhere, given rise to concern for protection of the environment. The state's Environmental Protection Agency is headed by a person with a "hard-nosed" stance, and he appears to have the complete support of the governor.

Georgia's environmental protection plan includes standards limiting air, noise, and water pollution; the regulation of surface mining; and controls for the preservation of scenic resources. Although there is no concerted effort to divert new industrial growth to rural areas, some decentralization is occurring naturally. Around Atlanta firms are following population movements to the suburbs and the metropolitan periphery, and to rural locations along Interstate Highways. In addition, the Department of Industry and Trade spends much of its efforts recruiting firms for nonmetropolitan areas. The Department, aided by the aggressive development efforts of the Georgia Power Company, differs from some comparable agencies in neighboring states in that stress is not placed on the availability of a pool of low-wage, nonunion workers. While it is freely admitted that Georgia wages are below the national average, this "inducement" is not emphasized. If "less desirable" firms, such as low-paying garment plants, are not discouraged, neither are they actively recruited. The Department of Industry and Trade is primarily interested in recruiting firms that would raise the earnings of Georgia workers. Increasing workers' skills, lessening underemployment, and broadening the state's industrial base are among the agency's principal concerns. Relatively high wage chemical firms are actively courted, as are electronics plants, which, while they often seek manual dexterity skills not unlike those of the garment industry, pay higher wages. Metal-working plants, which tend to pay relatively high wages and to upgrade workers' skills, also are actively sought.

Table 10-2
Absolute and Percentage Employment Change by Sector (One-digit SIC Code) in Selected Georgia Counties, by Population Change Category, 1964-69

	Total	Agricultural Services, Forestry, Fisheries	Mining	Contract Construction	Manufacturing
Absolute Change, 1964-69					
Loser	2,531	−29	−11	274	1,393
Stagnant Gainer	5,421	−6	32	491	2,320
Turnaround-Reversal	5,476	41	−92	554	2,584
Turnaround-Acceleration	16,521	46	179	1,212	11,736
Consistent Fast Gainer	12,709	248	7	912	5,311
Percentage Change, 1964-69					
Loser	15.52	−26.12	−5.55	60.88	13.03
Stagnant Gainer	16.28	−4.68	53.33	38.72	11.69
Turnaround-Reversal	22.51	14.74	−32.05	59.44	15.50
Turnaround-Acceleration	30.26	8.24	34.42	60.90	34.44
Consistent Fast Gainer	39.22	57.01	5.22	39.79	35.00

Table 10-2 (Continued)
Employment Change

	Transportation and Other Public Utilities	Wholesale Trade	Retail Trade	Finance, Insurance, and Real Estate (FIRE)	Services	Unclassified Establishments
Absolute Change, 1964-69						
Loser	114	155	514	77	99	36
Stagnant Gainer	331	243	692	265	946	34
Turnaround-Reversal	236	197	812	174	721	44
Turnaround-Acceleration	1,350	146	2,084	334	1,580	159
Consistent Fast Gainer	881	463	2,176	272	2,410	53
Percentage Change, 1964-69						
Loser	25.85	24.33	20.95	21.62	10.39	80.00
Stagnart Gainer	23.75	18.49	14.00	18.47	33.12	43.58
Turnaround-Reversal	31.50	31.57	29.34	43.93	46.24	59.45
Turnaround-Acceleration	89.74	9.15	27.80	26.42	49.54	105.29
Consistent Fast Gainer	54.14	26.09	38.02	16.72	71.64	23.98

Georgia is a "right to work" state. Most union membership is confined to the Atlanta metropolitan area; elsewhere, apart from a few sectors such as trucking and mining, unionization is minimal. Although lack of unions is attractive to some firms contemplating a Georgia location, the state does not make a point of this fact in its recruitment efforts. Moreover, the state has involved unions in various training programs, at least in an advisory capacity, and the Atlanta Manpower Planning Board has made efforts to gear its training to union standards in order to facilitate the entry of enrollees into a trade.[4]

The state of Georgia maintains a network of twenty-five area vocational-technical schools located within commuting distance of over 90 percent of the state's population. Courses are geared to current industrial demands, and emphasize such fields as air conditioning and heating, auto mechanics, business and personal services, building trades, metal fabrication, electronics, and food services. All twenty-five schools offer extension training. Industrial training coordinators at each school can establish courses in specific fields at the request of firms in their areas. Through the In-Plant Training Program, coordinators aid industries in establishing training courses to upgrade workers on the job. Quick Start, a totally state-supported program, trains workers for specific jobs in particular companies. The program is aimed at companies moving into Georgia, as well as Georgia companies expanding their operations. Employers determine skill shortages at their desired locations and specify the type of training desired. The state provides instruction to assure that the needs are met.

Excellent as Georgia's industrial training services are, the local tax structure hinders vocational education for young people. A number of Comprehensive Vocational High Schools, which train high-school students in the trades and provide them with industrial skills, are funded in part by the Department of Health, Education, and Welfare, or the Appalachian Regional Commission, with the state and localities providing matching funds. The matching funds, however, are not always readily forthcoming, because city and county governments must rely on property taxes. A recent grant of $322,000 to Barrow County from the Appalachian Regional Commission for the construction of a Comprehensive Vocational High School was lost when a bond issue to raise the local share was twice voted down. Reluctance to increase taxes is not the only reason for such reactions; many people have observed that young people tend to migrate to Atlanta or other cities that pay higher wages, once trained at local expense. On the other hand, the tax bases of Atlanta, Athens, and, to a lesser degree, Gainesville, have been seriously decreased by the migration of city workers to nonmetropolitan areas.

Whatever the problems connected with nonmetropolitan development in Georgia, it has benefited from one of the oldest and most effective delivery systems for planning and administrative services to be found in any state. Multicounty planning areas, called Area Planning and Development Commissions

(APDCs), have been the principal vehicle for the development of this system. The technical assistance and coordination functions of the state have been concentrated in the Governor's Bureau of State Planning and Community Affairs, which also has responsibility for coordinating federal programs with state objectives. Moreover, Georgia was one of the first states to recognize the need for multistate coordinated planning through the Appalachian Regional Commission. (It is one of only three states to participate in two regional commission programs; most of the southern counties are part of the Coastal Plains Regional Commission.)

Each APDC is guided by a board of directors made up of local leaders, including at least one representative from each member county and one from the cities within that county. They are often elected officials or their appointees. The board employs and directs a staff, which is usually composed of an executive director and professional specialists in such fields as city and regional planning, economic development, law enforcement and transportation. All but four of Georgia's 159 counties are members of one of the state's nineteen APDCs.

Each APDC is required to review and comment upon applications by units of local government within the area to state, federal, quasi-governmental, or private agencies for loans or project grants, and to prepare an Area Biennial Development Program, which is updated annually. The program includes an analysis of the current status of area development and an evaluation of the progress made under the previous program; a statement of the objectives of existing and recommended programs; six-year schedules of area capital improvements and other major program expenditures and activities based on a determination of relative urgency; and recommendations for possible changes in administration, organization, or procedures to bring about more efficient methods of operation. Each APDC conducts annual public hearings on its proposed programs and prepares forecasts of future needs and resources with respect to patterns of urbanization, uses of land, housing, transportation, commerce, industry, recreation, forestry, agriculture, tourism and human resources development.

The APDC's receive a ten- to twenty-five-cent per capita contribution from member counties and cities, matched by state and federal funds for planning. These planning dollars are multiplied many times over in terms of state and federal money brought in through plans made with APDC assistance. There are many examples of fruitful results from the APDC's work. For example, eight counties in an east Georgia APDC are sharing a central computer system to figure taxes and make out tax bills; what was once a month's work is now done more accurately in an hour. APDCs support nonprofit regional housing corporations that acquire funds and sites in order to build, rent, and sell houses to low- and middle-income families; local developers and banks have first priority in the program, for which APDCs provide facts, plans, and initiative.

APDCs also help to revitalize downtown business districts; take quick advantage of federal assistance for law enforcement; promote industrial expansion; and promote recreation and tourist attractions. Planning in the Atlanta area is providing a system of regional parks and solutions to metropolitan sewer problems. In parts of rural Georgia the APDCs are helping to develop "suburban" type residential areas where the new life styles are often more urban than rural. Whereas in the past much of rural Georgia felt dominated by urban power, chiefly in Atlanta, there is now a definite prospect that the latter will be balanced by a combination of central city and nonmetropolitan intersts.

Central Texas

Although population declines in the United States have been particularly marked in the Great Plains and many adjacent prairie counties from the Canadian border to the Rio Grande, there are a few relatively small areas in this vast space that have experienced reversal of population decline. One such area in central Texas was selected for examination here because of its proximity to Austin, where this volume was prepared and written.

Within a fifty-mile radius of Austin there are six Turnaround-Reversal and two Turnaround-Acceleration counties. Within the relevant BEA regions there also are three Consistent Fast Gainer counties and twelve Losers. (The San Antonio BEA region, part of which falls within the field of study, extends across an unusually wide distance, from the Rio Grande to the Gulf of Mexico; some counties in both the extreme east and extreme west were dropped from consideration here because they were judged to be quite different in character from the counties closer to Austin and San Antonio.)

Because the turnaround counties form a circle around the Austin SMSA (Travis County), it is necessary at the outset to examine the recent growth in the capital. Between 1960 and 1970 Austin was one of the fastest-growing cities in the nation. The SMSA population increased from 212,136 to 295,516, or by nearly 40 percent. Austin's favorable situation with respect to the Texas highway network has no doubt been an advantage. It lies on Interstate Highway 35 between the Dallas-Fort Worth region and San Antonio, and it is a focal point on two major state highways. However, other factors have certainly been more important in determining Austin's growth. (The Waco SMSA, further north on Interstate Highway 35, has been relatively stagnant despite an equally favorable situation with respect to highways.) Growth in state employment and the rapid expansion of the University of Texas have been major contributors to the overall growth of the city. But there also has been rapid expansion of other activities, many drawn by the area's amenities (a favorable climate, clean air, university activities, the presence of large lakes nearby) as well as by the fact that Travis County lies in the late Lyndon Johnson's congressional district. Thus major employers include a large federal office complex, a multistate regional Internal Revenue Service office, Bergstrom Air Force Base, large IBM, Tracor, and Texas Instruments facilities, a large boat manufacturing firm, and a number of smaller service and manufacturing firms. Slightly over one half of the Austin labor force is employed in the service sector; the next largest sector, retail trade, accounts for about 13 percent.

The dependence of the turnaround counties on Austin (and in one case San Antonio) is reflected in the data presented in Table 10-3, which shows employment changes at the one-digit SIC code level from 1964 to 1969. The Turnaround-Reversal counties had the lowest rate of total employment growth. The greatest absolute increases were in the manufacturing, retail trade, and services sectors, but the rate of change in each was not impressive. The two Turnaround-Acceleration counties had the highest rate of total employment growth despite a decline in manufacturing employment. The service sector had by far the highest rate of growth in these counties, and together with retail trade it accounted for 86 percent of the absolute increase in total employment.

One of the Turnaround-Acceleration counties, Hays, is located southwest of Travis County. San Marcos, the county seat, is thirty miles from Austin via Interstate Highway 35. Hays County grew by 39 percent during the 1960s as a consequence of the doubling of Southwest Texas State University's enrollment, recreation and retirement activities that have been developed along the Blanco River and tributary creeks in the Wimberly and Dripping Springs areas, and proximity to Austin. A survey made in 1970 in San Marcos, which has a population of 18,860, indicated that approximately 1200 residents of the city commute daily to jobs in the capital city. Moreover, interviews in the Wimberly-Dripping Springs and Kyle-Buda areas indicated that over half of their labor forces worked in Austin.

The other Turnaround-Acceleration county, Kendall, is located west of Hays County and north of San Antonio. Its county seat, Boerne, is thirty miles from downtown San Antonio and only fifteen miles from the city limit via Interstate Highway 10. Although Kendall County has no natural resources on which to base industrial growth, about fifteen families per month move there, mostly from San Antonio. In the past inmigrants were usually retired persons seeking a pleasant rural residence. Now, however, most of the inmigration is accounted for by young families. The heads of these households usually continue to work in San Antonio and commute each day.

The Turnaround-Reversal counties of Williamson, Bastrop, and Caldwell form an arc from north to south around the western part of Travis County. They bear much the same relationship to Austin as that of Kendall County to San Antonio. Although they have some manufacturing, their growth is largely attributable to availability of jobs in Travis County. Examination of population change in the subdivisions of these counties indicates a pronounced tendency for growth to take place within a thirty-mile radius of Austin; beyond this limit most areas have declined.

Table 10-3

Absolute and Percentage Employment Change by Sector (One-digit SIC Code) in Selected Central Texas Counties, by Population Change Category, 1964-69

	Total	Agricultural Services, Forestry, Fisheries	Mining	Contract Construction	Manufacturing
Absolute Change, 1964-69					
Loser	2,642	61	-50	485	683
Stagnant Gainer					
Turnaround-Reversal	1,906	23	-263	-184	494
Turnaround-Acceleration	3,197	23	15	264	-104
Consistent Fast Gainer	6,642	48	14	659	2,488
Percentage Change, 1964-69					
Loser	17.5	34.9	-8.0	44.5	24.4
Stagnant Gainer					
Turnaround-Reversal	19.6	23.7	-28.9	-22.7	23.5
Turnaround-Acceleration	62.5	127.8	16.7	30.2	-14.7
Consistent Fast Gainer	37.8	43.2	18.9	47.5	79.9

Table 10-3 (Continued)
Central Texas

	Transportation and Other Public Utilities	Wholesale Trade	Retail Trade	Finance Insurance, and Real Estate (FIRE)	Services	Unclassified Establishments
Absolute Change, 1964-69						
Loser	-3	71	701	73	647	-30
Stagnant Gainer						
Turnaround-Reversal	5	129	678	119	898	-1
Turnarund-Acceleration	136	69	770	111	1,968	-61
Consistent Fast Gainer	270	209	1,541	135	1,343	-65
Percentage Change, 1964-69						
Loser	-.2	7.5	13.3	10.0	32.4	-25.9
Stagnant Gainer						
Turnaround-Reversal	1.2	25.1	23.2	30.0	61.0	-1.4
Turnaround-Acceleration	63.3	26.5	48.2	40.5	192.9	-76.2
Consistent Fast Gainer	23.6	22.7	30.4	12.6	29.6	-50.0

Llano and Burnet, Turnaround-Reversal counties northwest of Austin, owe their growth to retirement and recreation living on the Highland Lakes. Both counties have less than 5 percent of the labor force in manufacturing. Llano city, the county seat of Llano County, is located 75 miles from Austin, a distance too great to encourage much commuting. Llano city has constructed a travel trailer, camper, and motor home park capable of handling up to 450 units at a time, and it has actively and successfully sought camper clubs and caravans to use this facility for extended periods. The service and retail trade sectors together account for over 60 percent of the county's employment. Burnet County is bounded on the west and southwest by Buchanan, Inks, and LBJ lakes. Most of the county's growth has occurred in those divisions bordering the lakes. Burnet city grew by 30 percent between 1960 and 1970, largely on the basis of expanded service and construction employment supporting the retirement and leisure-recreational living common to the area. Three hospitals also make Burnet the medical center of the upper Highland Lakes. The services and retail trade sectors account for over half of total employment in the county.

The final Turnaround-Reversal county, Gillespie, is the farthest from Austin. Over half of the county's population lives in Fredericksburg, about 80 miles from the capital. This area was settled largely by Germans and retains strong identification with its German history. Gillespie experienced an unusual amount of activity during the middle 1960s by virtue of being the county where the LBJ Ranch is located. As a result of being mentioned as a "safe place" to live in a recent book with that title, the Fredericksburg Chamber of Commerce has been receiving fifteen to twenty letters per month inquiring about living conditions in the area. However, most inmigrants are retired or semiretired persons, and it is questionable whether long-run growth can be sustained on this basis.

In sum, the turnaround region in central Texas has received little or no benefit from manufacturing decentralization. Rather, growth has resulted from the extension of the Austin (and to a lesser extent San Antonio) urban field, as well as rapid expansion of demand for leisure and recreation activities and retirement residences. It is expected that substantial growth will continue in the 1970s as Austin continues to have a high rate of population increase and as higher incomes and greater mobility generate increasing demand for recreation and dwellings along the major rivers and lakes.

Migration and Income Change
In Turnaround Counties

The Nature of the Data

This chapter examines the income gains (or losses) of migrants to and from turnaround counties.[1] The data were obtained from a 1 percent Social Security sample and were processed by David Hirshberg, Bureau of Economic Analysis, U.S. Department of Commerce. Social Security Administration (SSA) data are probably the best available for work force migration analyses, though there are technical limitations. The SSA maintains, on magnetic tape, an annual 1 percent sample of all Social Security records based on specific digits in a person's Social Security number. Because the same Social Security numbers are selected for inclusion each year, it is possible to establish a work history file for all relevant persons who worked in a given period.

The decennial censuses provide data for workers in given regional demographic categories at given periods in time, but they do not yield data for the same workers over time. The Social Security sample, in contrast, is longitudinal. It assigns to each worker one place of work; for multiple job-holders the location of the employer paying the highest wage determines the place of work. In the present study a migrant is defined as a worker who was employed in a given area in 1965, but worked in a different area in 1970. New entrants are persons who worked in 1970 but not in 1965; similarly, dropouts are persons who worked in 1965 but not in 1970. Nonmigrants worked in their category of county in both years.

The problem of statistical sampling errors in tabulations made from the 1 percent sample has been examined in a number of documents. They indicate that the sample yields reasonably reliable estimates of mobility so long as the number of workers tabulated in any group is not too small. Table 11-1 shows the variation in estimates for given sample sizes. The chances are nineteen out of twenty that the sample value will not differ from the true value by more than the specified percent variation.

Nonmetropolitan Migration

There is a pronounced tendency for migrants from the two turnaround groups of counties *to other nonmetropolitan counties in their respective BEA regions* to make more income than migrants *from these other nonmetropolitan counties* to

153

Table 11-1
Variation in 1 Percent Social Security Sample Estimates for Given Sample Sizes

Workers in Sample	Percent Variation	Workers in Sample	Percent Variation
5	87	1,000	6
10	63	2,500	4
50	28	5,000	3
100	20	10,000	2
500	9	50,000	1

Source: Bureau of Economic Analysis, U.S. Department of Commerce

the turnaround counties. In the Tennessee Valley, the biggest area in terms of size of labor force, the relevant inmigrants to Turnaround-Reversal counties increased their average income to $4444, or by 68.0 percent. However, outmigrants increased their average income to $5122, or by 56.8 percent. Similarly, inmigrants to Turnaround-Acceleration counties increased their average income to $5485 whereas outmigrants increased theirs to $5577. The latter increased their average income by 64.7 percent, as compared with only a 48.7 percent increase for inmigrants.

In the Ozarks, the region with the next largest labor force, outmigrants to other nonmetropolitan counties in the region did still better in comparison to inmigrants. Outmigrants from Turnaround-Reversal counties increased their average income to $7901, a 104.8 percent gain. In contrast, inmigrants had an average income of only $5794 in 1970, for a gain of only 67.4 percent. Outmigrants from Turnaround-Acceleration counties had an average income of $5554 in 1970, compared with $4393 for inmigrants; the corresponding rates of increase were 65.4 percent and 38.4 percent respectively.

In the Minnesota-Wisconsin Turnaround-Reversal counties inmigrants from nonmetropolitan counties made more in 1970 than did outmigrants; the respective figures were $6535 (a gain of 92.0 percent) and $5690 (a gain of 70.5 percent). However, outmigrants fared better in the case of the Turnaround-Acceleration counties. Average income in 1970 for the outmigrants was $6322, compared to $6023 for inmigrants. In each case the gain was slightly over 80 percent.

Outmigrants from Turnaround-Reversal to nonmetropolitan counties in the Vermont-New Hampshire region increased their average income by 115.9 percent, to $7124. In contrast, inmigrants made only $5794 in 1970, an increase of 58.3 percent. However, in the Turnaround-Acceleration counties, inmigrants made $6378 in 1970 (a gain of 86.7 percent) whereas outmigrants made $5557 (a gain of 101.0 percent).

In the Colorado-New Mexico region outmigrants from Turnaround-Reversal counties increased their average income by 140.1 percent (compared to 8.6 percent for inmigrants) and outmigrants from Turnaround-Acceleration counties increased theirs by 157.1 percent (compared to 80.0 percent for inmigrants). However, these comparisons must be qualified by the very small sample sizes for inmigration to Turnaround-Reversal counties and outmigration from Turnaround-Acceleration counties.

Among all regions migration between turnaround counties and other nonmetropolitan counties results in greater rates of income increase to migrants than to turnaround county nonmigrants, no matter what the direction of migration. However, inmigrants to turnaround counties usually make less than turnaround county nonmigrants (The Turnaround-Reversal counties in the Ozarks and the Minnesota-Wisconsin region are notable exceptions.). It is more difficult to generalize concerning the incomes of outmigrants relative to nonmigrants. Nevertheless, in the two largest regions, the Tennessee Valley and the Ozarks, outmigrants had higher average incomes in 1970 than did nonmigrants. For the large block of Turnaround-Reversal counties in the Ozarks, outmigrants to other nonmetropolitan counties had an average income of $7901 in 1970, compared to only $5400 for nonmigrants.

These results indicate that the growth of the turnaround counties is not providing relative advantages to migrants from other nonmetropolitan areas. If anything, the nonturnaround counties seem to be providing relatively greater opportunities for migrants from turnaround counties. In any case, both inmigrants and outmigrants have greater income gains than turnaround county nonmigrants.

Migration Flows with Regional SMSAs

Migrants to SMSAs in the relevant BEA regions from turnaround counties experienced greater percentage income increases than did nonmigrants. The only exceptions were the Turnaround-Acceleration counties in the Tennessee Valley, where migrants to SMSAs increased their average income by 42.9 percent, while nonmigrants had a corresponding increase of 49.3 percent; and the Turnaround-Reversal counties in the Colorado-New Mexico region, where the changes were practically the same (45.3 and 47.6 percent). Migrants from Turnaround-Reversal counties to regional SMSAs had an average income of $5881 in 1970, or 91.6 percent greater than their average 1965 wage. The comparable values for migrants from Turnaround-Acceleration counties were $6448 and 77.7 percent.

Migrants from regional SMSAs to Turnaround-Reversal counties had an average income of $6627 in 1970, or a gain of 44.7 percent. Migrants from regional SMSAs to Turnaround-Acceleration counties had corresponding values of $6414 and 55.6 percent. Thus, migrants from Turnaround-Acceleration counties to SMSAs had about the same 1970 income as migrants going in the reverse direction, but they improved their own relative position more. Migrants from Turnaround-Reversal counties had lower average incomes in 1970 than migrants going in the reverse direction, but they too improved their relative position more. However, on the whole there is no evidence that migrants from turnaround counties to SMSAs improved their economic status more than did migrants to other nonmetropolitan areas.

The evidence is also mixed with respect to the position of migrants from regional SMSAs vis-à-vis nonmigrants in turnaround counties. In the Tennessee Valley, for example, inmigrants to Turnaround-Reversal counties had lower average incomes in 1970 than did nonmigrants, and their rate of income increase over 1965 also was lower. But the opposite situation prevailed in the case of the Turnaround-Acceleration counties. In the Ozarks inmigrants from SMSAs earned more than nonmigrants in both categories of turnaround counties, though the rate of increase was lower than that for nonmigrants in the Turnaround-Acceleration group. In the Minnesota-Wisconsin region the migrants from SMSAs had a lower rate of income increase compared to nonmigrants in both categories of turnaround counties, but their incomes were higher in 1970 in the Turnaround-Acceleration counties. In the Vermont-New Hampshire region inmigrants from SMSAs have lower incomes than nonmigrants, but in the Colorado-New Mexico region the situation is mixed. These results appear to reflect the complex nature of migrants from regional SMSAs to turnaround counties. At one extreme are relatively highly paid executives who are transferred to turnaround counties; their relative gains in income may not be great but their income levels are higher than those of the resident populations. Skilled workers, some of whom may be return migrants, are in a similar position. On the other hand, some return migrants may have had little success in the city and are having little back home too.

Migration Flows with the Rest of the United States

Migrants to areas outside of the relevant BEA regions from both categories of turnaround counties in all regions had higher average incomes in 1970 than did nonmigrants. Moreover, in all but two instances (Minnesota-Wisconsin Turnaround-Acceleration and Vermont-New Hampshire Turnaround-Acceleration counties), migrants to the rest of the United States had higher incomes than migrants to regional SMSAs. The rate of income increase from 1965 to 1970 was greater in all cases for migrants to the rest of the United States than for nonmigrants. It was also greater than that for migrants to regional SMSAs in most cases. Overall, migrants from Turnaround-Reversal counties to the rest of the United States had average incomes of $6184 in 1970, an increase of 98.0 percent over 1965. The corresponding values for migrants from Turnaround-Acceleration counties were $6796 and 73.0 percent.

Inmigrants from the rest of the United States to Turnaround-Reversal counties had average incomes of $5465 in 1970, an increase of 42.0 percent. Comparable values for migrants to Turnaround-Acceleration counties were $6820 and 46.6 percent. There is a pronounced tendency for inmigrants from the rest of the United States to have lower rates of income increase in relation to turnaround county nonmigrants, but to have higher incomes in 1970. This suggests that migrants from the rest of the United States, rather than less qualified local workers, are taking advantage of opportunities in turnaround counties.

Summary and Conclusions

The migration flow and income data indicate that both outmigrants to and inmigrants from other nonmetropolitan counties have greater income increases than do nonmigrants in turnaround counties. However, the turnaround counties, on balance, provide no more opportunities for migrants from other nonmetropolitan areas than the latter do for migrants from the turnaround counties. Indeed, if any generalization can be made from the mixed evidence, it is that other nonmetrpolitan areas provide relatively greater opportunities for migrants from turnaround counties.

Though there are exceptions, migrants from turnaround counties to regional SMSAs tended to have higher incomes in 1970 than nonmigrants. In terms of rate of income increase it was clear that migrants to regional SMSAs did considerably better than nonmigrants. Migrants from turnaround counties to the rest of the United States had higher incomes in 1970 than did migrants to regional SMSAs, but the rate of income increase was about the same because this group had higher base incomes in 1965. Thus, despite reversal of population decline or accelerated growth in turnaround counties, those workers who migrated to other areas were still better off economically than those who did not.

The position of inmigrants from regional SMSAs and the rest of the nation relative to local workers varies considerably by region. In the Tennessee Valley, which accounts for a high proportion of all such inmigration, the data indicate that inmigrants from the rest of the United States have higher 1970 incomes than either migrants from regional SMSAs or turnaround county nonmigrants, though they have the lowest percentage increases in incomes because of their high 1965 base. This suggests, in line with data presented in chapter 7, that the region is importing managers and skilled workers and exporting relatively unskilled workers.

In contrast, in the Ozarks Turnaround-Reversal counties, which account for most of the remaining total inmigration, inmigrants from regional SMSAs have the highest rates of income gain and the highest incomes in 1970. Inmigrants from the rest of the United States have lower rates of income increase and lower 1970 incomes than even local nonmigrants. This phenomenon is possibly a result of large-scale return migration of marginal workers from the rest of the United States, coupled with importation of mangers and skilled workers from regional SMSAs.

The situation in both the Minnesota-Wisconsin and Vermont-New Hampshire regions resembles that in the Tennessee Valley, though workers in these regions work in higher-paying sectors. The Colorado-New Mexico region presents a more complicated picture. The Turnaround-Reversal counties have a high number of relatively affluent migrants from both regional SMSAs and the rest of the United States, but in the Turnaround-Acceleration counties, these migrants have low incomes in relation to the resident population. The reason for this phenomenon is not readily apparent.

Finally, it may be noted that in all regions new entrants to and dropouts from the labor force have considerably lower earnings than resident workers employed in both 1965 and 1970.

12 Summary and Conclusions

The population of the United States is becoming increasingly concentrated not only in metropolitan areas, but also in a relatively few metropolitan regions, of which the northeastern "megalopolis" is perhaps the most familiar. While some view this phenomenon with alarm, others find it to be quite consistent with the objective of increased opportunities for most of the nation's population. William Alonso, for example, points out that German and Japanese data show that the gross regional product of metropolitan areas is rising faster than public costs, and that per capita income in the United States rises sharply with urban size. He argues:

Urban size is a measure of the opportunities to which an inhabitant or enterprise has access. Interestingly, per capita income is also strongly correlated to population potential, which is a mathematical measure of the accessibility available to residents of the city to the population of the rest of the country. Thus, a small metropolis in an area of high population potential will usually have as high a per capita income as a larger but more remote metropolis. This phenomenon may account for the emerging megalopolitan pattern, which consists of constellations of metropoles. The nineteenth century city, which had a single dominant center of activity, has given way to a much larger metropolis, whose structure is a complex counterpoint of multiple nuclei which permit the advantages of concentration and specialization while keeping functional distances relatively small. The megalopolis, for all the negative associations this term has gathered in journalistic usage, seems to be a further adaptation permitting specialization and high connectivity among urban areas, while avoiding some of the penalties of excessive size.[1]

In keeping with this line of reasoning Brian Berry maintains:

Proper regional strategies can contribute to self-sustaining urban growth and also to efficient allocation of resources by facilitating equalization of returns at the margin by easing migration out of the interstices and periphery under the condition that the migration stream is not directed at the big city ghettos. But these results will only be possible when regional economic development policies are explicitly urban in orientation, urban in content, urban in result. To try to keep people down on the farm, or in the small town, is to condemn regional policy to failure.[2]

Nevertheless, federal policies with respect to the development of a national spatial growth policy continue to emphasize small towns and rural areas. A summary of 1971 legislative and executive actions in this regard concludes that

159

"perhaps the most active component of national urban growth policy in 1971 was concern for the development of smaller urban centers as an option to present metropolitan growth trends."[3]

In view of this concern for rural areas and small towns the present study has examined the nature and general significance of cases where recent reversal of rural stagnation and decline has occurred spontaneously. Of particular interest is the relevance of these cases to regional development and manpower policies.

In chapter 2 it was pointed out that the "metropolitanization" of the American population may be perfectly consistent with population growth in previously stagnant or declining nonmetropolitan counties. The fundamental reason is that for many people a metropolitan life means more than merely living and working in an SMSA. Just as the compact nineteenth-century city gave way to the metropolitan area, so today the SMSA is giving way to urban fields which may include whole regions within a two-hour driving radius of the central cities. Increased incomes, leisure, and accessibility have permitted a growing number of persons to avail themselves of opportunities and amenities throughout their respective urban fields. Thus, many persons who work in SMSAs may reside in nonmetropolitan areas where residential amenities are more agreeable, and many persons who live and work in SMSAs regularly go to nonmetropolitan areas for tourism, recreation, second homes, and retirement. Indeed, this broader spatial framework has made it ever more difficult to really distinguish between what is properly "rural" and what is properly "urban." Moreover, urban fields need not be limited to areas contiguous to SMSAs. Areas with attractive recreation-tourism-retirement-second-home features may expand because of demand generated by metropolitan residents who live well beyond commuting range.

The phenomena described here are clearly seen in all of the regions studied. Turnaround-Acceleration counties in particular are relatively concentrated around major SMSAs and many smaller ones. Moreover, while employment expansion in these counties includes a considerable amount of manufacturing activity, it also includes a relatively large amount of workers in non-goods-producing sectors usually associated with metropolitan areas. The Interstate Highway System has helped to expand urban fields, but its role has primarily been to reinforce processes already at work. Moreover, while the presence of Interstate Highways and other major highways may accelerate commuting or even attraction of economic activity, the evidence indicates that they are neither necessary nor sufficient for economic development, and that their lack does not preclude development. Although many nonmetropolitan counties have benefited from the continuous extension of urban fields from SMSAs, others have grown on the basis of the leapfrogging of metropolitan demand for amenities conducive to recreation, tourism, and retirement and second homes. This is particularly seen in the Colorado-New Mexico, Vermont-New Hampshire, Minnesota-Wisconsin, and Central Texas regions. The impact of this demand on local employment and income is difficult to establish.

County Business Patterns employment data relate to mid-March of each year, a time that falls between the winter and summer peak employment seasons; and the 1 percent Social Security sample is subject to a large amount of statistical variation in these cases. Nevertheless, there are indications that while tourism and related activities bring undoubted satisfactions to metropolitan populations and profit to many metropolitan-based developers, their positive impact on the local nonmetropolitan labor force is often less certain. The tourist industry does not have strong linkages to other industries and usually does not lead to the growth of complementary activities. Moreover, the kinds of skill required by the tourist industry are not those that would be likely to lay the bases for new industry; rather, what is usually needed are low-level skills utilized in retail trade. It has been aptly remarked that "the promotion of tourism, while it may win political support from local chambers of commerce dominated by the owners of retail establishments, is not likely to have much of a multiplier effect on the state economy such as the promotion of most other industries can be expected to have."[4] The local impact of recreation employment is illustrated in the following analysis of counties in the northern halves of Vermont and New Hampshire:

The economic impact of the recreation industry cannot be dismissed as inconsequential. It supports many small businesses, most of them of the proprietorship variety, and some larger ones. The local and state tax dollars it generates help to ease the tax burden on all residents, including those who have no direct connections with this industry. But the seasonal employment it generates appears only to create ripples on the tides of employment and unemployment. Answers to the problem of a low rate of job creation . . . need to be found elsewhere than in an acceleration of recreational activity.[5]

Interviews with local and state officials in the regions concerned also indicated that poorer residents of amenity-rich nonmetropolitan areas often end up worse off as a result of the influx of persons from metropolitan areas. Their employment and income opportunities are too rarely improved as a result of the factors causing population turnaround. This situation is partly a result of human resource development and manpower program deficiencies, of which more will be said below. Moreover, the poor frequently feel the brunt of local price inflation and are denied access to recreation opportunities that they once took for granted, as more and more territory falls into the "off-limits" domain of the more affluent. The case studies also pointed up widespread concern over damage to the environment that has been largely responsible for population growth; it is to be hoped that this concern will be translated into effective controls for preserving unreproducible scarce resources. In any event, it is apparent that although the omnivorous appetite of metropolitan residents for nonmetropolitan amenities may cheer local Chambers of Commerce the blessings are perhaps at best mixed.

It was suggested in chapter 2 that in addition to the expansion of urban fields, the principal cause of reversal of nonmetropolitan decline or stagnation would be decentralization of manufacturing. Wilbur Thompson's hypothesis of industrial filtering in the national system of cities maintains that invention, or at least innovation, takes place more than proportionally in the larger metropolitan areas of industrially mature regions. However, as industries age and their technology matures, skill requirements fall and competition forces them to relocate to lower-wage areas. The lower an urban area in the skill and wage hierarchy, the older an industry tends to be when it arrives, and the slower its national growth rate. Intermediate-level places tend to fashion a growth rate somewhat above the national average out of growing shares of slow-growing industries, but in smaller places the positive change in share weakens and erodes to zero, leading to slower-than-average growth and net outmigration, or even to absolute employment and population decline in the smallest places.

The evidence in the present study supports Thompson's hypothesis. With the exception of the Colorado-New Mexico and central Texas regions, all of the regions considered have benefited from industrial decentralization. In some instances, e.g. Minnesota-Wisconsin, Vermont-New Hampshire, and the Atlanta BEA region, nonmetropolitan turnaround has resulted from a combination of extension and intensification of urban fields on the one hand, and industrial decentralization on the other. However, in the two largest regions in terms of number of workers affected — the Tennessee Valley and the Ozarks — industrial decentralization has been the principal cause of growth. Both of these regions, but especially the Ozarks, have a relatively high proportion of Turnaround-Reversal counties. In general, the growth of Turnaround-Reversal counties, which usually are located farther from SMSAs than are Turnaround-Acceleration counties, depends most on industrial decentralization and least on urban field expansion.

Although industrial growth in rural hinterlands is by no means a universal phenomenon, the fact that it *is* occurring in some regions has given rural development advocates some cause for rejoicing. But here too what appears to be "success" must be qualified. In the first place, it could be argued that many of the Turnaround-Reversal counties are at best only nominally successful by any standard. A net loss of fifteen people in one decade and a net gain of a dozen in the next is scarcely an impressive performance even in terms of demographic criteria, since obviously net outmigration has barely been outweighed by natural increase. This argument would be telling with respect to one or a few counties, but loses credibility when urged against whole regions such as the Tennessee Valley, the Ozarks, and northern Wisconsin and Minnesota, where large blocks of counties have experienced significant reversal of often severe population decline. Growth, even small growth, must be acknowledged as significant when it occurs over such large areas. Nevertheless, it remains true that these regions do not have the relative security that characterizes metropolitan areas with more diversified economic activities.

Agricultural employment still is considerably above the national average and the few manufacturing sectors are frequently in the low-wage, slow-growth (and often heavily subsidized) class.

Moreover, rural workers have been among the most neglected segments of the nation's population in terms of manpower and other domestic policies. One promising organizational development was the change of the Farm Labor Service to the Farm Labor and Rural Manpower Service in 1969, and then to the Rural Manpower Service (RMS) in 1970. Whereas the Farm Labor Service seemed preoccupied with the needs of agricultural employers, the RMS has attempted to be more responsive to workers in the total rural setting rather than in agriculture alone. It also is developing programs geared specifically to rural areas rather than transferring programs developed mainly in an urban context. Nevertheless, rural manpower programs remain hampered by scarcity of manpower experts, low population densities, limited training facilities, and an urban bias in manpower legislation and programs. For example, it is estimated that in 1971 rural areas accounted for 31 percent of the national population and an even larger proportion of all poor persons, yet they received only 23 percent of manpower outlays. In addition, the rural employment service staff amounted to only 16 percent of the total. The RMS is attempting to obtain a greater share of manpower funds for rural areas and to be an advocate for rural manpower within the Department of Labor, but it still must contend with its poor image among many rural workers and with employer-oriented influences that often permeate its field operations.[6]

On the other hand, regional development, if it takes place at all, must begin somewhere. And there are indications that despite deficiencies in public policies and programs the process of industrial filtering does eventually lead to the upgrading of both manpower qualifications, types of industry, and incomes. These phenomena are clearly in evidence in the South. The industrialization of the South was initiated in large measure by the movement of textile mills from New England and other northern areas into the Piedmont region of the central Carolinas. The textile mills in turn generated other activities. For example,

by 1970 there were 214 establishments in the South producing *machinery* for the textile industry. In addition, there were 65 chemical plants involved in producing synthetic fibers; the bulk of these plants were in the states where substantial textile production has concentrated. Suppliers of dyes and other processing chemicals were also stimulated by the movement of the textile industry.[7]

The growth of manufacturing in the Carolinas, especially North Carolina, was followed by similar expansion into Georgia. Decentralization next spread to the Tennessee Valley, which has managed to achieve a higher degree of industrial diversification than either the Carolinas or Georgia. More recently, the states of Mississippi and Arkansas have entered the lower rungs of the filtering process. Interviews with state and local officials and university personnel in these states reflected these transitions. Although Georgia is actively recruiting northern industrial firms, it is not attempting to "sell" the state on the basis of a labor force willing to work for low wages; that era has passed. Tennessee officials take a certain pride in the fact that they no longer need to tempt firms with the subsidies available in Arkansas and Mississippi. Arkansas and Mississippi are gratified with industrial growth based on low-wage, slow-growth industries, though stirrings for something better are apparent and probably will be realized.

The southern turnaround counties that have been the primary beneficiaries of industrial decentralization are overwhelmingly white in racial composition. The largest block of Turnaround-Reversal counties in the nation is that in the Ozarks. The remarkable industrial growth taking place in Mississippi is concentrated in a few counties in the northeastern part of the state; similar expansion is occurring in northern Alabama. Some of the most impressive manufacturing growth in the nation is in Tennessee (apart from some southwestern counties), northern Georgia, and the Piedmont. These areas have one element of homogeneity that is even more striking than their industrial expansion: although they are southern they have proportionally fewer blacks than the nation as a whole.

It was noted earlier that the reversal of population stagnation or decline has been obvious around southern SMSAs as a consequence of the extension of urban fields. The one notable exception, Memphis, is surrounded by counties (in three states) that are essentially black and rural.

The obvious general lack of extension of employment opportunities to areas with a high proportion of blacks has been rationalized on a number of grounds. Many employers believe that blacks are less productive and more inclined toward organization by unions. A prominent local official in northeastern Mississippi, commenting on the failure of the industrial growth characteristic of his area to spread to the Black Belt, stated that firms seeking a large pool of relatively cheap labor may need to go as far south as northeastern Mississippi, but no farther. Whatever superficial merit these arguments may have it cannot be denied that racial discrimination plays a part in the failure of firms to locate in "black" areas. However, the issue is not solely one of overt racism on the part of those who decide where firms will locate. Past and present discrimination against blacks in the provision of manpower services and health, education, and other human resource investments has created a labor force that may really be relatively less productive, and marginal firms in particular cannot afford experiments based on social concern.

The plight of rural blacks is seen particularly in data on educational attainment. Over half of all black males displaced from agriculture in the South between 1950 and 1969 had less than four years of schooling, and 75 percent of the blacks over twenty-five years old who remained on southern farms in 1970 had eight years or less of schooling.[8] The disadvantage at which the black finds himself in competition for jobs in nonfarm labor markets is apparent. Moreover, too many vocational schools in rural areas still continue to give disproportionate emphasis to agricultural skills for which the need is decreasing. In view of the continuing migration of large numbers of blacks from the rural South it clearly would be in the national interest to substantially upgrade the means for developing the region's black human resources.

This is not to suggest that manpower and related programs would be a panacea for the problems of rural blacks or other groups concentrated in economically lagging regions, e.g. Mexican Americans in south Texas, Appalachians in eastern Kentucky, and Indians on the reservations, and especially not for those who choose to remain in these regions. There is a tendency for better educated and better trained workers to leave poor rural areas for more attractive opportunities elsewhere. (It was shown in chapter 11 that even in the turnaround counties outmigrants improved their economic status in relation to nonmigrants. Turnaround counties also tend to provide relatively little economic advantage to inmigrants, though there are regional differences in this regard.) I would also hasten to agree with Peter Doeringer:

There is clearly a connection between education and income, as has been ably demonstrated by the work of scholars such as Denison, Schultz, and Becker, but the causal mechanisms underlying this association are complex and only poorly understood at present. For example . . . a high-wage industrial structure may encourage greater education and training rather than the reverse. Or, as can be seen in the case of the black work force, reducing the educational differential with respect to the white work force does not necessarily lead to a corresponding decline in income differentials.[9]

In the Minnesota-Wisconsin and Vermont-New Hampshire regions, the nonmetropolitan labor forces have clearly benefited from a relatively long process of mutual upgrading of education and manpower training on the one hand, and industrial composition on the other. Understanding of this process may have more to do with social and cultural factors than with those of a purely economic nature. The South, though it is rapidly rejoining the rest of the nation economically, still retains its uniqueness.[10] Nevertheless, capital deepening and higher wages have accompanied the simultaneous industrial filtering and labor-force upgrading process that has moved through the Piedmont, northern Georgia, Tennessee, and the white counties of Arkansas and northern Mississippi and Alabama. One is tempted to speculate on which region will be the next to enter the lowest step of the industrial decentralization escalator. West Texas is making a strong bid; despite its almost exclusively Anglo-Saxon population it will probably have more last picture shows than factories. Kentucky would also seem a likely candidate. The industrialization of the white South has curiously bypassed much of the Bluegrass State, and particularly its unemployed and underemployed Appalachians. Yet another possibility — maybe the most likely — is that industrial filtering will spread to foreign countries rather than major lagging regions of the United States. In this event the United States would tend to become an international center of tertiary activities, with secondary activities being increasingly relegated to countries with low wages. Of course, whatever the economic rationality or feasibility, constraints of a political and military nature would no doubt eventually be placed on such a process. In any case, within the nation tertiary activities will remain concentrated in or very near metropolitan areas while manufacturing continues to decentralize to nonmetropolitan counties in urban fields, or even beyond. But without subsidies on a scale not likely to be politically feasible, lagging rural *areas* with large concentrations of minority groups will remain poor. Yet the *people* of these areas can be given the option of employment in viable urban "growth centers," preferably not too big or too distant from the regions where the relocatees feel they have their roots. If a federal subsidy can accelerate growth in a center that is already growing, and if this subsidy is made conditional on providing opportunities for residents of lagging areas, then it would be more efficient to try to tie into the growing area than to attempt to create growth in stagnant areas that are basically unattractive economically. It should be emphasized that this approach has little to do with the prevalent notion that a growth center should, for policy purposes, be a generator of beneficial "spread effects" to its hinterland; there is little evidence that such a policy really works in large lagging rural regions. It might be preferable to refer to our growth centers as migration centers, which link external economies of urban growth to human resources development in lagging areas. Assisted labor mobility also would have an important role in such a strategy.

The lack of a permanent program of comprehensive worker relocation assistance represents one of the greatest deficiencies in public policies directly affecting spatial resource allocation.[11] The data in table 12-1 show the relative

Table 12-1
Public Cost for Creating Each New Job for Rural Workers

Public employment ($5000 per year for 10 years with 40 percent productivity)	$30,000
Industry location through tax write-offs	10,000
JOBS program ($2000 per job, two-thirds retention rate)	3,000
Subsidized migration ($500 direct payment plus $500 for administration and counseling)	1,000

Source: Luther Tweeten, *Research Application in Rural Economic Development and Planning* (Stillwater, Okla.: Oklahoma State University Agricultural Experiment Station Research Report No. P-665, July, 1972), p. 13.

public costs associated with the creation of each new job for rural workers by means of public employment, industrialization motivated by tax write-offs, the JOBS program, and subsidized migration. The first two alternatives are clearly very expensive. The JOBS program, which is run by the National Alliance of Businessmen, is supposed to combine the efficiency of private industry and incentives provided by the public. However, it has only very limited applicability in rural areas, simply because there are not enough jobs available. The $1000-per-job figure for subsidized migration is somewhat above the norm for pilot labor mobility projects sponsored by the Department of Labor,[12] and it apparently fails to take account of unsuccessful moves. Despite the lack of hard evidence concerning the rate of success in these projects, a reasonable estimate of 50 percent would imply that subsidized migration is relatively efficient.[13]

A related manpower issue is whether rural workers should receive training in their home areas or in urban places. No simple answer can be given because of the wide variety of circumstances that occur. Nevertheless, the case for coordinating training in rural areas with local economic development activities is strong where such areas are benefiting from manufacturing decentralization. A study of relocation projects in Michigan and Wisconsin, for example, indicated that while migrants apparently received little benefit from training, workers who remained at home during training were helped considerably.[14] South Carolina's efforts to integrate a manpower inventory system and worker training program with industrial expansion has proven quite successful. When a firm demonstrates an interest in a given locale, the recruitment, selection, classification and training of the local labor force are carried out to meet the specific requirements of the firm. On the other hand, training in urban areas would be more feasible when training facilities and employment opportunities are lacking in rural areas.

Whatever the merits of these approaches it is clear that they would affect a relatively small proportion of the nation's total population. The turnaround regions that are now growing spontaneously as a result of the extension of urban fields and manufacturing decentralization also involve only a fraction of the total population. Thus, even if the nation's largest cities are too big in some meaningful if not yet quantifiable sense, it seems clear that solutions to problems of the spatial distribution of population and economic activity will have to be explicitly urban — broadly defined to include urban fields. This is not to assert that the vast number of people living in hinterlands of urban fields and in interstitial areas must either construct high-rise buildings and international airports or else move to metropolitan areas. But they should learn to cooperate in at least simulating some of the advantages that firms find in metropolitan areas. In this regard it would be advisable to redelineate the local office jurisdictions of the Rural Manpower Service to conform with rational labor market areas. Current office areas are not always logical and sometimes obstruct the placement of rural workers in jobs within reasonable commuting distance from their homes. When the Ottumwa, Iowa jurisdiction was restructured to conform to a functional economic area — defined on the basis of trading patterns, transportation facilities, and other factors integrating small towns — placements of rural workers were substantially increased.[15]

It is significant that the turnaround regions lie wholly or mostly within the areas covered by the regional commissions created in 1965 by the Public Works and Economic Development Act and the Appalachian Regional Development Act. In addition, the turnaround regions have profited in varying degree from the activities of the Economic Development Administration and from planning efforts carried out within the context of state-designated multicounty planning units. Few would claim that these federal and state initiatives have been responsible for the growth of the relevant regions. The agencies involved have had too little money, too little time, and no coherent and systematic strategies for development. In many cases they also have neglected the human resource and manpower development needs of the poor. Nevertheless, their presence has undoubtedly been a positive factor in inducing and orchestrating the growth that has taken place. In the future it may be hoped that such efforts will concentrate not only on *regional* development, but also on the plight of those disadvantaged persons whose economic status remains deplorably low even by the most modest standards of equity.

Chapter 1
Introduction

1. Economic Research Service, U.S. Department of Agriculture, *The Economic and Social Condition of Rural America in the 1970's*, Part 1 (Washington, D.C.: Government Printing Office, 1971), p. 30. This report was prepared for the Senate Committee on Government Operations, 92nd Congress, 1st session.

2. Ibid., p. 16.

3. For a good discussion of the urban and rural dimensions of manpower policies see *Manpower Report of the President, 1971* (Washington, D.C.: Government Printing Office, 1971), pp. 83-146. An excellent overview of the issues involved in national growth policy is found in *Population and the American Future: The Report of the Commission on Population Growth and the American Future* (Washington, D.C.: Government Printing Office, 1972).

4. A group of counties surrounding Atlanta were included with the Tennessee Valley throughout the research for this volume. However, it was decided near the completion to break them out for separate analysis, adjusting employment change in the Tennessee Valley accordingly. For this reason the Georgia counties in the Atlanta BEA region are not considered separately until chapter 10.

Chapter 2
Factors Determining the Location of Economic Activity
in Metropolitan and Nonmetropolitan Areas

1. An excellent review of these factors is given in David M. Smith, *Industrial Location: An Economic Geographical Analysis* (New York: John Wiley and Sons, 1971).

2. The term "external economies," as used here, applies "to services or facilities which exist outside the firm, which serve to reduce its operating costs, and which are available because other economic activities have already brought them into being. It is conceptually useful to say that external economies so conceived are *external* to the *firm,* but *internal* to the *region*." Boris Yavitz and Thomas M. Stanback, Jr., *Electronic Data Processing in New York City* (New York: Columbia University Press, 1967), p. 12. For more detailed discussion see, for example, Smith, op. cit., pp. 82-88; and Edgar M. Hoover, *An Introduction to Regional Economics* (New York: Alfred A. Knopf, 1971), pp. 77-86, 148-51, 277 81.

169

3. Joseph J. Spengler, "Some Determinants of the Manpower Prospect, 1966-1985," in Irving H. Siegal, ed., *Manpower Tomorrow: Prospects and Priorities* (New York: Augustus M. Kelley, 1967), p. 91.

4. Wilbur R. Thompson, "Internal and External Factors in the Development of Urban Economies," in Harvey S. Perloff and Lowden Wingo, Jr., *Issues in Urban Economics* (Baltimore: The Johns Hopkins Press, 1968), p. 53.

5. Mathew Shane, "The Flow of Funds Through the Commercial Banking System, Minnesota-North Dakota," University of Minnesota, Department of Agricultural and Applied Economics (August 1971), p. 19.

6. Mathew Shane, "The Branch Banking Question," University of Minnesota, Department of Agricultural Economics, Staff Paper P 70-6 (April 1970), p. 12.

7. "The Availability of Capital in Central Appalachia," *Appalachia,* Vol. 3, No. 2 (September 1969), p. 1.

8. Committee on Business Financing, *Adequacy of Business Financing in Virginia* (Richmond: Advisory Council on the Virginia Economy, 1964), pp. 15-16.

9. Shane, "The Branch Banking Question," p. 2.

10. Ibid., p. 9. See also R.W. Hooker, Jr., "The Effect of the Financial Community's Structure on the Commercial Bank's Role as a Financier of Regional Growth," Program on the Role of Growth Centers in Regional Economic Development, Discussion Paper No. 5, Center for Economic Development, University of Texas (February 1970), pp. 11-12.

11. Shane, "The Branch Banking Question," p. 13.

12. See, for example, Ibid., pp. 15-19; Hooker, op. cit., pp. 26-30; Surveys and Research Corporation, *Capital Markets and Regional Economic Development* (Washington, D.C.: U.S. Department of Commerce, 1968), p. 131; Irving Schweiger and John S. McGee, "Chicago Banking," *The Journal of the University of Chicago,* Vol. 34 (July 1961), p. 254. Shane (p. 19) estimates that $161 million worth of extra loans would have been made in Minnesota in 1968 if all banks in the state had performed as well as the holding company affiliates.

13. Shane, "The Branch Banking Question," p. 18. See also Mathew Shane, "Elements of Banking Performance," University of Minnesota, Department of Agricultural Economics, Staff Paper P 70-21 (December 1970).

14. Roland I. Robinson, "Unit Banking Evaluated," in Dean Carson, ed., *Banking and Monetary Studies* (Homewood, Illinois: Richard D. Irwin, Inc., 1963), p. 298.

15. Cited in an address by Orville Freeman to the Conference on Rural-Oriented Industry, Washington, D.C., May 13, 1968.

16. The entire survey will be analyzed in papers by A.E.K. Nash, S. Mazie, and D. Wolman. The papers will appear in research volumes to be published by the Commission in 1972.

17. James L. Sundquist, "Where Shall They Live?" *The Public Interest,* No. 18 (Winter 1970), p. 90.

18. Wilbur R. Thompson, "The Economic Base of Urban Problems," in Neil W. Chamberlain, ed., *Contemporary Economic Issues* (Homewood, Illinois: Richard D. Irwin, 1969), p. 11.

19. Wilbur R. Thompson, "The National System of Cities as an Object of Public Policy," *Urban Studies,* Vol. 9, No. 1 (February 1972), p. 108.

20. Cited in National Area Development Institute, *Area Development Interchange,* Vol. 2, No. 6 (March 15, 1972), p. 2.

21. Dennis Durden, "Use of Empty Areas," in *Future Environments of North America* (Garden City, New York: Natural History Press, 1966), p. 484.

22. John Friedmann and John Miller, "The Urban Field," *Journal of the American Institute of Planners,* Vol. 31, No. 4 (November 1965), p. 314.

23. Ibid., p. 313.

24. *U.S. News and World Report,* April 17, 1972, p. 42.

25. Friedmann and Miller, op. cit., p. 316.

26. *U.S. News and World Report,* April 17, 1972, pp. 42-45.

27. U.S. Bureau of the Census, *Statistical Abstract of the United States: 1971* (Washington, D.C.: Government Printing Office, 1971), p. 217.

28. Claude C. Haren, "Employment, Population and Income Growth in the South's Metro-Nonmetro Areas, 1960-70," paper presented at the 1972 annual meeting of the Southern Regional Science Association, Williamsburg, Va., April 13-14, 1972.

29. Thomas E. Till, "Rural Industrialization and Southern Rural Poverty in the 1960's: Patterns of Labor Demand in Southern Nonmetropolitan Labor Markets and their Impact on Local Poverty," unpublished doctoral dissertation, University of Texas, August 1972.

30. Thompson, "The Economic Base . . .," op. cit., p. 8.

31. Ibid., p. 9.

32. Brian J.L. Berry, "Labor Market Participation and Regional Potential," *Growth and Change,* Vol. 1, No. 4 (October 1970), p. 3.

33. Ray Marshall, "Manpower Policies and Rural America," *Manpower* (April 1972), p. 15.

34. *State and Local Finances* (Washington, D.C.: Advisory Commission on Intergovernmental Relations, 1968), pp. 104-11.

35. Economic Research Service, U.S. Department of Agriculture, *The Economic and Social Condition of Rural America in the 1970's,* Part 1 (Washington, D.C.: Government Printing Office, 1971), p. 29. This study was prepared for the Senate Committee on Government Operations, 92nd Congress, 1st session.

Chapter 3

The Role of Highways

1. George W. Wilson, et al., *The Impact of Highway Investment on Development* (Washington, D.C.: The Brookings Institution, 1966), p. 3.

2. John A. Kuehn and Jerry G. West, "Highways and Regional Development," *Growth and Change,* Vol. 2, No. 3 (July 1971), p. 23. See also Claude Abraham, "L'étude économique des investissements routiers," *Revue économique* (September 1961), pp. 762-80.

3. For detailed discussions of the growth center concept see Niles M. Hansen, ed., *Growth Centers in Regional Economic Development* (New York: The Free Press, 1972); and Antoni R. Kuklinski, ed., *Growth Poles and Growth Centers in Regional Planning* (Paris and The Hague: Mouton, 1972).

4. Carl W. Hale, "The Mechanism of the Spread Effect in Regional Development," *Land Economics,* Vol. 43, No. 4 (November 1967), p. 437.

5. Albert O. Hirschman, *The Strategy of Economic Development* (New Haven: Yale University Press, 1958).

6. E.K. Hawkins, *Roads and Road Transport in an Underdeveloped Country: A Case Study of Uganda* (London: Her Majesty's Stationery Office, 1962).

7. Kuehn and West, op. cit., p. 24.

8. Howard L. Gauthier, "Geography, Transportation, and Regional Development," *Economic Geography,* Vol. 46, No. 4 (October 1970), p. 614.

9. See, for example, Niles M. Hansen, "Regional Planning in a Mixed Economy," *Southern Economic Journal,* Vol. 32, No. 2 (October 1965), pp. 176-90; and "Unbalanced Growth and Regional Development," *Western Economic Journal,* Vol. 4, No. 1 (Fall, 1965), pp. 3-14.

10. See, for example, Robert W. Raynsford, Jr. and Curtis C. Harris, Jr., "Foundation for a National Policy on Local Growth and Location of Federal Expenditures," *Review of Regional Studies,* Vol. 2, No. 1 (Fall, 1971), pp. 5-22; Niles M. Hansen, *Intermediate Size Cities as Growth Centers* (New York: Praeger, 1971), pp. 71-77; Kuehn and West, op. cit.; and Economic Research Service, U.S. Department of Agriculture, *The Economic and Social Condition of Rural America in the 1970's,* Part 3 (Washington, D.C.: Government Printing Office, 1971). This study was prepared for the Senate Committee on Government Operations, 92nd Congress, 1st Session.

11. Hirschman, op. cit., pp. 84-85.

12. Ralph R. Widner, "Appalachia after Six Years," *Appalachia,* Vol. 5, No. 2 (November-December 1971), p. 19.

13. Much of this section is based on Niles M. Hansen, *A Review of the Appalachian Regional Commission Program,* a report prepared in November 1969 for the U.S. Department of Commerce.

14. John M. Munro, "Planning the Appalachian Development Highway System: Some Critical Questions," *Land Economics* Vol. 45, No. 2 (May 1969), p. 149.

15. Ibid., p. 156.

16. From a letter in Hansen, *A Review of the Appalachian Regional Commission Program,* op. cit., Appendix 1.

17. *Effects of Federal Expenditures on the Economy of Johnson County, Kentucky* (Washington, D.C.: General Accounting Office, 1972).

18. Ibid.

19. Quoted in Bill Peterson, "The Poverty War," *Louisville Courier-Journal,* June 8, 1972, p. 1.

20. *Effects of Federal Expenditures . . . ,* op. cit.

21. Quoted in Bill Peterson, "Impoverished Still — The Poor Seem to Have Lost the War on Poverty," *Louisville Courier-Journal,* June 4, 1972, p. 1.

22. Hank Burchard, "U.S. Highway System: Where to Now?" *Washington Post,* November 29, 1971, p. C1.

23. Dick Netzer, *Economics and Urban Problems* (New York: Basic Books, 1970), p. 149.

24. William Bradford, "Superhighways Net to Leave Few Counties Unlinked," *Louisville Courier-Journal,* April 13, 1969, p. B7.

25. Peterson, "Impoverished Still . . .," op. cit.

26. Kuehn and West, op. cit., p. 26.

27. Ibid., p. 27.

Chapter 4
Changes in Employment Structure

1. U.S. Bureau of the Census, *Statistical Abstract of the United States: 1971* (Washington, D.C.: Government Printing Office, 1971), pp. 219-20.

2. Ibid.

3. Ibid., pp. 220-21.

4. Ibid., p. 221.

5. Ibid.

Chapter 5
Minnesota and Wisconsin

1. The preceding material in this section is derived from *Minnesota,* a survey of industrial development opportunities in the state prepared by Conway Research, Inc., for the Minnesota Department of Economic Development.

2. *Minnesota's New and Expanded Industries: 1970* (St. Paul: Minnesota Department of Economic Development, 1971), p. 1.

3. *Minnesota,* op. cit., pp. 14-15.

4. Minnesota Department of Economic Development, *Crosby and Brainerd Community Profiles,* no dates.

5. Bureau of Commercial Recreation, Wisconsin Department of Natural Resources, *A Program for Snowmobiling in Wisconsin* (Madison: Bureau of Commercial Recreation, n. d.), p. 1.

6. *Minnesota,* op. cit., p. 15.

7. Minnesota Department of Economic Development, *Thief River Falls Community Profile,* n. d.

8. *Minnesota,* op. cit., p. 15.

9. John R. Borchert and Donald D. Carroll, *Minnesota Settlement and Land Use: 1985* (St. Paul: Minnesota State Planning Agency, 1970), pp. 10-13.

10. Per capita income data by county are from "Qualitative Economic Growth in Minnesota: The Per Capita Income Aspect," unpublished paper prepared by the Minnesota Department of Economic Development, 1971.

11. U.S. Bureau of the Census, *Statistical Abstract of the United States: 1971* (Washington, D.C.: Government Printing Office, 1971), p. 121.

12. *Minnesota,* op. cit., p. 9.

13. Specific information on Wisconsin counties is derived in part from county economic profiles prepared by the state Department of Economic Development. These are available for only half of the counties at this writing. Supplemental data are available in Philip Sundal and Richard Kotenbeutel, *Geography of Wisconsin Manufacturers* (Madison: Department of Local Affairs and Development, 1970). Interviews with Mr. Sundal and Jim Jackson of the Wisconsin Employment Security Division were also valuable in this regard.

14. William H. Dodge, *Influence of a Major Highway Improvement on an Agriculturally-Based Economy* (Madison: University of Wisconsin Bureau of Business Research and Service, 1967), p. 20.

15. U.S. Bureau of the Census, op. cit., p. 121.

16. *Experiences, Opinions, and Attitudes of Company Officials and Community Leaders Related to Non-Metropolitan Branch Plants* (Minneapolis: Experience, Inc., 1972).

Chapter 6
The Ozarks

1. Forrest H. Pollard and Kenneth D. Jones, *Arkansas Population Migration Estimates, 1960-1970* (Little Rock: University of Arkansas Industrial Research and Extension Center, Research Memorandum RM-43, 1971), pp. 1-3.

2. Gordon D. Morgan, "Some Observations on the Rural Black Arkansas Population," unpublished paper submitted to the Commission on Population Growth and the American Future, 1971, pp. 7-8.

3. *Arkansas' Manpower Needs* (Little Rock: Arkansas Employment Security Division, 1970), p. 9. Emphasis added.

4. Ibid.

5. *State and County Economic Data for Arkansas* (Little Rock: University of Arkansas Industrial Research and Extension Center, 1971), p. 9.

6. *Arkansas Average Covered Employment and Wages, 1970* (Little Rock: Arkansas Employment Security Division, 1971), p. 55.

7. "Statement of Russell A. Thomas, Director of Industrial Relations of Wolverine Toy Division of Sprang Industries, Inc. for the Commission on Population Growth and the American Future," June 8, 1971, unpublished paper.

8. Ibid.

9. Lloyd D. Bender, Bernal L. Green, and Rex R. Campbell, "Trickle-down and Leakage in the War on Poverty," *Growth and Change,* Vol. 2, No. 4 (October 1971), p. 40.

10. Charles F. Floyd, *The Changing Structure of Employment and Income in the Ozarks Region* (Washington, D.C.: Economic Development Administration, Office of Economic Research, 1970), pp. 10-13.

11. "Testimony of the Honorable Winthrop Rockefeller, Former Governor of Arkansas, to the Commission on Population Growth and the American Future, June 1, 1971," unpublished paper, p. 14.

12. Ibid., p. 15.

13. Alfred W. Stuart, *Rural Industrialization and Population Growth: The Case of Arkansas* (Oak Ridge, Tennessee: Oak Ridge National Laboratory, 1971), p. 16.

14. *Annual Report, 1971* (Little Rock and Washington, D.C.: Ozarks Regional Commission, 1972), special section, p. iv.

15. *Arkansas River and Tributaries: Multiple-Purpose Plan, Arkansas and Oklahoma* (Little Rock and Tulsa: U.S. Army Engineer District, 1968), n.p. (map format).

16. Ibid.

17. Robert S. Kerr, *Land, Wood, and Water* (New York: Fleet Publishing Corporation, 1960), pp. 299-300.

18. Frontiers of Science Foundation of Oklahoma, Inc., *Project to Plan for Orderly Development of Arkansas-Verdigris Waterway Area* (Oklahoma City: Frontiers of Science Foundation of Oklahoma, Inc., 1971), II, appendix F, p. 1.

19. Letter from David L. Burrough, Chief, Planning and Reports Branch, Little Rock District, U.S. Army Corps of Engineers, Little Rock, June 5, 1972.

20. For more detail in this regard, see Curtis D. Toews, "The McClellan-Kerr Arkansas River Navigation System: A Study of Attempted Ex Post Facto Development Planning," University of Texas Center for Economic Development Discussion Paper No. 51 (Septermber 1972).

Chapter 7
The Tennessee Valley

1. U.S. Bureau of the Census, *Statistical Abstract of the United States: 1971* (Washington, D.C.: Government Printing Office, 1971), p. 18.

2. *Tennessee Comprehensive Manpower Plan, Part A, Fiscal Year 1973* (Nashville: Tennessee Manpower Council, 1972), p. 6.

3. Ibid.

4. U.S. Bureau of the Census, op. cit., p. 314.

5. *Tennessee Comprehensive Manpower Plan,* op. cit., pp. 48-59.

6. *Basic Industrial Data For the State of Tennessee* (Nashville: Staff Division for Industrial Development), n.p.

7. Data supplied by the Tennessee Staff Division for Industrial Development, Nashville.

8. Ibid.

9. These and most of the following data on local industry and employment are taken from *Basic Industrial Data* sheets, published by the Tennessee Staff Division for Industrial Development, for the communities discussed.

10. *Tennessee Comprehensive Manpower Plan,* op. cit., p. 54.

11. Ibid.

12. Ibid., p. 16.

13. *First Stage Overall Economic Development Program* (Nashville: Mid-Cumberland Development District, 1971), Appendix E, p. E-11.

14. *The Southwest Area Comprehensive Manpower Plan, Part A, Fiscal Year 1973* (Nashville: Southwest Manpower Planning Board, 1972), p. 3.

15. *First Stage Overall Economic Development Program* (Cookville: Upper Cumberland Economic Development District, 1969), pp. 70, 73.

16. *The First Tennessee Comprehensive Manpower Plan, Fiscal Year 1973, Part A* (Johnson City: First Tennessee Manpower Planning Board, 1972), pp. 12, 45.

17. Ibid., pp. 13, 14.

18. This section is based on Roger A. Matson and Wesley G. Smith, "Some Policy Implications of Labor Mobility in the South with Special Reference to the Tennessee Valley Region," unpublished paper presented to the 1972 annual meeting of the Southern Regional Science Association, Williamsburg, Virginia. The data used by the authors were based on a 1 percent sample of Old Age,

Survivors, and Disability Health Insurance records contained in the Social Security Administration's Continuous Work History Sample.

19. The low-wage sectors referred to here are tobacco, textiles, apparel, lumber and wood, furniture, leather, and miscellaneous.

20. The high-wage sectors referred to here are ordnance, chemicals, petroleum, primary metals, nonelectrical machinery, transportation equipment, and instruments.

21. Ibid., p. 16.

22. *The Population and Economy of the TARCOG Region* (Huntsville: Top of Alabama Regional Council of Governments, 1972), pp. 9-10,

23. Ibid., p. 20.

24. Ibid., pp. 163-66.

25. U.S. Bureau of the Census, Census of Population: 1970, *General Social and Economic Characteristics,* Final Report PC(1)-C2 Alabama (Washington: Government Printing Office, 1972), pp. 197, 376-77.

26. *The Population and Economy of the TARCOG Region,* op. cit., p. 166.

27. U.S. Bureau of the Census, op. cit., pp. 160, 380-85.

28. U.S. Bureau of the Census, Census of Population: 1970, *General Social and Economic Characteristics,* Final Report PC(1)-C26 Mississippi (Washington: Government Printing Office, 1972), pp. 145, 311-17.

29. Thomas E. Till, *Rural Industrialization and Southern Rural Poverty in the 1960's: Patterns of Labor Demand in Southern Nonmetropolitan Labor Markets and their Impact on Local Poverty,* unpublished dissertation, University of Texas, 1972, pp. 198-206.

30. Ray Marshall, "TVA and Social Development," University of Texas Center for the Study of Human Resources, unpublished paper (1972), pp. 2-3.

31. Claude C. Haren, "Rural Industrial Growth in the 1960's," *American Journal of Agricultural Economics,* Vol. 53, No. 3 (August 1970), p. 436.

Chapter 8
Colorado and New Mexico

1. Sigurd Johansen, *Population Changes in New Mexico* (Las Cruces, N.M.: New Mexico State University Agricultural Experiment Station Report No. 191, June 1971), p. 5.

2. Los Alamos is in fact a small federal enclave not associated with any New Mexico county, though it is usually listed separately when county data are presented. Its population rose dramatically during the 1940s because of atomic research activities centered there, and it has continued to grow on this basis. In 1967, about four fifths of wage and salary payments in Los Alamos was accounted for by the government sector, and nearly all of this amount was attributable to the federal government. For specific data see *New Mexico*

Statistical Abstract, 1970, Vol. 1 (Albuquerque: University of New Mexico Bureau of Business Research, 1970), pp. 44-45.

3. *Development Issues and Alternatives for North Central New Mexico* (Sante Fe: North Central New Mexico Economic Development District, 1972), pp. 35-36.

4. *New Mexico* (Sante Fe: New Mexico Department of Development, Tourist Division, n. d.), p. 12.

5. Data supplied by the Bureau of Business Research, University of New Mexico.

6. *New Mexico Statistical Abstract, 1970,* op. cit., p. 47.

7. Ibid., p. 16.

8. Ibid., p. 17.

9. *Development Issues and Alternatives,* op. cit., p. 24.

10. *Colorado Preliminary State Development Plan* (Denver: Colorado State Planning Office, 1969), p. 15; and *First Report* (Denver and Grand Junction: Colorado Rural Development Commission, 1971), p. 2.

11. Colorado Division of Planning, *Colorado Population Trends,* Vol. 1, No. 2 (Spring 1972), p. 2.

12. Colorado Division of Planning, *Colorado Population Trends,* Vol. 1, No. 1 (Winter 1972), p. 1.

13. *Western Mountain Region Study* (Boulder: University of Colorado Business Research Division, Graduate School of Business Administration, n.d.), pp. 115-16.

14. *Colorado Business-Economic Outlook Forum* (Boulder and Denver: University of Colorado Graduate School of Business Administration and Colorado Division of Commerce and Development, 1971), pp. 25-26.

15. Gerald L. Allen, *Colorado Ski and Winter Recreation Statistics, 1971* (Boulder: University of Colorado Business Research Division, Graduate School of Business Administration, 1971), pp. 64-70.

16. Ibid., p. 93.

17. Ibid., p. 51.

18. *The 12 Districts of Colorado* (Denver: Colorado Division of Planning, 1972), p. 71.

19. *The Aspen Times,* August 17, 1972, pp. 11-B.

20. Frank E. Smith, *The Politics of Conservation* (New York: Random House, 1966), p. 297.

21. Ibid., p. xi.

22. *Western Mountain Region Study,* op. cit., pp. 186-91.

23. Ibid., pp. 187-88.

24. U.S. Bureau of the Census, Census of the Population 1970, *General*

Social and Economic Characteristics, Final Report PC(1)-C7 Colorado (Washington: Government Printing Office, 1972), pp. 143, 161.

Chapter 9
Vermont and New Hampshire

1. *Third Annual Report of the New Hampshire-Vermont Development Council, Inc.*, p. 1.

2. *Vermont: Social and Economic Characteristics* (Montpelier: Vermont State Planning Office, 1971), p. 110. Unless otherwise indicated, the materials on Vermont in this chapter are based on this excellent source, as well as interviews related to it.

3. Brian J.L. Berry, "The Geography of the United States in the Year 2000," *Transactions*, No. 51 (November 1970), pp. 47-49.

4. George K. Lewis, "Population Change in Northern New England," *Annals of the Assocation of American Geographers*, Vol. 62, No. 2 (June 1972), pp. 312-13.

5. U.S. Bureau of the Census, *Statistical Abstract of the United States, 1971* (Washington, D.C.: Government Printing Office, 1971), p. 13.

6. *Vermont: Social and Economic Characteristics*, p. 5.

7. Matteson Associates, *Challenge and Opportunity*, Cycle III, Vermont Public Investment Plan (Montpelier: State of Vermont Planning and Community Services Agency, 1970), p. 17.

8. Ibid., pp. 26-27.

9. *Newsweek*, July 10, 1972, p. 86.

10. Lewis, op. cit., p. 322.

11. *Third Annual Report*, p. 4.

12. Matteson Associates, op. cit., pp. 103-104.

13. *Newsweek*, July 10, 1972, p. 86.

14. Ibid.

15. *Vermont Adopted Land Capability Plan* (Montpelier: Vermont State Planning Office, 1971).

16. *Newsweek*, July 10, 1972, p. 86.

17. Keith Warren Jennison. *Vermont is Where You Find It.* Kennebunkport, Maine: Durrell Publications, 1954.

Chapter 10
Northern Georgia and Central Texas

1. U.S. Bureau of the Census, *Statistical Abstract of the United States, 1971* (Washington, D.C.: Government Printing Office, 1971), p. 15.

2. Kenneth P. Johnson, *Georgia County Migration Patterns, 1960 to 1970* (Atlanta: Office of Planning and Budget, State Demographic Data Center, 1972), pp. iv-vii.

3. *Atlanta Area Manpower Plan, Fiscal Year 1973,* 1972, n.p.

4. *Atlanta Area Manpower Plan,* op. cit.

Chapter 11
Migration and Income Change in Turnaround Counties

1. In this chapter the Atlanta BEA region is included with the Tennessee Valley and central Texas is omitted because of the smallness of the sample size. Breakdowns by age, sex, race, and employment sector are not considered because sample sizes would in most cases have been too small to permit meaningful generalizations.

Chapter 12
Summary and Conclusions

1. William Alonso, "The Question of City Size and National Policy," Center for Planning and Development Research, Institute of Urban and Regional Development, University of Califronia, Berkeley, Discussion Paper No. 125 (June 1970), pp. 3-4.

2. Brian J.L. Berry, "Labor Market Participation and Regional Potential," *Growth and Change,* Vol. 1, No. 4 (October 1970), p. 10.

3. Norman Beckman, "Toward Development of a National Urban Growth Policy: A Legislative Review," *Journal of the American Institute of Planners,* Vol. 38, No. 4 (July 1972), p. 232.

4. Alfred S. Eichner, *State Development Agencies and Employment Expansion* (Ann Arbor, Michigan: University of Michigan and Wayne State University Insitute of Labor and Industrial Relations, 1970), pp. 41-42.

5. Third Annual Report of the New Hampshire-Vermont Development Council, Inc. (Hanover, N.H.: New Hampshire-Vermont Development Council, Inc., 1971), p. 4.

6. Ray Marshall, *Rural Manpower Problems and Programs* (Austin, Texas: University of Texas Center for the Study of Human Resources, 1973), pp. 116, 185-86. This study is in preliminary draft form.

7. John H. Zammito, *Dynamics of Southern Growth* (Memphis: Morgan, Keegan and Company, 1972), p. 24.

8. *Potential Mechanization in the Flue-Cured Tobacco Industry* (Washington, D.C.: U.S. Department of Agriculture, Economic Research Service, Agricultural Economics Report No. 169, 1969).

9. Peter B. Doeringer, review of Niles M. Hansen, *Rural Poverty and the Urban Crisis, Journal of Human Resources,* Vol. 7, No. 3 (Summer 1972), p. 396.

10. See, for example, Marvin K. Hoffman and James E. Prather, "The Independent Effect of Region on State Governmental Expenditures," *Social Science Quarterly,* Vol. 53, No. 1 (June 1972), pp. 52-65.

11. See Niles M. Hansen, *Location Preferences, Migration and Regional Development* (New York: Praeger, 1973).

12. Charles K. Fairchild, *Worker Relocation: A Review of U.S. Department of Labor Mobility Demonstration Projects* (New York and Washington: E.F. Shelley and Co., 1970), p. 105.

13. Fairchild's review of the pilot projects found that three fourths of relocated workers remained in the areas in which they were placed, if not in the same jobs, during the standard two-month followup period. Fairchild, op. cit., p. 12. Similar results are reported in Ray Marshall, *Policy and Program Issues in Rural Manpower Development* (Austin, Texas: University of Texas Center for the Study of Human Resources, 1971), p. 26. An investigation of one of the larger projects indicated a "success" rate of 48 percent after a six-month followup survey. Carol Pfrommer, *Employer Assessment of Assisted Labor Mobility: A Study of the STAR Project* (Austin, Texas: University of Texas Center for Economic Development, 1973), p. 13.

14. Gerald G. Somers, *Labor Mobility: An Evaluation of Pilot Projects in Michigan and Wisconsin* (Madison: University of Wisconsin Industrial Relations Research Institute, 1972).

15. Daniel W. Sturt, "The Need for Rural Labor Market Information at the National Level," in Collette Moser, *Labor Market Information in Rural Areas* (East Lansing: Michigan State University Center for Rural Manpower and Public Affairs, 1972), p. 16.

Index

Index

Aerospace industries, 103-104
Agriculture, 9, 17, 36, 37, 61, 70-71, 85, 97, 101, 103, 106, 115, 163
Alabama, northern, 103-105
Alonso, William, 159
Appalachia: capital flows in, 9; highway construction in, 21-25, 31
Appalachian Regional Commission, 21-25, 102, 146, 147
Appalachian Regional Development Act of 1965, 168; objectives of, 21-22
Apparel industries, 48
Area Planning and Development Commissions (Ga.), 146-148
Arkansas, 80-83
Arkansas Department of Labor, 81
Atlanta Manpower Planning Area Board, 142, 146
Atlanta Regional Commission Data Center, 142

Beale, Calvin, 4
Berry, Brian, 16, 129, 159
Branch banking, 9-10
Branch plants: in selected nonmetropolitan communities, 73-75; in Tennessee, 96
Bureau of Economic Analysis: definition of economic areas, 4-5; see also 91, 153, 154

Caudill, Harry, 25
Central place theory, 5, 8
Chamber of Commerce, 62, 75, 96, 100, 161
Chittendon County, Vermont, 133-135
Coastal Plains Regional Commission, 147
Colorado, 117-123; Labor mobility, see also, Work force migration analysis
Colorado Rural Development Commission, 121
Commission on Population Growth and the American Future, 10, 11, 82, 85
Commuting, 137, 142, 143, 149
Counties studied: and proximity to highways, 25-30; definition of, 4; employment change in, 36-55; in Alabama, 103; in central Texas, 148; in Colorado and New Mexico, 111; in Minnesota, 57, 65; in Mississippi, 106; in northern Georgia, 141; in the Ozarks, 77; in the Tennessee Valley, 91; in Vermont and New Hampshire, 125; in Wisconsin, 57

Denver Research Institute, 118
Doeringer, Peter, 165

Eau Claire State University, 72
Economic base theory, 8
Economic Development Administration, 24, 25, 96, 125, 168
Employment, change in: by population change category for selected counties, 36-40; in apparel industries, 48; in selected Colorado and New Mexico counties, 111-114; in selected Georgia counties, 142-145; in selected Minnesota and Wisconsin counties, 57-61; in selected New Hampshire and Vermont counties, 125-130; in selected Ozarks counties, 77-80; in selected Texas counties, 149-151; in selected TVA counties, 91-94; in Tennessee, 94-96; in the Arkansas-Verdigris Basin, 86-90; see also, Service-related employment, Manufacturing employment
Environment, concern for, 117, 120-123, 135-139, 143, 161
External economies of agglomeration, 8, 16, 19, 88, 89

Financing rural development: problems of, 9-10; rural banks, 8
Friedmann, John, 12

Gallup poll, 10
Gauthier, Howard, 20
Georgia, 141-148
Georgia Department of Industry and Trade, 143
Growth centers, 17, 166; and transportation, 19-20, 65, 133

Haren, Claude, 110
Hawkins, E.K., 20
Highways: and decentralization, 143; and economic growth, 31-32; 160; and population growth in central Texas, 148; and population growth in New Hampshire and Vermont, 130-133, 137, 139; and population growth in selected counties, 25-32; and regional development programs, 21; in Appalachia, 21-25
Hill-Burton Act, 52
Hirschberg, David, 153
Hirschman, Albert 20
Hunter, Holland, 20

Income change and migration, 153-158
Income gap, 83-84
Interstate Highway System, see Highways

Investment in human resources, 16, 21, 22, 23, 66, 161, 163-168; *see also* Manpower programs; Vocational and technical training

Jennison, Keith Warren, 139, 140
JOBS Program, 167
Johnson, President Lyndon, 148, 152

Kuehn, John, 20

Labor mobility: assisted, 166-168; in TVA region, 102-103; *see also,* Work force migration analysis
Labor unions, 96-97, 106, 107, 146
Leisure and recreation, 12, 13, 64, 67, 69, 70, 71, 73, 85, 101, 118-120, 129, 135-139, 148, 149, 152, 160, 161
Location theory, 8

McClellan-Kerr Waterway, 85-90
Manpower programs, 163, 165; and relocation, 166-168; in Georgia, 146; in northern Alabama, 104
Manufacturing: decentralization of, 12, 14-15, 71, 73-75, 143, 152, 162-167; earnings in, 50-51, 82, 108-109; employment change in selected counties, 37-38, 40-45, 48-52, 55; employment change in U.S., 13-14; in Arkansas, 81-83; in Chittenden County, 133-134; in Minnesota, 61, 62, 63, 64; in northeastern Mississippi, 106-107; in northern Alabama, 103; in Tennessee, 95-103; in the Ozarks, 77-78, 80; in the TVA, 108-110, 162; in Vermont and New Hampshire, 128-129; in Wisconsin, 68; tax breaks to firms, 17
Marshall, Ray, 107, 110
Migration: and income change, 17, 153-158; and race in Georgia, 141-142; in U.S., 17
Miller, John, 12
Minnesota, 9, 57-66, 73-75; Labor mobility, *see,* Work force migration analysis
Minnesota Department of Economic Development, 63
Mississippi, northeastern, 106-107, 164
Munro, John, 22, 23

National growth policies, 159-160
Negro migration, 80, 102, 141-142
Netzer, Dick, 28
New Hampshire, 125-133, 139, 161
New Hampshire-Vermont Development Council, 125
New Mexico, 114-117, 123; Labor

mobility, *see* Work force migration analysis
Nodal-functional concept, 5
Nonmetropolitan development: and human resources, 163-168; and local banking, 8-10, 100-101; and manufacturing decentralization, 162-167; and metropolitanization, 160-162; and race, 97-98, 105, 106, 107, 164-165; barriers to, 8-10, 85; cost of job creation, 166; financial inducements, 16-17; rationale for, 1-2
Nonmetropolitan financial markets, 9
Nunn, Governor Louie, 31

Office of Economic Opportunity, 23
Opinion Research Corporation, 10
Ozarks, 77-85, 162; Labor mobility, *see* Work force migration analysis
Ozarks Regional Commission, 84, 85, 89

Per capita income: by residence, 1-2; in Minnesota, 65-66; in northern Alabama, 104; in Tennessee, 95; in the Ozarks, 83; urban size, 159; *see also* Income change and migration
Population potential, 159
Population trends: and proximity to SMSA's, 159, 164; in Alabama, 103; in Arkansas, 80; in central Texas, 148, 149, 152; in Colorado, 117-118, 120-122; in Georgia, 141-142; in Minnesota, 64, 65; in New Hampshire and Vermont, 139-140; in New Mexico, 114-115, in Tennessee, 94-95; in U.S., 2, 7; in Wisconsin, 70, 71
Poverty: by residence, 2-3; in Colorado, 123; in New Mexico, 116-117, 123; in northern Alabama, 104; in rural areas, 163
Public Works and Economic Development Act, 168

Railroads, 20
Recreation, *see* Leisure and recreation
Residential location preferences, 10-12, 16
Retirement, 70, 72, 149, 152, 160
Rockefeller, Winthrop, 85
Rostow, W. W., 20
Rural job creation: cost of, 166
Rural Manpower Service, 163, 167

Service centers, 17
Service related employment: change in selected counties, 45-47, 52-54; change in U.S., 13-14; growth of, 114, 129, 136-137, 149, 152; *see also,* Employment, change in

Small Business Administration, 62
Smith, Adam, 19
SMSA's: and migration flows, 153-158; and urban fields, 141, 152, 160, 164; as nodes of BEA economic areas, 5, 14; definition of, 1; growth effects of proximity to, 26-32, 54-55, 60, 65, 91, 111, 118, 121, 125, 160, 164; in the South, 14; poverty in, 2-3
Snowmobiles, 62, 64
Social Security Administration Work Force Sample, *see* Work force migration analysis
Social Security Coverage Status, 33-34
South: growth of manufacturing in, 14-15, 163-164
Southwest Texas State University, 149
Spread effects, 19-20, 166

Take-off stage of economic growth, 20
Tennessee, 94-103
Tennessee Manpower Council, 98
Tennessee Technological University, 100
Tennessee Valley, 91-110; Labor mobility, *see* Work force migration analysis
Tennessee Valley Authority, 86, 89, 91, 98, 104, 107-110
Texas, central, 148-152
Textiles, 95, 96, 163
Thompson, Wilbur, 8, 11, 15, 48, 85, 162
Till, Thomas, 14, 106
Top of Alabama Regional Council of Governments, 103-105
Transportation: and economic growth,

19-21, 31-32, 65, 67, 71, 73, 131-133, 160
Tweeten, Luther, 166

U. S. Bureau of Standards, 120
U. S. Bureau of the Census, 3, 7
U. S. Department of Agriculture, 4, 74
U. S. Department of Commerce, 5, 33, 153
U. S. Department of Health, Education, and Welfare, 34, 146
U. S. Department of Labor, 167
U. S. Department of the Interior, 13
U. S. Department of Transportation, 25
University of Colorado, 120
University of Minnesota, 66
University of Texas, 148
Urban fields, 12-13, 54, 71, 73, 74, 85, 118, 123, 128, 152, 160, 162, 164, 167

Vermont, 125-140, 161; Labor mobility, *see,* Work force migration analysis
Vermont State Planning Office, 133
Vocational-technical schools and training, 66, 73, 104, 146, 164-165

West, Jerry, 20
Western State College, 119
Widner, Ralph, 23
Wisconsin, 57-61, 66-75; Labor mobility, *see* Work force migration analysis
Wisconsin Department of Transportation, 69
Wisconsin Division of Economic Development, 67, 68
Work force migration analysis, 153-158

About the Author

Niles M. Hansen is Professor of Economics and Director, Center for Economic Development, at the University of Texas. He is the author of *French Regional Planning, France in the Modern World, Rural Poverty and the Urban Crisis, Intermediate-Size Cities as Growth Centers, Location Preferences, Migration and Regional Growth,* and the editor of *Growth Centers in Regional Economic Development.* He also has contributed numerous articles to professional journals in economics and the social sciences. Professor Hansen is a member of the Board of Editors of *Growth and Change, Review of Regional Studies,* and *Regional and Urban Economics.*